MAKING MARRIAGE WORK

MAKING MARRIAGE WORK

Avoiding the Pitfalls and Achieving Success

Rob Pascale and Louis H. Primavera

ROWMAN & LITTLEFIELD
Lanham • Boulder • New York • London

Published by Rowman & Littlefield
A wholly owned subsidiary of The Rowman & Littlefield Publishing Group, Inc.
4501 Forbes Boulevard, Suite 200, Lanham, Maryland 20706
www.rowman.com

Unit A, Whitacre Mews, 26-34 Stannary Street, London SE11 4AB

British Library Cataloguing in Publication Information Available

Library of Congress Cataloging-in-Publication Data

Names: Pascale, Rob, 1954- | Primavera, Louis H., 1943-
Title: Making marriage work : avoiding the pitfalls and achieving success /
Rob Pascale, Louis H. Primavera.
Description: Lanham : Rowman & Littlefield, 2016. | Includes bibliographical
references and index.
Identifiers: LCCN 2015030327| ISBN 9781442256972 (cloth : alk. paper) | ISBN
9781442256989 (electronic)
Subjects: LCSH: Marriage. | Communication in marriage.
Classification: LCC HQ734 .P9197 2016 | DDC 306.81--dc23 LC record available at http://
lccn.loc.gov/2015030327

Printed in the United States of America

To our wives, Lynne Pascale and Anne Primavera,
for their many years of tolerance, patience,
understanding, and affection
as well as their outstanding editing.

CONTENTS

I

INTRODUCTION

Mark and Judy had been married about eighteen years and wanted to find out if counseling could improve their marriage. During the initial sessions, I asked a lot of questions about their relationship to uncover what might be at the heart of their issues. As we met over the following weeks, both claimed there wasn't a specific problem that kept cropping up. In fact, they said they almost never argued. However, they also rarely engaged in any forms of intimacy. Their broader issues—that is, what was causing their lack of intimacy—remained very much under the surface.

One day Mark arrived before Judy and told me that going to therapy was Judy's idea. From his perspective, he was just going through the motions. He already had a girlfriend and was really just working out the best time to leave. He believed his marriage was too far gone, and regardless, he had no interest in fixing it. Therapy for him was a way to end their relationship, not a way to repair it. Judy, on the other hand, was committed to turning things around and was completely unaware of Mark's intentions.

A lot of couples come to marriage counselors to get permission to leave. One or the other has already made up their minds before the first session, and going to therapy makes it look as though they tried, but it's a way to alleviate their guilt. What's truly unfortunate is that many of their problems could have been solved, and if they don't try, they might end up facing many of the same issues in future relationships.

Marriage as an institution seems to be at risk, or at least that's what recent statistics suggest. At present, somewhere between 35 percent and 50 percent of marriages are expected to end in divorce at some point, and only about seven out of ten couples will make it to their tenth anniversary. Additionally, young people are not flocking to marriage the way they used to. While getting married in the past was something of a rite of passage into adulthood, people today are waiting longer to get married. More couples also seem to regard living together outside of wedlock as a better way to go, possibly because it's less complicated, less restricting, or just less scary because the door is always a little open.[1]

For some contemplating marriage, such statistics and social trends can be downright depressing. They suggest that, despite how hard we worked to find the right person, we don't have a very good chance of long-term success. Others may take a more cynical perspective. Having grown up with friends living in single-parent households or experiencing that arrangement themselves, they may expect their own marriages to fail. Either way, it's not unreasonable to question whether taking that step makes sense. Maybe the institution is obsolete and no longer relevant to the way we live now.

That, of course, is not the case. Being married is still how people prefer to live, and within all cultures it's one of the most valued institutions. Most of us eventually end up married at least once in our lifetimes, and rare is the totally committed bachelor or bachelorette. It's predominance in our individual and social psyches is demonstrated by how much press the subject receives. As of this writing, an online search of library abstracts cites more than forty thousand scientific articles just from the fields of psychology and sociology, and the Amazon.com website lists more than nine thousand books on how to make your marriage better.

But if marriage is so cherished and so culturally ingrained, why are couples more likely today to end up divorced? From our perspective, what the statistics actually reveal is not that marriage isn't valued, but that it's much harder today to keep one intact. There's evidence, for example, that relationships have more conflicts nowadays. That's not to say that marriages were happier years ago. The truth is there was probably a lot of suffering in silence. Yet these couples stayed married, mostly because there wasn't much choice if you wanted to be accepted in the community. However, those in the Baby Boomer and later generations have had to marry in the face of social changes that have made it much easier to walk away.

One factor that has worked against the stability of the institution is the adoption of no-fault laws in the late 1960s. As a result of such legislation, couples no longer need to explain why they are divorcing. A marriage can be dissolved for any reason or no reason at all. However, as an unintended consequence, the government has actually helped to legitimize divorce. These laws are an acknowledgment by the state that breaking up a marriage is acceptable and the reasons for doing so is nobody's business. In effect they have removed the negative stigma, so couples can split up and still retain their standing in the community.

Then there's the women's movement. Women now have more and better employment opportunities and are more in control over their own lives. Although their salaries lag behind those of men, a job still provides them with a good amount of independence, and they no longer require a husband for financial security. So they can now wait longer to get married, and don't have to stay married if they're not satisfied with their partner. Without feeling trapped in bad marriages, women may have less of a need to work through marital problems because they're better equipped to make it on their own.

Along with greater equality, the roles held by men and women are no longer clearly delineated. As a result, there's been a reduction in interdependency. Before the 1960s, husbands and wives held complementary roles. One was the breadwinner, providing safety and financial security for the family; the other was responsible for maintaining the home, raising children, and fulfilling other social and family duties. Because each partner filled a specific and highly defined role, couples had functionally different and very useful reasons for staying together. In contrast, today there's a good deal of overlap in terms of who brings home the bacon and who manages the household. The blurring of roles means each partner doesn't provide to the other a unique set of benefits that they did in past generations, which weakens the need to stay together.

The movement toward gender equality has also affected the balance of power within marriages. Because power is a zero-sum game, an increase in status for women means there's an equivalent loss of status for men. Prior to the 1960s, men held the power in marriage. They had a housekeeper, a cook, a regular sex partner, and freedom of movement, all with little or no responsibility inside the home. Although men still get more out of marriage than they give, they're not quite the kings of their castles as they used to be. In some marriages, there can actually be an on-going power struggle, as men strive for control and their wives fight for equality. The point here is that, for men, the loss of much of their status may have made starting or staying in a marriage less attractive.

Women's entry into the job market has affected men in other ways. They've added another layer of competition for jobs, thereby reducing men's career opportunities and earning potential. Furthermore, while men still don't carry an equal load at home, they do more today than did husbands in the past. Having to dedicate more time to household maintenance may have forced some men to focus less exclusively on their careers, and that may have slowed or limited their ability for advancement. With their weakened status and increased home responsibilities, both men and women might not see marriage as advantageous in today's world.[2]

More liberal attitudes toward sex may have also chipped away at marriage. While only about 30 percent of adults felt premarital sex was acceptable in the 1950s, that percentage has grown to about 75 percent today. As it is no longer a prerequisite for sex, marriage has lost one of its more popular and exclusive benefits. There's also been a change in attitudes toward out-of-wedlock births. It's much more acceptable now to have children without being married, even without a live-in partner. More than 40 percent of all births in the United States in 2007 were outside of marriage, compared to less than 5 percent in 1950. The estimates are that more than half of all children today will spend their formative years moving in and out of different households and living in different kinds of family structures, some with two adults, some with only one, and others with two same-sex partners. The net result is that there's no longer a need to marry in order to raise a family.

There has also been a rise in secularism. Religious beliefs and doctrines had a powerful influence on how people thought and acted before the last few decades. For many, the teachings of their church made divorce untenable. Even today, couples who are more connected to their religion are less prone to get divorced. But fewer people today look to their religion for personal guidance, so it's not as effective in persuading as many couples to stay together.

Couples from earlier generations may have also thought differently about marriage. They tended to regard the institution as sacred and their marriage as permanent, and they stayed married regardless of how each partner felt about each other. Their happiness and personal needs were sublimated to the needs of the marriage. It's not that love wasn't important, but they may have been more concerned about conforming to social standards, following the rules, and being an accepted member of the community.[3]

Changes in social conditions may have also led to, or at least were accompanied by, changes at the personal level. With the 1960s' civil rights and social reform movements, people have become more open-minded. Today we're more accepting of minorities and alternative lifestyles, and we care more about social injustices. Some consider the period of the last fifty years to be the most prolific in fostering social equality and a growth in free thinking. As a by-product of these reforms, there has been a shift away from conformity and a greater focus on personal growth and exploration. People today spend more time searching for ways to achieve their own emotional well-being and establish personally satisfying lifestyles. The evidence suggests that we think more about ourselves and our personal needs today than did past generations.[4]

Many of us would agree that paying attention to our psychological needs is a good thing. However, it's possible we may have gone too far. Some argue that our quest for personal growth nowadays looks a little too much like narcissism. There's evidence that the general population's scores on this trait have risen dramatically in recent decades. Narcissism is the tendency to focus on one's self and to put personal needs above all else. Highly narcissistic people have inflated opinions of themselves and of their importance, and have few positive qualities. They tend to have higher self-esteem, are more extroverted, are less prone to depression or feelings of loneliness and isolation, and are generally happy with how they live.

However, narcissists also exhibit quite a few negative characteristics, some of which are especially counterproductive when it comes to personal relationships. Narcissists don't often develop emotionally close ties to other people. They tend to lack empathy, so they have a hard time understanding or caring about the issues or problems of others. They also look to establish relationships with people who can enhance their own status, and generally look to exploit personal relationships to their own advantage. Additionally, narcissists prefer to establish relationships with others who validate who they are, that is, very important people. When they feel insulted or rejected, or they're with someone who is critical or disagrees with them, they tend to react with aggressive or verbally abusive language.

If narcissism is more prevalent and we're just more self-absorbed, it's easy to see how that can work against marriage. We're likely to put our personal interests ahead of those of our relationship. If we feel our own interests are threatened or unsatisfied, we may be more inclined to think the relationship isn't working rather than adjust what we expect to get out of it. When considered in combination with the social changes we talked about earlier, we can see why marriage has gotten a lot harder.[5]

Dave and Maria had been married for less than a year. Typically, couples who come to marriage counseling do not reveal much in the first session or two, and some probing is needed to uncover their problems. Not so with Dave and Maria. Within fifteen minutes of the first session, they were on the attack, accusing each other of a range of misdeeds and disappointments. As often happens in such relationships, an accusation by one leads to a counter-accusation from the other, which then leads to further counterattacks.

Their issues for both came down to unfulfilled needs and expectations. Each was highly protective of their personal well-being, and believed it was extremely important to achieve their individual goals. All that Dave and Maria had to say focused on what each was not getting from the other. Their expectations as to what each was personally entitled were strongly imbedded in their belief systems, so they could only react with anger at the hint of those expectations not being satisfied. Interestingly, not once did either talk about their relationship in terms of "we," nor did they talk about what each was getting from the other.

The truth is both Dave and Maria felt emotionally supported by each other, helped each other when needed, were connected and involved with each other's lives and families, and had an active and enjoyable sex life. However, their personal needs overwhelmed and clouded their thinking, and that made it difficult for them to see that their marriage was actually providing a lot of benefits. These weren't apparent because they dwelled mostly on how disappointed they were in each other.

Looking at things broadly, many couples today really have two goals they pursue simultaneously. They want to be married, but they also want to fulfill their own personal needs. Such a perspective is certainly reasonable, and in fact it's psychologically healthy, but it can also put a relation-ship at risk. When our personal goals and the demands of our marriage are at odds with each other, we find it easier, and probably regard it as a personal responsibility, to walk away. Many of us are just not willing to sacrifice our individual goals for the sake of the institution. Author Steph-anie Coontz sums it up pretty well: "Marriage has become more joyful, more loving, and more satisfying for many couples than ever before in history. At the same time it has become optional and more brittle. These two strands of change cannot be disentangled."[6]

That's not to say that couples today aren't highly invested in their relationships. They actually will go to great lengths to try to work out their problems and keep their marriages intact. In fact, most couples who end up divorced believed that would be the eventual outcome, but still they hold out for ten or more years before they actually get to that point. Throughout that time they keep evaluating and reevaluating, searching for evidence that the good outweighs the bad so that they can justify staying together. They want it to work, and it's only with great reluctance that they ultimately throw in the towel.

The dramatic growth of the marriage counseling industry over the past few decades also provides evidence that couples truly want their mar-riages to be successful. Sadly, though, even professional intervention hasn't been that helpful. Many couples who go through that process find their problems returning later on. In fact, the relapse rates are so high that some pundits argue that marriage counseling just doesn't work at all.[7]

However, we believe that this criticism is not entirely appropriate. When one considers who seeks marriage counseling, it's no surprise at all that the success rate is low. Typically, couples try to work through prob-lems on their own, and it's only when the relationship is on its last legs that they try a marriage counselor. But by then it's often too late—one or both partners may already have at least one foot out the door. Counseling is then more of a formality; a process to follow that alleviates guilt and permits both partners to feel as though they tried.

With such clientele, marriage counselors don't stand much of a chance. However, we should point out that physicians treating various kinds of physical illnesses wouldn't fare much better. We would not, for example, regard cancer specialists as ineffective if they only treated pa-tients who were in the final stages of the disease. To avoid high failure rates, the medical profession has put a lot of effort into telling us about the early symptoms of illnesses and recommends that we see our doctor at the first sign of these symptoms.

Reading the early warning signals is just as critical for a marriage. The problems that many couples face emerge early, often before the marriage takes place. We develop patterns of interacting, and the subsequent direction a marriage takes is usually determined by these early patterns. Some of these destructive patterns are not always easy to detect, or may be hard to admit to, and some we may not even recognize as potential problems. Most importantly, problems that start out small may become worse over time if not handled effectively. Minor annoyances can turn into major sources of resentment and anger. When that happens, they can cloud how each partner views the other and they can infect other parts of the relationship. Problems that are left unchecked will eventually turn into bad habits, and that makes them increasingly harder to fix.

From all we've discussed so far, a sane person might conclude marriage just isn't worth it. It's too hard, if not impossible, to do it well. We agree that it's difficult, but even with its pitfalls, marriage can be fulfilling if it's approached the right way. The fact is marriage has the potential to offer a wide range of benefits. Despite all its problems, the majority of couples who stay married eventually find there is something in their partner that's worth hanging around for, even if their relationship isn't as exciting as when they first met. Indeed, even couples who divorce, while they can list the reasons why they ended up that way, also remember the good parts: the stability, companionship, and security it provided. We should also mention that we didn't begin this project as completely committed advocates for marriage, but we moved in that direction after compiling the evidence for and against it.

Of course, not all marriages can be saved and a few should end in divorce. They may be damaged beyond repair, or partners may be so mismatched from the start that they should never have gotten together in the first place. Regardless of whether they believe they still love each other, partners will suffer more harm than good if they stay in bad marriages. But that doesn't describe most marriages, including those that seem to have a lot of problems, and probably quite a few that split up. It's very easy to think the grass is greener when you're in the midst of difficult times, or to think that things would be so much better with a different partner. The reality, however, is that it's usually not.

Furthermore, while staying together may be hard, it can be a lot harder to break up. Most of us have heard enough war stories about divorce to know it is an extremely painful process. So, as bad as you think your marriage might be, it has to be weighed against that experience. Just in case you're unsure as to whether it may be easier to walk away than to try to work on your marriage, we thought a quick review of what happens in divorce may make you better informed.

For one, divorce typically brings financial hardships to both partners. Their incomes and financial reserves tend to decline substantially, leading to a much lowered standard of living. For some, they might actually dip below the poverty line. When people live together, they share fixed costs, such as housing or home repairs, but these costs double when they live separately.

Women are especially likely to suffer financially from a divorce. We mention this because, interestingly enough, it is women who are especially prone to think about and initiate divorces. Women tend to take a more analytical approach to their relationships, and so are more sensitive to their problems. They also don't typically benefit as much from marriage as do men, so they may believe they have less to lose if it's dissolved.

The psychological consequences to each partner can be especially severe. Individuals who end up divorced often suffer a variety of physical and emotional problems. Many are likely to go through periods of depression, and of course there's a lot of anger. As Dr. Primavera put it when asked if he'd witnessed any good divorces, "It doesn't matter how well they start out, sooner or later they all end in rage." Those who are going through divorce are also likely to experience a loss of stability and security, bouts of loneliness and disconnectedness, a sense of having failed, and a fear of committing to future relationships.

We also have to consider the impact on our social circle. Divorces affect not only the lives of partners but all of their friends and family members as well. Each one suffers the loss of the partner that's been dropped. That's especially the case for children. The evidence suggests that those who grow up in a divorced household are more likely themselves to take that same path as adults. They may develop a belief from their parents that divorce is acceptable and can be survived. They might also develop a fear of commitment, or will learn negative styles of interacting that make them less effective in their adult relationships. [8]

Recovery requires a good deal of time, although how much can depend on your role in the decision. Typically, no one wants to take responsibility for a failed marriage. Couples typically blame their partners and not themselves, and self-preservation may be the reason why. When we blame ourselves, we might hold a stronger emotional attachment to our spouses than if we blame them. Blaming them gives us reasons for leaving. We're also more prone to feel guilty or remorseful, because we might be forced to admit that it could have worked if we were better partners or better people. However, while blaming yourself is more painful, you may actually have a faster recovery if you can do that. If you blame your spouse, you're likely to stay angry and resentful because you believe your marriage could have been saved if your partner wasn't such a jackass. Holding on to anger and resentment makes it difficult to put our former partners out of our minds, and that makes it harder to accept our non-married lifestyle.[9]

Given the realities of divorce, if you're on the fence, it might be better to take a closer look at how your relationship can be repaired before you decide to call it quits. You should also keep in mind that, while you might feel at times your marriage is just not worth the effort, there's a good chance other relationships you have will follow the same path. The ways we think and act in marriage are learned. So if you have learned ineffective relationship skills, these might be what are beneath your marital problems. In other words, if your marriage has problems and you don't try or don't know how to fix it, there's a chance your next relationship will end up in pretty much the same place. Sometimes it's not the person you're with; it's the kind of person you are.

Our point of all this is that, while marriage requires a lot of hard work, we can do ourselves a major disservice if we don't try to find a way to make it successful. By success we mean not just co-exist without wanting to kill each other, but to get to a point where we actually enjoy our partner and our relationship has real personal value. For some, that may seem easier to say than to accomplish. Problems can be so pervasive or overwhelming that it's difficult to know where and how to proceed. When marriages reach that stage, not knowing how to make them better can be frustrating if not downright depressing. Nevertheless, paths to success are available with a little guidance.

That brings us to our objectives. In the upcoming chapters we present the reasons why some marriages work well and others don't. We haven't just relied on our personal opinions or experiences. Instead, we have based our comments on the findings of hundreds of research studies conducted by social scientists on marriage. We've also incorporated some of the experiences of Dr. Lou Primavera from his twenty-five years in private practice as a marriage counselor. Through his exposure to many marriages in various stages of disrepair, Lou has developed a solid understanding as to what makes for good marriages, and what may actually be behind marriages that suffer from chronic problems. Note that we've tried to cover as many of the lifestyle and emotional aspects of relationships as we could in a single volume, and surely we've missed more than a few. Nevertheless, we hope that what we have included is enough to be of some value to a good percentage of couples. All the anecdotes related in these pages are from actual people; however, names and other identifying features have been changed to protect their identities.

Along with pointing out problem areas, our intention was to provide some guidance as to how to make marriages better. To those already married, we have tried to point out ways they can make adjustments to their relationships. For those planning to marry, we hoped to create a sense of what it really means to be married, and to point out the many obstacles and pitfalls they might face so that they won't be blindsided. All along the way, we try to provide information that can temper expectations, a key ingredient for keeping a marriage moving on the right path. Researchers propose that those who repeatedly get divorced and remarry may in part have inaccurate expectations about intimate relationships and how they evolve over time. With realistic expectations, both those already married and newlyweds-to-be may have an easier time avoiding disillusionment and destructive patterns.[10]

We should mention that, although it's a hot topic now that was always in the back of our minds while writing, we didn't cover gay marriages specifically. This was so primarily because it's a new phenomenon, so there's very little research that has been conducted at this point. That said, where it made sense throughout the book we talk about partners, that is, we purposely left out gender identification. While many of the issues that arise in marriage are a result of the social and psychological differences between men and women, some are just the result of two people interacting daily in an intimate relationship. So while we did not specifically reference gay couples, they're likely to face many of the same problems as do heterosexual couples. Time will tell whether or not this will actually bear out, but we're pretty confident it will, because, well, people are people.

2

MARRIED, LIVING TOGETHER, AND LIVING ALONE

The social changes we discussed in the first chapter have affected each of us. Importantly, they've given us options, and options make life more complicated. Today we can choose to stay single, marry, or forgo the ceremony and just live with someone. Of course, we've always had these options, but social customs have nudged us down the more conventional path of marriage. While most still look to marry, both living alone or with someone else are now perfectly acceptable. The latter has actually become a step taken by many couples before they get married.

So, before we talk about what makes marriages succeed or fail, we thought it would be useful to examine each of these lifestyles. Specifically, we wanted to find out whether one is a better way to live than the others, and by that we mean has a more positive impact on our long-term physical and psychological health.

On the face of things, each lifestyle has specific defining features. Broadly speaking, marriage provides for more security and stability, living together provides companionship and shared living minus the contract, and staying single allows for more independence of thought and freedom of movement. If we're trying to decide which way to live, we might be tempted to just consider these salient features. All we have to do is determine which benefits are most personally meaningful and then choose the corresponding lifestyle. However, there are many more nuances to these three lifestyles than appears at a single glance, and some of these differences can have a dramatic impact on how one's life turns out.

Joey and Liz were married a little less than two years when they started counseling. Prior to getting married, they had lived together for almost seven years. Throughout that time, their relationship was stable and happy. They shared a lot of activities and interests but also had time to pursue their own interests. So they had a good balance of time together and time on their own.

Shortly after getting married, the relationship began to run into problems. These were minor at first, but gradually turned into bigger issues. By the time they began therapy, Liz complained that Joey had become emotionally distant and impatient, and seemed to have lost interest in her. Joey, on the other hand, felt Liz had become too demanding of his time and attention and seemed to find a lot of reasons to be angry with him.

Despite all their years of living together, marriage had changed how Joey and Liz interacted with each other. For Liz, she had a set of rules and expectations as to how a husband and wife should act in marriage, and these were different from what she expected when they were just living together. She wanted a greater commitment of his time to home and family, and to her. Joey, on the other hand, was just not prepared for the emotional commitment that came along with marriage. He also regarded her new rules as demands, and these led him to feel restricted and pressured by the relationship, and those feelings affected how he felt about and treated Liz.

As we looked into the more subtle differences among these lifestyles, it became clear that the balance of strengths and weaknesses tipped in favor of one over the others. Cutting right to the chase, marriage emerged as the qualified winner. Living together outside of marriage can be either good or bad, depending on how couples end up in that arrangement, but it's not as good as marriage when both are at their highest quality. Staying single seems to be the least desirable option. This lifestyle leaves us open to the possibility of a variety of problems and relatively few advantages over the long term, especially for men.

When it's done well, marriage offers the best chances for a high quality of life and personal well-being. We've mentioned that it provides for security and stability, but it also seems that marriage is associated with better health. Specifically, individuals who are married are less likely to suffer chronic diseases, disabilities, and long-term illnesses, and even have fewer physician visits as compared to those who are single or living together. If you're married, you also have a better chance of surviving a catastrophic event, such as a heart attack, and you'll recover faster from such events.

We can't definitively say there's a cause and effect, that is, that marriage directly leads to better health. It may also be the case that those who are healthy feel good about their lives, and that helps them have a better marriage. Nevertheless, it is reasonable to assume that the security provided by marriage helps us feel good about ourselves, and that lets us feel good about our marriage.

These health benefits are believed to result from features that are unique to the husband-wife relationship. Married couples are more likely to monitor each other's behavior. Each partner makes sure the other gets to the doctor for regular checkups, stays on their medications, and has follow-ups with doctors if there are problems. Married couples are also more likely to have certain habits that contribute to good health, such as healthy diets and regular exercise, and tend to have fewer unhealthy ones, such as substance abuse and poor sleep habits.

Better mental health may also come from supportiveness. When we believe we're supported, we feel better about ourselves and can cope better with stressful events and situations. Married couples have been found to experience fewer depressive symptoms, are generally happier, and are emotionally more stable than those who are single or living together. Marriage may also have a restorative effect for some people who have experienced emotional problems in the past. For example, among many who had suffered bouts of depression prior to marriage, they have been found to have fewer such episodes after they get married.

These health benefits tend to be especially pronounced for husbands. That's because wives are so good at watching their husbands' behavior and making sure they follow healthy regimens. Left to themselves, men are not as attentive to their health regimen. Their wives understand that, and so they watch out for them, and they do that more so in marriage than in other living arrangements. Unfortunately, wives can't rely as much on their husbands for monitoring their health. Nevertheless, they're still better off than women who are not married.[1]

Married men also look to their wives to keep them socially connected. Men in general tend to have fewer and less emotionally close relationships with other people. Consequently, they can become socially isolated without wives to maintain outside relationships for them. Feeling connected to the outside world is essential to a healthy state of mind. Friendships and group memberships can be the bases for our identities and are sources of self-esteem, not to mention giving us something to do. In fact, social isolation is just as bad for you as other major risk issues, including smoking, high blood pressure, obesity, and lack of physical activity. Taken together, the benefits of feeling emotionally supported and being socially connected give husbands a sound health advantage, as compared to men who are not married.[2]

As a primary defining feature, and its major shortcoming, live-together relationships lack durability. About five out of ten split up in less than five years. In comparison, only about two out of ten marriages end in divorce within that same time frame. It's extremely rare for a couple to live together for as long as those who are married, which is often more than twenty years.

One reason for their brevity is the lack commitment. By that we mean a sense that your partner will not leave; that when you face problems, even severe ones, you will try to work them out. Relative to marriage, cohabitating couples are less bound to each other, which is what both partners probably intended for their relationship. Possibly because they're less committed, partners often give their relationship lower priority, and they don't have their personal identities tied up in each other as is typical for married couples. They also tend to have more socially liberal views, which often include greater openness to divorce and a belief that relationships aren't necessarily supposed to be permanent. Instead, they value their freedom and individualism, and these attitudes cut into their willingness to invest in long-term relationships.

Their lack of commitment often leaves live-together couples feeling more at risk. Partners know they're susceptible to a breakup, so the relationship is more stressful. Because they're more vulnerable, it's harder for partners to establish trust and intimacy, and that inhibits their ability to communicate openly. The net result is to make it more difficult for them to resolve conflicts. These communication problems aren't easy to fix. Even if they eventually marry, they don't seem to be quite as effective at working through their problems as couples who are committed to marriage from the start.

Many women are reluctant to enter a live-together arrangement for precisely this reason. While they are equally devoted to their relationship regardless of whether or not they're engaged, they worry about a man's commitment when there are no firm plans to marry. To them, living together delays the possibility of marriage because it reduces her partner's incentive to take that step.

Men also worry about commitment, but their worries are in the opposite direction. They fear the loss of their freedom. They can no longer pursue alternative sex partners and can no longer control how they use their time. However, such freedom goes both ways, and men realize that. While they might consider extra-relationship affairs, they also have to worry about their partner doing the same thing. They understand that without giving a commitment to marry, their partner may be on the look out to look for a man who is willing to do so. Note that it seems their worries are not groundless—those living together are more prone to cheat on each other as compared to married couples.[3]

Living together is also a more narrowly defined lifestyle. These couples are less likely to have their finances comingled, have weaker relationships with each other's families, and are less dependent on each other socially and emotionally. Partners have to be careful about getting too close because they understand their relationship might not last.

The narrowness of the live-together lifestyle is also exemplified by the kinds of rewards these relationships provide. Relationships can give internal or intrinsic rewards, such as love and emotional support, and more practical or extrinsic rewards, such as shared expenses, a roof over their heads, and sex. Initially, relationships provide mostly extrinsic rewards, but as they develop and mature, they give more intrinsic rewards. Intrinsic rewards indicate a deeper connection between partners and give them stronger reasons for staying together. If relationships remain mostly driven by external benefits and less by emotional bonds, the odds of success drop substantially.

Marriage typically gives partners both types of benefits. However, because live-together partners are less committed to each other and the relationship is more fragile, it's harder to get the intrinsic rewards. That means they have a harder time withstanding many kinds of pressures. If a husband loses his job, he and his wife will try to come up with a way to deal with that problem. She might go back to work, or they will cut down on unnecessary expenses. Or if one partner feels they're not having sex as often as they would like, that situation will be tolerated for quite some time. Those who are living together, on the other hand, are less likely to survive these problems because the only reasons for staying together, that is, the extrinsic benefits, are not being satisfied.

Couples who live together can also face other kinds of pressures. They might feel less integrated into society or receive less support from family and friends. People from their social circle might question whether the relationship will last, so they may prefer not to get too connected to a partner. Furthermore, children born to cohabitating couples also don't seem to fare as well. There's a lack of stability in the household because of the likelihood of a breakup, so these children are at a greater risk of being raised in broken homes.[4]

Of course, not all live-together relationships are destined to fail. In fact, there are circumstances in which living together works well, providing many of the same benefits of marriage. The good ones are made up of couples who are committed to their relationship, the two partners tend to have similar traits and backgrounds, and they take on a more or less equal share in household responsibilities. They also work hard at their relationship. They might be aware their relationship has no legal bonds and can be ended without much difficulty, so they put the extra effort in to keep it intact.

Older couples also have an easier time living together. Those in their mid-fifties and older don't have as many pressures working against them, such as young children or limited finances. Their priorities are focused on finding a companion and a sex partner rather than love, so they have different expectations about their relationship. As a result, these couples place fewer demands on each other, so the relationship is more relaxed. Additionally, they don't have as many options that could lead them astray. With fewer potential sex partners available, they will worry less about losing their partner and can feel secure in their relationship.

Living together also works if marriage is pre-planned. Engaged couples have already made the long-term commitment, and living together is a short-term arrangement that will end at the altar. They're usually happy living together, and their marriages are as successful as those who married without living together first. Honestly, these couples are generally so close to marriage that we're not sure they even should be classified in the live-together category. They just don't face the same emotional issues that can interfere with other live-together relationships.

Note that when we say pre-planned, we mean two people are totally committed to each other, not just considering a commitment. Some couples might try living together to find out if they want to make the commitment. However, that's not likely to be an effective test of compatibility or the durability of the relationship. If partners have such questions, they're probably sensing their relationship has problems. In some cases one or the other partner may have personal traits that interfere with their ability to have an intimate relationship. Living together won't fix these problems.

The truth is a successful live-together relationship does not necessarily translate into a successful marriage. Marriage and living together operate by very different sets of rules, and being good at one doesn't mean we'll be good at the other. In marriage, partners have to be supportive of each other, are less independent, must be more accepting and compromising, and because there's no easy way out, have to work harder at their relationship. We have a very different list of things we expect and want from a spouse than from someone we are just living with. It's interesting to note that couples who decide to marry after living together often end up with poorer-quality marriages. They tend to have a good deal of conflict, and they're more likely to divorce.[5]

The last of these, staying single and living alone, may be the least desirable option. In this lifestyle we lose all the benefits of an intimate relationship, such as a steady companion and intimate partner, and are more likely to experience bouts of loneliness. Relative to marriage, we might sacrifice certain health benefits, and we run the risk of becoming socially isolated. Health and social isolation can be particular problems for men, since many of them don't monitor their health issues well and don't put the effort in to maintain emotionally satisfying relationships.

Of course, there are some benefits to being single. We can pursue our own interests, have many opportunities for personal growth, and have fewer responsibilities. If we have a wide network of friends who share our lifestyle, we're less susceptible to isolation and the problems that can cause, such as depression. Having friends with the same lifestyle is also important because they share our interests and concerns, and often have the same time availability for activities.

Unfortunately, it's hard to maintain a network of single people because most people are paired off with someone. Even when we find single friends, there's always the chance we'll lose them if a suitable person comes along. The truth is the social network for single people can be extremely fluid, and we can be required to expend a great deal of effort to stay active and involved. When we're young, we have the energy and the inclination to meet people and find things to do with our time, but we might not be quite as motivated when we get older.

As we've pointed out at the beginning, marriage is a qualified winner. Now, here's the major qualifier. We've been referring to good marriages. A bad marriage not only lacks the benefits we talked about, it's probably more harmful to your health than other lifestyles. You're likely to experience more chronic health problems and more heart issues, such as high blood pressure. Bad marriages can also exacerbate a health problem, or at the minimum impede your speed of recovery. Couples in distressed marriages are more likely to report chronic pain and pain-related disabilities, and seem to have a harder time coping with all kinds of pain. Even common colds can occur more frequently and last longer among those in unhappy marriages versus those in happier situations.

Wives are especially likely to suffer from bad marriages. Men are generally better off married regardless of the quality of their marriage, but women are only better off if their marriages are happy. Additionally, women tend to be more emotionally invested in their marriages, and that makes them more vulnerable to a downturn in its quality.

The primary impact on women seems to be depression. The lack of emotional support and intimacy are part of the reason, but it can also spring from feelings of powerlessness. Very often a wife in a bad marriage will feel she cannot make it better and as a result feel she has no control over her life. Furthermore, the relationship between depression and marital quality is such that one feeds on the other: a poor marriage is likely to lead to depression, and depression tends to make them feel even worse about their marriage. That in turn can lead to even more intense feelings of depression.[6]

A bad marriage is one that has a lot of conflict and a lot of anger. Arguments and disagreements occur frequently. But it's not just about fighting; it's the accompanying hostility and the lack of resolution. When conflicts can't be resolved, couples can either keep on fighting or avoid issues and/or each other. Abusive behaviors such as criticism, interruption, blaming, sarcasm, disgust, or withdrawal will generally produce a continuing downward spiral in the quality of the marriage and the emotional well-being of each partner.

As its most damaging side-effect, sustained conflict leads to chronic stress. That's probably the most accurate way to define a bad marriage.

It's not boredom or growing apart, a less than perfect sex life, lack of shared interests, believing in greener pastures, or even regular arguing. Some of these may be a reason to break up a marriage, but unless a spouse is a source of chronic stress, the marriage is not truly bad. In one respect, social scientists think of marriage in terms of stress versus social support. Marriage can be a source of one or the other, and most marriages produce both, depending on the day. When relationships are mostly supportive, the impact on health is positive, but when negative, the effect is to keep both partners in a general state of chronic stress.

Couples in bad marriages have about twice as much stress as other couples. The situations that cause stress are almost always present. An argument is not always needed as a trigger. Just thinking about a spouse or the last argument is sufficient to raise stress levels. Additionally, typically there's spillover that occurs from these relationships. The tension coming from their marriage is retained and can affect how partners treat their children and other family members, how they perform on their jobs, their interest in personal activities, and how they feel about themselves.

The problem with chronic stress is that it can interfere with the immune system. That makes us more susceptible to certain kinds of illnesses and infections. It also affects our cardiovascular system, causing elevated blood pressure and hypertension. Prolonged stress also disrupts circadian rhythms, which causes abnormal elevations in cortisol, the effect of which is to slow down healing from wounds. In a study among college students, their cuts healed about 40 percent slower when under the pressure of exams, as compared to when the same students were on summer vacation. And the effects are cumulative: the longer we stay in a prolonged stressful environment, the greater will be the negative effects on our health. Interestingly, couples in marriages that eventually end in divorce show physiological effects before they consciously admit that their marriage isn't working. It seems our bodies let us know we are running into problems without being aware of them ourselves.[7]

The health risks are enough to suggest you're better off leaving a chronic stress marriage. Along with eliminating the source of their stress, those who have left such marriages tend to have higher overall satisfaction with life in general and have better self-esteem than those who stay in these marriages. Many who stay in bad marriages do so because they would feel like failures if they left, believe they cannot be successful in another relationship, or believe they cannot make it on their own. Such reasoning often springs from poor self-esteem, but it is the marriage itself that can undermine how they feel about themselves and weaken their resolve to take control of their lives.

If the decision is made to leave a bad marriage, what follows is the traumatic process of divorce, the difficulties of which we discussed in chapter 1. Nevertheless, we eventually recover, and then we're faced with having to make another decision: we can remarry, stay single, or live with someone. While some may question whether marriage is the wisest choice, most take that path, and they do it quickly. On average, people remarry within four years after their divorce, and three in ten do so within the first year.[8]

Rob and Katie have been married for almost five years. This was the second marriage for both of them and both had children from their first marriage. Prior to their marriage, Katie had been divorced about eight years, while Rob was divorced about three years. By the time they married, their children were all adults, and all lived nearby.

Their difficulties stemmed from their children and not from their relationship per se. More specifically, the problem was how Rob's children felt about Katie. Katie's children had accepted Rob from the beginning, but Rob's kids held Katie responsible for Rob divorcing their mother. This is in spite of the fact that Rob and his first wife could not get along at all, which the children were well aware of, and that Katie and Rob only met about a year after Rob's divorce. The result was they treated Katie badly, ignoring her at times and treating her with open hostility and contempt at other times.

The truth is Katie was able to deal with his kids. She would have preferred a better relationship, but she accepted it as it was. However, she had a major problem with Rob's handling of the situation. He would not step in or confront them about their behavior. As a consequence, his relationship with Katie was floundering. She resented him for his lack of support for her, and these feelings came out in how she acted toward him and felt about her marriage.

Rob felt powerless to fix the problem. He regarded his relationships with his children as fragile, and he was afraid that a confrontation would mean an end to these relationships. Unfortunately, he was faced with choosing between two evils. He could do nothing and risk losing his marriage, or he could confront his children and risk losing them. He

could not accept the fact that his relationship with his children was actu-
ally unhealthy, and if it wasn't changed, it would always cause difficulties
for him, regardless of his marriage. Consequently, while he really had no
choice but to confront them and deal with the consequences, he could not
take that step, and so his marriage could not be improved.

Given how often it happens, we thought it would be useful to look at remarriages to examine whether things are easier or better the second time around. There are two opposing outcomes that seem reasonable. First, we might expect that people fine-tune their skills. From their first marriage, they've figured out what they want and don't want in a mate and can use those new criteria for their next marriage. They've also learned what they should and should not do, so they should be better partners. From this perspective we would predict second marriages should be successful.

However, it's also reasonable that they would be worse, or at least no better. We might go into a second marriage mistrusting people and anxious about our prospects for success. These thoughts and feelings can get in the way of committing to a new relationship. Or we may have personal characteristics that make it difficult to establish any long-term relationship, and practice has not made us any better. Additionally, because we're older, we might not have as many potential partners to choose from, so we might have to settle on someone who doesn't exactly meet our criteria.

Unfortunately, the latter perspective tends to prevail. Second marriages have a higher rate of failure than do first marriages. The divorce rate for first marriages is somewhere between 35 and 50 percent, but for second marriages it's estimated to be as high as 65 percent. They also tend to end more quickly, possibly because partners are better at reading the signs that the relationship isn't working, or because having gone through it before, they're less fearful of taking the step to divorce. Interestingly, men get divorced the first time most often because of an affair, and they usually marry the one with whom they had the affair. The divorce rates for these marriages are estimated to be as high as 80 percent. It would seem that cheating partners don't make the best marriage partners.[9]

Second marriages can have a lot of obstacles to overcome. The failure of first marriages can affect people in a number of ways. As we've mentioned, people may be fearful about making the required emotional commitment. They may still harbor anger, resentment, or feelings of betrayal, which they bring into their next relationship. That can make it hard for them to connect with their new partner. This is especially true if they did not want or seek their first divorce. Those who had divorce thrust on them take longer to recover from the trauma and suffer more emotional problems, which can leave them ill prepared for a new relationship.

First marriages can also affect how partners treat each other. Men actually do learn to change how they view their marital roles, making more concessions and taking more responsibility around the house. Women feel more empowered in their second marriage, learning from their prior relationship to stand up for themselves. However, their stronger sense of independence can make their new husbands feel insecure and emasculated. There's also a tendency for partners to be more vocal in expressing criticism and anger, and to be more protective of their rights. Consequently, there are more opportunities for conflict, and that can keep both partners on edge.

Second-time couples also have to cope with the reactions of their social circles. The more their social network supports the move, the greater will be the couple's adjustment to the second marriage. But sometimes they're not supportive. Some family and friends will have strong opinions about a couple's divorce and remarriage, and more than a few of these may be voiced. They may prefer the first spouse, or they may feel one of the new partners caused the break-up of the first marriage. When family and friends aren't supportive, they put the relationship on shaky ground. Partners may question whether they made the right choice in remarrying, or they may resent their new partners because they may regard them as the reason why they're rejected by their circle. [10]

The first spouse can also be a sore point. Despite anger and resentment, some may actually still feel a connection to their former partner even after remarrying. That sense of attachment can go on even if both partners have negative feelings about each other. Almost one-third of formerly married partners still feel connected to their former spouse even a year after divorcing, and about the same proportion of second wives claim to be jealous of their husband's ex-wife. If we sense that our spouse is still emotionally tied to their former partner, we're likely to feel insecure, and those feelings make it hard for us to commit fully to our new relationship. Prior spouses can especially be a problem if only one partner has one. The never-married may not understand the issues that follow their previously married partner from their first marriage. They're also more likely to expect exclusivity, and any ties to a former spouse, financial or otherwise, can interfere with the new marriage. A first-time married partner can feel threatened by the prior relationship, especially if the two former spouses have reasons to interact regularly, such as when they share children. Such situations are harder to tolerate and more likely to be a source of conflict than if both partners had been married before. That may be the reasons why these second marriages are less prone to work, as compared to marriages with two previously married partners.

For some couples, there may be alimony payments or other forms of asset loss. Money that has to be given to a former spouse can put a strain on a second marriage. Many remarried wives claim to run into more financial problems in their second marriages than in their first, and while they usually did not intend to remarry for money, financial hardships are often cited as the reason their second marriage failed.[11]

Probably the number one issue working against second marriages is stepchildren. Two families trying to meld into one can be extremely difficult. Most remarried husbands and wives feel their marriage would be better if there were no stepchildren. Stepchildren have been found, in fact, to be a major reason why second marriages fail at a relatively fast rate. One key factor is whether or not they all get along with each other. If there are poor relationships between a stepchild and a stepparent, that will undermine how a parent feels about their spouse. This is especially true for women: remarried wives evaluate the quality of their marriages primarily by the relationship she and her husband have with his and her children.

It's also hard to be a parent to someone else's child. It's not uncommon for couples to argue about what each child is entitled to, how they should be raised, and who's responsible for what in their care. Each parent also keeps a watchful eye to make sure their own child is being treated fairly. If they feel they're not, they might react with anger or even vengeance against their partner or the stepchild, or may question whether to stay in the marriage.[12]

Certainly quite a few second marriages remain together. However, we're not sure that many of these couples have actually improved their quality of life. There is no evidence that people are happier remarried versus staying single, and their marriages aren't necessarily any better than their first marriages. Alternatively, if they decide to just live together without a commitment to marrying a second time, they're likely to run into the same problems as those who live together without a commitment to a first marriage. Furthermore, they can feel pressure to keep the second marriage intact even if it's not what they wanted because failing again can be even more psychologically damaging. Partners might feel worse about themselves than after the collapse of their first marriage. Their sense of failure will likely be magnified, leaving them to question whether they have the skills or mind-set to make a marriage work at all. [13]

Considering the evidence with respect to the quality of life they produce, we would rank happy first-time marriages as the best lifestyle by a pretty wide margin. While many of us decide to marry because it's what is normally done in our culture, it turns out to be the best option and is likely to be for the foreseeable future. Next we would rank living together if you're older or have definite plans to marry. Regarding the remaining lifestyles, it's a toss-up as to which come next in the hierarchy. Each one has a few strengths but many weaknesses. Living as a single person has its freedom of movement and independence, but may lead to a gradually deteriorating quality of life and health. Living together outside of marriage limits commitment and simplifies a break-up, but there's no certainty as to its longevity, and that makes it hard to establish real intimacy and trust.

Understanding the advantages and disadvantages of each lifestyle is extremely important, because the one we choose will have a profound impact on our personal well-being and the quality of our lives. While marriage seems to be best, not all of them work out. A truly bad one has chronic stress as its defining feature, and unless that can be eliminated, it may be best to end it. However, chronic stress isn't found in most marriages, and if there isn't chronic stress, a marriage may not be as bad as you think. The reality is those who believe they would be happier with a different person or lifestyle will likely face a few unpleasant surprises. There's a chance they'll fail again, or if their marriage holds together, they could have a more complicated living arrangement, or worse, end up in a marriage that's no better than their first one. Our point here is if you believe your marriage isn't good enough, but at the same time it's not physically or psychologically harmful, you might be better off trying to make some improvements instead of just walking away. Finding a way to get there is what we will discuss in the upcoming chapters.

3

TRANSITIONING FROM LOVERS TO PARTNERS

The most important point to keep in mind about marriage is that it's a long-term relationship. That might seem like a trivial point, but it's really not. The way a marriage starts out is not what it eventually becomes. The relationship evolves, and how well we handle the transition depends on a lot of factors. One set of these factors has to do with our thought patterns. By that we mean our overall beliefs about marriage; what we need, want, and expect from a prospective partner; and the broader values and principles by which we live. In this chapter we focus on how these cognitive issues can determine the course and quality of our relationship.

One that falls into this class is how we think about love, possibly our most valued emotion. There is nothing else in the human experience that comes close to what happens when we fall in love. Being in love is wonderful because it makes us feel so good. There's the physical chemistry and feelings of ecstasy. The world and everyone in it is perfect, but even if it isn't, it wouldn't matter anyway because we only see the person we love. Our self-esteem is soaring because someone we think is the greatest person alive actually loves us back.

That's phase 1 of an intimate relationship, and unfortunately it usually doesn't last very long. In the next phase, the relationship evolves from one of absorbed lovers to partners, and for some couples that transition can be difficult. We have to adjust to a life that is completely shared with and in full view of another person. Doing it well entails acceptance of your partner's idiosyncrasies, acceptance of your own idiosyncrasies by your partner, lots of compromise, and an extremely thick skin. Above all, it requires that we adjust our thought patterns so that they are more in line with what marriage is really all about.

This isn't a revelation for couples even just a few years into their marriages. But for some couples just starting out and still thinking in terms of romance, they may not realize what's in store for them. Without having actually experienced a day-in-day-out relationship that extends on for years, there's no way to know what will be thrown at them and what it takes to make such a relationship successful. Newly married couples may also not entirely understand how love evolves over the long term. They will come to define their feelings toward each other less in terms of passion and more in terms of comfort and security.

Making the adjustment to the second phase is very much affected by how we think about it. We bring with us our personal perspective on what a relationship is supposed to be like. Among other things, this perspective includes our wants, needs, and expectations. It is these that can be problematic because many of the difficulties that couples face are a result of thinking the wants, needs, and expectations we hold onto are not being met.

The reality is we have lots of baggage we bring into our intimate relationships. From a very young age, we begin to develop patterns of thinking and behaving, much of which is learned from our parents, but it also includes the things we've experienced from other relationships. What we observed and experienced in our formative years sets the stage for how we think about many aspects of our own marriage. For example, if our parents divorced when we were a child, we may question the permanence of marriage, consider divorce as perfectly acceptable, or be skeptical about our chances of having a happy marriage.

From our past experiences and observations we also develop belief systems. These are the things we hold to be true about ourselves, our partners, and relationships in general. Belief systems are essentially a set of hard facts we live by. They guide how we act and think, and are the cornerstone of our values. When it comes to relationships, they give us standards for how we treat others, as well as expectations for how we want others to treat us. In effect, our belief systems are what are beneath our wants, needs, and expectations.

Michael and Jamie were in their mid-twenties and had been married about five years when they first came to therapy. As with many couples, they started out very happy and very much in love. However, about three years or so into their marriage, Jamie started to feel unhappy. She no longer felt attracted to Mike and wasn't sure she still loved him. Many of his traits that she used to regard as cute idiosyncrasies and habits now irritated her. As a result she had become much more critical and intolerant. She began questioning whether or not she made the right decision in marrying Mike.

Mike could not understand what was wrong with their marriage. He tried to find ways to make her happy but nothing seemed to work. That left him feeling insecure about their relationship, but at the same time he was frustrated and angry. He resented her constant criticisms, and he tended to react to these with his own criticisms of her, and that would lead to fighting and bad feelings. Jamie admitted that she thought Mike was actually a good husband and a caring individual, and really hadn't changed much from when they first were dating. Yet she was very disappointed with how her marriage had turned out and wasn't very motivated to fix it.

Jamie's disappointment stemmed from inaccurate expectations about marriage. She was just not emotionally prepared for how their feelings toward each other would change and become less passionate, and how these changes would affect how they treat each other. She didn't realize just how much married life can become routine and at times boring, that there are a lot of added responsibilities, and that at times a partner won't do or say what we want or expect. She also didn't recognize that it wasn't Mike or marriage per se that caused their relationship to change, it was the amount of time they were together. She would have experienced the same changes in her feelings in any other long-term relationship, so getting out of her marriage was not a solution.

Some beliefs are useful, but others can be wrong-headed. The latter ones can block us from making decisions that are in our best interests or from interpreting situations accurately. Some social scientists refer to these as dysfunctional or constraining beliefs. Renowned psychologist Albert Ellis, the founder of Rational Emotive Behavior Therapy, called them irrational beliefs. They include ideas that really have no basis in reality, but we still hold onto as unquestionable truths. The problem with such beliefs is that we won't readily give them up, even when there's proof that they're inaccurate.[1]

Constraining or irrational beliefs can interfere with our relationships even before we enter into them. For example, they can affect our decision as to whether, or to whom, or when, to marry. We might think we can't get married at a given point in our lives because we're not ready emotionally or we need our careers in a better place. Or we may feel we must get married right away because everyone we know is married, we're running out of time to have children, or we're worried we'll end up alone. When we feel pressure to marry, we might set standards so low that anyone who isn't already married or dead is a potential candidate. Or if we're afraid we might make the wrong selection, we may use such strict criteria that not even the gods would make the cut.

These beliefs are irrational because they don't describe an actual person. You may have very good reasons for not wanting to get involved with a particular individual, but that should have everything to do with the characteristics of that person and little to do with your general beliefs. The truth is we are all completely ready, and never ready, for marriage. And there's really no sure way to predict whether a relationship will ultimately work out, regardless of all the precautions we take when we are looking for a partner.[2]

After we've become involved with another person, some wrong-headed beliefs can interfere with our relationship progressing. These are the things we hold in our minds that affect how we interpret interactions with our partner. Here are a few examples of irrational things we might believe: couples should never argue; each partner should know what the other is thinking; love conquers all; people cannot change how they behave; men and women are inherently different and can never get along; and sex should always be perfect. For some couples, a few of these beliefs, or others like them, can be held onto well into their marriage.

Of course, we can see the irrationality of these beliefs. Arguments are unavoidable, and all couples argue. In fact, arguments can be quite healthy for a relationship. Confrontation is how we get clarity as to our partner's needs and give us a forum for presenting our own needs. And it's only the very naïve who believe love can overcome hardships—a few children or unpaid bills are usually enough to quash such thoughts. Sometimes sex is fantastic, and sometimes it's just okay. It can depend on the kinds of pressures or time constraints that are affecting each partner at the time. People may not be able to change their personalities much, but they can change how they act if they choose to, and actions are the way personality is expressed.

An important point about irrational beliefs is that it is difficult to resolve the problems they can lead to. It may not be easy to convince your partner that it's ok to argue if he or she is committed to the opposite point of view. Because they're not easy to deal with, such beliefs are detrimental to a relationship. They can work against emotional bonding because they affect how we evaluate our relationship and how we view our partner. They can also lead to disappointment because they set up unrealistic expectations about how two people should act and think in a relationship.

Another constraining belief we mentioned in the previous chapter is that we can test whether a marriage will last by living together beforehand. Unfortunately, that won't work because living together has characteristics that make it very distinct from marriage. How our relationship functions under that arrangement won't necessarily mirror how things will go as a married couple.

Another that's widely held is that romantic love is the main ingredient of marriage. In fact, romantic attachment is not a good criterion on its own for getting married, and its role in a long-term relationship is pretty limited. It's not that being in love is a bad reason to marry, it's just not good enough, and there are likely to be other features of a relationship that are much more important in later years.[3]

There are a number of reasons why romantic love is of only partial value to a long-term relationship, but first and foremost, as we pointed out early on, it's because it doesn't last very long. However, that doesn't mean love is not important at all, particularly in the early stages. In fact, the neurological events that occur when we experience love act as a motivator, leading us to pursue that person. Romantic love, or the thoughts and emotions that we experience as romantic love, might actually be the way our brains tell us we have found someone whom we should consider as a partner.

When we fall in love, the sections of the brain that contain high concentrations of dopamine become active. Dopamine is associated with rewards and motivates us to obtain rewards. When dopamine is released in our brains, we experience feelings of euphoria. Because of how that makes us feel we are driven to focus our attention and energy on the person who triggers that reaction. That's the motivational quality of romantic love. Through the release of dopamine, we become obsessed with the idea of being with the person who is causing us to have ecstatic feelings.

The same chemical reactions occur when we eat chocolate, take cocaine, or have an opportunity to make money. These are things that are highly rewarding and can be addictive to some people, and we feel addicted because of the chemical events they cause in our brains. When we're in love, we feel addicted to the target of our affections and want to be with them all the time, because of how good we feel when we're together, or more precisely, because of what happens in our brains. It's also the reason why it hurts so much for two people in love to be apart.

The brain in love also produces higher levels of oxytocin and vasopressin. These are involved in bonding between individuals, and they work to focus our sexual desires to one person. Oxytocin also works to keep our blood pressure and heart rate more controlled. Consequently, in the face of stressful events, we don't feel quite as agitated. That may be the reason why lovers seem to be happy with everyone and everything, not just each other. As a side note, some researchers propose that people who are suffering from unrequited love can be helped by drugs that inhibit the brain's release of oxytocin and vasopressin. If these chemicals can be suppressed, it might be easier to break the emotional attachment. Love also leads to increased production of nerve growth factor (NGF). This chemical is important for overall health, and is believed to play a role in a variety of illnesses and disorders such as heart disease, Alzheimer's, and diabetes, and has been found to speed up the healing process for cuts and bruises.

So, romantic love can enhance our physical health and emotional well-being. But it can also be debilitating. The expression that love is blind has a good deal of truth to it. When we're in love, the frontal cortex becomes less active. This section of the brain affects our ability to behave in a socially acceptable manner, make decisions that are in our best interests, and be aware of the consequences of our actions. When the frontal cortex is not operating at its full potential, we're not able to think as clearly as we normally might, so we're more prone to relax our judgment in sizing up other people. Unfortunately, that also means we may be less accurate in judging the person we're in love with. Many of us have been in love with someone and years later we can't figure out how or why we ever felt that way. A love-impaired frontal cortex may have been the reason.

Passionate love's relatively short lifespan—about two to three years for most people—is a result of habituation, the process of getting used to something. In time, any stimulus, including a loved one, loses its ability to dazzle. It's not necessarily that we get bored, although that could happen; it's just that the brain stops being overactivated, so we no longer feel the thrills as in the first stages. It's the same thing that happens when we do too much of anything. As a positive, however, couples can think more clearly when this phase ends. Then they can find out if they make as good companions as they do lovers. They might still make mistakes in assessing their compatibility, but it won't be due to neural malfunctioning.[4]

What's truly dangerous about romantic love is that it can cloud how we evaluate our relationship. When emotions settle down, we might think the relationship is coming to an end. However, in successful long-term marriages, the emotional connection between partners actually evolves from romance into what is best described as companionate love, which includes a mix of friendship and passion. Couples are comfortable but still affectionate to each other. While the passion may not be what it once was, many believe they have reached a higher form of love. They may also feel their relationship is easier to handle because it's not quite as emotionally charged.

Some couples might find the transformation from passion to companionship hard to accept. They may not realize the evolution is unavoidable. If they look to define their marriage primarily from a romantic perspective, they're likely to end up dissatisfied because the passion is hard to sustain. Worse yet, if they rely too heavily on emotions, they may not put in the right amount of effort before marrying to find out if they are compatible in other areas and if they like being with each other.[5]

The concept of "soul mate" is another dysfunctional belief about romantic love. This is the idea that there is only one person in the world with whom we are completely connected. Those who adhere to this notion believe no one can substitute for a soul mate: it is with that person alone that we have a special sense of relatedness and understanding.

As much as we'd all like to believe we have a soul mate, it's a dubious proposition. For one, the vast majority of us marry someone who comes from our own neighborhoods. In fact, propinquity—our tendency to marry someone who lives near us—may have more to do with whom we end up with than anything else. If we acknowledge the role of proximity, then we have to consider the astronomical odds of ending up with our soul mate. It would be a miracle if each of us would be able to find that one person in our own back yards. So if you feel you haven't married your soul mate and that makes you unhappy, keep in mind that the odds of actually meeting that one person are greater than 1 in 3 billion, and he or she might not even speak your language.

If lottery-type odds aren't enough, some researchers argue that a soul mate wouldn't necessarily make a good partner. The emotional and physical connection that is central to the idea of soul mate cannot be sustained indefinitely. As we pointed out, our brains won't cooperate. Furthermore, life events such as children, finances, household chores, and various other sources of conflict will affect how spouses feel about each other. When we don't feel quite as passionate or connected, we may then question whether the person we thought was our soul mate truly is. We then leave ourselves open to disillusionment.[6]

Our point is romantic love—soul mate or otherwise—is nice, but couples have to acknowledge the inevitability that their feelings for each other will move to lukewarm and their love will evolve. We have to accept the evolution from less passionate to more companionate as normal, not an indication of a love gone bad. The fact that you are no longer head over heels is not a reason to be disappointed, nor does it necessarily mean you are not right for each other. When you feel a passionate connection with someone, enjoy it while it lasts, but keep in mind that it's more important that you like that person's company, and that you will have things you can share in the future.

In fact, it's easier for couples to make the transition from lovers to companions when they have similar interests and perspectives. We tend to be more comfortable with someone who has the same values and beliefs, as well as religion, ethnic background, and education. When you and your partner share these characteristics, you eliminate them as sources of conflict. You also have an easier time communicating about many topics because you can relate to each other's point of view. You also may find your relationships more fulfilling when you enjoy the same activities and participate in them together. Similar interests can go further than romantic love in keeping two people connected to each other.

Couples are also better off if they have the same views on the roles of husbands and wives. Couples generally fall into one of two camps: They will either hold the traditional perspective of male breadwinner/female homemaker, or the more contemporary view that men and women are equal and have shared responsibilities. Whether partners hold onto traditional or egalitarian roles doesn't matter much, or at least not as much as being in sync. However, when one partner holds one perspective and the other partner the opposite one, they can have a hard time as they progress into their marriage. They have a lot of opportunities for conflict, especially if the husband holds onto a traditional male role and his wife expects gender equality. Over time they might come to feel they have little in common with each other.[7]

The age at which we marry can also affect the relationship's long-term success. Being similar in age is a good thing, because you go through various life stages together. However, it's also important that couples marry at the right age. If we marry too young, say, in our late teens or early twenties, the odds are we'll have a harder time keeping the marriage together. These are still the formative years, and very young couples may lack the emotional maturity and the skills to keep a relationship on an even keel. Additionally, it's questionable whether we could really know at a young age the qualities we want and need from a lifelong partner. If we guess wrong, there's a chance we'll grow apart. What might seem like a good match in youth might not be when we're older and more established.

Too young is problematic, but it may not be better if we marry much older. The difficulties for first-time-marrying forty-plus-year-olds relate to selection and habits. The longer we take to find a mate, the fewer are available, so we might find ourselves settling for someone who is less than right for us. And as we get more set in our ways, it can become harder to tolerate someone who doesn't match our own views and lifestyles.

For some who marry when they're older, there may be other factors that work against their marital success. There may have been something in their personalities or their belief systems that prevented them from getting married when they were younger. They may have had problems making the necessary commitment to marriage, or had unrealistic standards as to what they expect in a spouse. Any of these raise the question as to whether they have the right mind-set to make a good marriage partner.

Of course, not all marriages among the old or very young fail. It really depends on the personal characteristics of the partners. Some older people

remain flexible and open-minded, and some young couples end up growing together rather than apart. Generally speaking, however, the odds tend
to be against them. It seems the optimal age to get married is between the
late twenties to early thirties. By then you should have emotional maturity
and a sense of your own needs, but you're not so settled into habits that
you lack flexibility. Additionally, because your contacts and environment
are more expanded, you're more likely to find the right person rather than
just settling on someone who happens to live down the block. [8]

The idea that partners with similar traits and backgrounds might have
better long-term relationships raises the question of whether opposites
attract. However, we would consider this to be another wrong-headed
belief. Two people who have just fallen in love won't feel stressed by
their differences, because, well, they're thinking with their love brains.
They might find their dissimilarities to be interesting or refreshing, or
even exciting. However, they're not likely to feel that way later on in
their relationship. As they become more acclimated to each other, their
differences will become more apparent and obstructive. They may not
like to participate in the same activities, have different views on how to
manage their social lives, or they may not want to live in the same places.
Many of these couples will gradually feel that they haven't got much in
common, and that will get in the way of building a solid connection. [9]

*Roger and Cheryl have been married for about seven years. They
grew up in the same neighborhood and knew each other since they were
children, but they were very different people. Roger was an extremely
independent person with definite opinions on how he wanted to pursue
his life and what he expected of his marriage. He pursued his own interests and expected Cheryl to do the same. He did not want to complicate
his life with unnecessary responsibilities such as raising kids or owning a
house. Cheryl held a more conventional view of married life. She expected to spend a lot of time with their families, raise their own families,
and buy a house in a neighborhood close to where they grew up.*

*One of Roger's passions was gambling. He did not have a gambling
problem; he bet fairly small amounts, and he would never use money
earmarked for bills or other expenses. Cheryl, on the other hand, did not
gamble at all. In fact, she hated it. When they were still dating, Cheryl
was well aware of Roger's interest in gambling. At times she would even
accompany him to the track or a casino and would occasionally make*

bets. Before they married, she also knew how he felt about owning a house and raising children, and Roger was just as familiar with Cheryl's views on marriage.

Early on into their marriage, Cheryl began putting pressure on Roger to gamble less, take part in the activities that she liked, and raise a family. Roger remained adamant about not having children, and while they did buy a home, this became an added problem because he would not dedicate the time or effort to make repairs and improvements. Cheryl's demands that he change his priorities and "act like a normal husband" led to intense arguments and bad feelings.

Cheryl and Roger were angry and frustrated with each other because neither was willing to budge on what they wanted. Without being willing to compromise or to change their beliefs and expectations, their problems could not be resolved and their marriage could not improve. The truth is, however, that compromise was not a realistic option. There were too many important beliefs and expectations that each would have to give up. In effect, one or the other would have to become a completely different person. Both knew beforehand that they held extremely different views, yet both expected the other would change their perspective after they were married, or would at least be tolerant of their differences. They divorced about six years later.

Some couples might think that it's okay if they're very different because they will be able to change things after they marry. They believe they will be able to get their partners to act or think the way we want them to. That's another type of irrational belief. There are just some things that are beyond our control, and one of them is other people.

Each of us cherishes our right to make our own choices. No one can force us to change, and we have the right, within reasonable bounds, to choose our own paths. But just as we have this right, we must also acknowledge that our partners have the same right. The only things that we can control with any degree of certainty really come down to our own personal thoughts, behaviors, and emotions. These are the things that we personally own, and it is entirely reasonable and rational to believe we can control them.

However, that might not stop some people from trying to control their partners. We might believe things would be better if they would just do things the way we want them to. However, while we might believe we know what's best, the truth is we probably don't, and even if we did, there's no guarantee our partners will see it that way. Nor should they, because they have their reasons as to why they think and act as they do. Each of us thinks and acts a certain way because we get benefits and rewards from doing so. When someone requires us to behave differently, they remove the opportunity for us to get those rewards, and that can leave us feeling frustrated and resentful.

This is not to say that we can't influence our partners. However, influence means that we present information so our partners can understand our issues and needs. They can then use that information to make their own decision as to whether or not they want to make any changes so our needs can be fulfilled. Control, on the other hand, means that we tell our partners what to do or say and not give them an opportunity to make the decision on their own.

Trying to change our partner is not only unreasonable; it can be harmful to the relationship. Typically the spouse who wants the other to change continues to be disappointed, and that can cause them to stay frustrated and angry. The ones who have pressure to be different will likely regard their marriage as stressful and might resent their partners for making them feel that way. Such problems can't easily be resolved because partners are really working toward opposite objectives. Without resolution, they're likely to hold onto their anger and resentment even when they're not arguing about who should change what.

Besides, even if we could change our partner, it might not be in our best interests to do so. When we try to control another person, we are deciding we know the best way for that person to live. However, our way of thinking or acting might not be the best way for another person. Additionally, while we may believe we have our partner's interests at heart when we want them to change, we really don't. We are working from our own interests, and we want them to think and act in a certain way because it fills our own needs, not theirs. Finally, if you try to get someone to behave according to your needs, you become responsible for the outcomes they experience. That's a responsibility you should be happy to avoid, because when things don't go according to plan, you also end up sharing their problems and getting the blame.

In marriage, we don't have much choice but to accept that what we see in our partners is very often what we have to live with. If they have traits we don't like, we can suggest changes, but then we must leave it up to them to make their own decision as to whether such changes are in their own interests. If they decide not to, we are left with the choice of either accepting them with their faults and keeping them in our life, or breaking off our relationship. Turning them into something different is not an option. Acknowledging this fact is a good thing, since it may help to avoid disappointments and frustrations, and it takes quite a bit of pressure off of us to fix our partner's life and lets us dedicate more time to fixing our own. After all, if one of our major goals is to make our partner into someone different, it's possible that we have a few issues of our own to work out.

Beyond irrational beliefs, there are a few other factors that can affect how well couples adjust to a long-term relationship. One is how committed they are to the idea of marriage before they get married. If partners believe marriage is permanent, divorce is much less likely to be a consideration. There can be mitigating factors, such as physical abuse, which might force you to rethink your beliefs. However, beyond extreme events, your marriage has a better chance of succeeding because you'll put more effort into it. Couples who believe in the permanence also tend to minimize marital problems because they are less focused on their own needs and more on maintaining harmony in their relationship. [10]

Another is the characteristics we look for in a marriage partner. We already discussed the importance of similarities, but our search for a candidate also usually includes a comparison to an ideal. Each of us has a standard or a set of criteria we take into account for the ideal mate. We might want someone who is capable of intimacy, is attractive, or has a certain social and financial status. When we consider a potential candidate, we will size them up against our ideal. The more a person's qualities or traits are in line with our ideal, the more we're likely to think that person is a good match.

Unfortunately, not many of us end up with a perfect match. Some may come close, but there are usually one or more traits we're not crazy about. So we go through a process of aligning what we dreamed of with the actual characteristics of a potential partner. Being able to relax our criteria is important because people are pretty much stable. Who they are won't change dramatically, but ideals are adjustable. The alignment process between an ideal and reality requires that we make trade-offs. If a potential partner is especially warm or sensitive, we may forgive his or her lack of attractiveness, even if attractiveness is something that's important to us.

The trick is to make sure you can live with the trade-offs. If you can't, you may eventually come to feel conflicted about your relationship because you will continually compare your partner to a standard you hold in your mind. That might also mean your partner will be conflicted about you. They will sense your disappointment and will probably react with anger, resentment, and concern about the future of the marriage. With both of you feeling disillusioned, you will probably find yourselves in continual conflict. Quite often such conflicts are hard to resolve, because they will be about who you are as people rather than a particular issue.[11]

We defined ideal standards above as a set of parameters we use when we are trying to find a mate. Expectations are another type of standard. Both derive from our belief systems and are part of the mind-set that we bring to a relationship. However, expectations are also affected by what we learn about our partner as we get to know them better. We watch how they behave in different situations, and from there we have an idea as to how they will act when faced with other situations. Our expectations can guide how we think about partners, and can affect how we treat them.

Most couples enter marriage with positive expectations about their partner and their future together. Positive expectations have important benefits. When we expect our partners to say and do good things, we tend to interpret their words and actions favorably, even when they say or do things that are not so positive. We also tend to project a more positive attitude toward our partner, and that leads to better interactions and better feelings toward each other. Unfortunately, the reverse is also true. If our expectations are negative, we can project a negative attitude, and that can provoke negativity in return from our partner.

Positive expectations can be a problem when they're too positive. In *The Retirement Maze*, we found that people's expectations of retirement before they retire can affect how well they adjust after they actually leave the workforce. When they're too positive, very often the reality of retirement doesn't measure up. Some retirees are not as happy out of their jobs as they thought they would be, and those who feel that way tend to become disenchanted with their new lifestyle. Such disappointments can have harmful consequences. We're likely to experience a variety of negative emotions, including depression, and these emotions make it hard for us to get motivated because we don't think we can make our lives more fulfilling. Instead, we might look to get rid of our disappointment by getting out of the situation.

The same holds true for marriage. Exceedingly high expectations can be hard to satisfy, and when that happens we can become disappointed. Disappointment in turn can lead to demotivation about building the relationship further, but also to concerns as to whether marrying that person was the right decision. We should also note that, like romantic love, overly positive expectations can be blinding. Because we expect the best, we might initially overlook our partner's shortcomings, and only find out later that he or she isn't the person we thought we married.[12]

Expectations are also problematic when we use them as a measuring rod that guides our emotions. Here we are referring to wishes and *shoulds*—you should do this and not that, you should earn more, I wish you wouldn't say that, I wish you were a better cook, and so on. We might compare our partners' words and actions to what we expect, and then gauge how we feel or treat them based upon whether or not they measure up. But somewhere and somehow they will eventually fail the test. When that happens, the relationship is fine if we are forgiving (or at least not overly disappointed) and then adjust our expectations to fit better with how our partner actually behaves. If, on the other hand, our expectations are deeply imbedded and we have difficulty adjusting, we might be perpetually dissatisfied and our partner will be perpetually annoyed and resentful.

For both standards and expectations, it comes down to realism and flexibility. Keep an optimistic outlook and a positive perspective, but at the same time keep your eyes and your mind open. If you expect your partner to be a certain way or your relationship should follow a certain path and it doesn't, you might have to acknowledge that your expectations are too high and you need to make adjustments. Additionally, avoid using your expectations to judge your partner. Be aware that he or she will not always perform to your standards, but neither will you.

Here's another point to keep in mind to manage expectations. Marital satisfaction declines, and pretty early on. For most marriages they do so at varying rates of intensity throughout its course. The most dramatic drop-offs occur within the first few years or so, then again after seven to eight years, and then again when the first child enters their teen years. This latter period is usually when many couples are at their lowest point. Of course, not all suffer the same rates and depths of decline, and some may settle at a plateau after a few years. However, they never reach the high point of the first few months, and there doesn't seem to be later-year upswings. Furthermore, marriages don't just decline for couples with children. All marriages typically follow the same pattern, so going childless won't ensure you and your partner will be happier.

Nevertheless, on the positive side, the inclination to divorce goes down with the years. Most marriages that haven't dissolved after thirty years are either good enough or at least not bad enough to put up with the hassles of divorce and a single lifestyle. Besides, long-term marriages often leave couples' lives so intertwined that keeping a spouse might come to be seen as a lesser evil than a break-up.

However, it's not just that divorce becomes too difficult. Older couples may be better equipped psychologically to handle the demands of marriage. As people age, they operate less at an emotional level in virtually all of their relationships. With less emotional volatility, their marriages become more stable. Long-term marriages may still have the same annoyances and sources of irritation, but these rile partners less, while the benefits of companionship and a history together come to matter more. [13]

Our point is that, while a decline in quality is normal, many older couples feel their marriages are worth keeping. Certainly their relationship is different from the early days; but still they find a level of happiness that is fulfilling. By acknowledging that a drop-off is likely and that all relationships follow the same path, there's a better chance your expectations will be grounded in reality. When they're realistic, couples are less likely to experience disappointments, and more likely to keep a positive perspective about their partner and their marriage.

4

THE FOUR CORNERSTONES

In our opinion, there are four fundamental elements to a successful marriage. In and of themselves, these cornerstones won't guarantee success. Yet without them there's not much certainty that a relationship will be permanent, and there's little chance that it can withstand the problems that couples will face as they go through the course of their lives. They really form the foundation upon which everything else in a relationship is built. When they're missing, a marriage is characterized by unhappiness, insecurity, and emotional pain, and is as fragile as a house of cards.

COMMITMENT

Commitment is an unwavering allegiance to a relationship and a partner. Central to the idea of commitment is the conviction that regardless of what happens you are bound to your partner. Commitment helps to sustain a marriage, and the lack of it is one of the top reasons for its failure. In fact, even if couples think things aren't working out right at the moment, they're likely to feel better about it later on if they can stay committed to each other.

Commitment builds in a relationship as partners spend time together. It also comes in different forms, and while each form contributes to the stability of a relationship, certain types of commitment do more to strengthen the emotional connection between partners. As one of the more basic forms, people can be committed to their marriage for moral reasons. These couples typically have religious beliefs or social norms that compel them to stay in their marriage. There can be a sense of duty, concerns about how others might react if they were to divorce, or a need to follow the guidelines of their religion.

Another is practical or structural commitment. We become practically committed to our partner through intermingling of our resources. Together we accumulate money and other material possessions, have children, establish a social life, and come to have our personal identity defined as a member of a couple. In effect, practical commitment entangles partner's lives together, and it can do it to such an extent that it makes it easier to stay in a relationship than to leave it.

For both moral and structural commitment, partners believe they have no choice but to stay married. They have agreed not to shirk their responsibility to the relationship, regardless of whether or not they're happy. These forms of commitment also rely on external factors to keep the marriage together. Partners are bound to their marriages because of children, finances, morals, and so on. They do not take into account individual desires, nor do they imply that partners are personally connected to each other. Instead, the marriage is held together by things that are not directly part of their one-on-one relationship. [1]

A third form is personal commitment. This one is much more complicated than just entangled lives, and is most important for the success of a marriage. As its defining feature, personal commitment has an emotional component not necessarily found in moral or structural commitment. Personally committed partners see their relationship and their emotional bonds as the most important thing in their lives. They genuinely care about each other and stay married because they want to, not out of necessity or a sense of duty and responsibility.

The emotional aspect of personal commitment helps to make a marriage better because how we feel about each other regulates how we treat each other. Personally committed couples work harder to keep their relationship on solid ground. When they're dealing with conflict, they will try to diffuse the situation and not let it get out of control. Emotional commitment also makes us more accommodating. We're more willing to sacrifice our own needs and desires so that we can pursue ones that serve us as a couple. We're also more likely to hold onto positive thoughts about our marriage and be supportive of our partner, and because we cherish our relationship, we're less likely to be unfaithful, and we're more prone to regard our relationship as better than that of other couples.

As another distinguishing characteristic, partners who are personally committed are interdependent. By that we mean they rely on each other to fill their individual needs. As a result of having these needs satisfied, interdependent couples become psychologically attached to each other. They come to think of themselves not as individuals but as a member of a team, sharing aspirations, thoughts, and interests, all of which strengthen their desire to stay in the relationship.[2]

Interdependency is not dependency. In a dependent relationship, needs are also filled by a partner. However, the need-filling goes in only one direction, that is, one person provides and the other receives. Dependency also doesn't necessarily mean commitment. You can be dependent without being committed to that person. If the reasons why you're dependent on someone no longer exist, you may or may not stay in that relationship. If you stay in a marriage for financial reasons, and you win the lottery, you're no longer financially dependent and you can choose to leave that relationship.

We can have all three forms, but the one that really matters is personal commitment. While moral and structural commitment may keep couples together, they really don't say much about how couples feel about each other. When we feel we have no choice but to stay married, we may be dedicated to our marriage, but we won't necessarily be dedicated to our partners. That means we might not put in a lot of effort trying to make the marriage happy. Furthermore, because we're committed to the idea and not the person, we might not express much interest or affection for our spouse. The truth is, as hard as they might try not to, couples who are only morally or structurally committed are at greater risk of divorce than those who are personally committed.[3]

Still, any form of commitment is better than none. All three suppress one of the major threats to marriage—options. Here we are referring to holding onto thoughts that there's a better way to live, either with other partners or in another lifestyle. Typically these emerge during conflicts, or boredom, or when feeling overburdened, and they work to break down a relationship because they present a way out that might seem better at the time.

Rich and Joann came to therapy after eleven years of marriage. They believed their problems had to do with communication. Whenever there was an issue, it would turn into a shouting match, with each taking turns accusing the other of some wrongdoing. These arguments rarely produced solutions, and their ill feelings toward each other usually lasted long after the arguing ended.

During one session, they got into a heated exchange. They stopped arguing when Rich shouted out, "I don't need this nonsense!" When they calmed down, I asked Rich what he meant by that. He explained that he considered their arguments to be a waste of time because they didn't get anywhere. He also mentioned that his past relationships were never as contentious and their arguments weren't so filled with hostility, and sometimes he thinks he would have been better off not getting married. Rich also admitted that he occasionally thought about being single, even when he and Joann were getting along fine. When they argued, however, these thoughts came up much more often.

Their difficulties had less to do with communication styles than with Rich's thought patterns. His comments about leaving his marriage suggested he was not thinking about the problem they were arguing about. They also couldn't solve their problems because he was usually focusing on a way out rather than a way to make their marriage better. And because they couldn't come to solutions, they would stay angry at each other.

Fueling their problems further was Joann's reaction to Rich's comments about "not needing this nonsense." As soon as he said something to that effect, she would no longer think about their problem and instead would think that he doesn't want to be married to her. She interpreted his comments as rejection of her and their marriage. She kept them in her mind long after the arguing stopped and would stew over them for days. That would leave her feeling perpetually angry and frustrated, and she would express these strong feelings whenever there was even the smallest provocation. Rich was not aware that he had never made a complete commitment to his marriage and that was what was causing the hostility.

Couples who are truly committed to each other work hard to prevent alternative partners or lifestyles from being considered. If they find themselves in situations where they're tempted, they might rely on mental tricks to drive such thoughts out of their minds. One of these is devaluation. They will think about that person or lifestyle in less than flattering ways or make comparisons to their current relationship. They will work this out in their minds in such a way that the alternative will always fall short.

Devaluation is a better way to handle such situations than just denial. If, for example, we see an attractive person and we just say no, we are trying to deny ourselves something we think is pleasurable, yet we will still find the person to be tempting. However, if we change how we think about that person by critiquing them as less attractive or damaged in some way, we avoid having to make a difficult choice. In that way we give ourselves peace of mind by eliminating that person as someone worth pursuing.

Dismissing options is an extremely important point because when we don't, they can affect how we act in our relationship. However, some people may not even be aware that they have options floating around in their heads, or they believe having such thoughts is harmless. For example, if during a conflict we say out loud or to ourselves something like "I don't need this aggravation" or "I should get a divorce," we may not try too hard to fix a problem because we're not convinced that we have to stay with our partner. Couples may also find that when they consider alternatives, they will argue more often and their tone is more hostile. That's because they might harbor anger and resentment just below the surface as a result of feeling stuck in their marriage, and these feelings can emerge when things are not going well.[4]

As we've mentioned, personal commitment grows over time. However, time is not the only ingredient: it really depends on how that time is used. Whether or not couples actually achieve the level of personal commitment essential for marital success depends on the qualities of their relationship. It becomes stronger as we become more intimate and as we grow together with our partner. It's also strengthened if partners feel and act positively toward each other. Additionally, partners' attitudes tend to feed on each other. If one is expressly committed, that can get the other to move in the same direction. Of course, one person's commitment doesn't guarantee their partner will feel that way, but there's a very strong chance that if one hasn't committed, neither will the other. On the other hand, marriages characterized by negativity or conflict, those that are thought to be unfair or one-sided, or those that leave a partner's needs unsatisfied are not likely to get a spouse to want to stick around for the long term.

Furthermore, commitment can decline over time: even if partners start out highly committed, they might become less so if the relationship has other problems.

It's not just marital conflicts or negative interactions that block personal commitment. Some people have trouble making a commitment because they can't connect emotionally with others. Without that connection, personal commitment can't happen. Additionally, some may not realize just how important personal commitment is, or that what seems like harmless daydreaming about alternatives can work against it. Of course, occasional daydreaming or fantasizing is harmless, but it's not if it becomes a habit. Whatever the reason, without total personal commitment, couples may not have as rewarding a marriage as they could and may experience more difficulties than they need to.[5]

Working to strengthen your personal commitment is in your own best interests. Posing a few questions to yourself can give you an idea where you stand: When things get tough, do you wish you were somewhere else or with someone else? Do you stay in your marriage because you want to or because you have to? Do you see yourself mostly as part of a couple or as an individual? If you find you're not as committed as you can be, you can fix that by making the appropriate adjustments to your thought patterns (since you own your thoughts, you can change them if you want to). If you cannot adjust your perspective, be aware that your partner will likely be less committed to you and that can weaken both of your resolves to achieve a happy marriage.

As we pointed out, treating each other with kindness and consideration helps partners feel committed to each other. When things are tough, a relationship can be kick-started again by a random benevolent action, one that has no strings attached. Simple acts such as bringing home flowers or a small gift, or doing something that your partner enjoys, are seen as demonstrations of commitment and caring, and that can lead to reciprocal feelings from your partner. Of course, we should also point out that you can't buy commitment. Random acts of kindness will not be enough if you're not kind most of the time, or if your relationship lacks any of the other cornerstones.

TRUST

Trust goes hand in hand with personal commitment and is essential for the stability of any relationship. Trust lets us feel secure about our marriage because we believe our partner has our back and is loyal through thick and thin. Trust is also what lets us display our thoughts and feelings openly and honestly, without worrying that our partner will judge, ridicule, or reject us.

Some researchers argue that trust comes after commitment. When we become committed to another person, we think of our own interests as secondary to those of our new partnership. From personal sacrifice and positive interactions, partners realize they can rely on each other, and that leads them to trust each other. However, it's also possible that things happen the other way around. Once you feel you can trust someone, you can then decide whether or not you want to commit to them. Regardless of which one comes first, the two tend to be reciprocal. Improvements in one will often lead to improvements in the other.[6]

Trust, like commitment, builds slowly as we learn about our partner and they become predictable to us. Predictability is important because when we have an idea of what will happen in a given situation, we feel more in control of our lives. By learning how our partner thinks and acts, we can figure out whether or not he or she has our best interests at heart. If they have consistently acted like they do, we can believe they will continue to do so in the future, so we can trust them. There's also an element of faith operating with trust because we really can't know what our partner might do or say before the fact. Having faith in our partner, meaning we believe they will do right by us before they do it, is considered to be a pretty good indicator of a trusting relationship.

As we mentioned, relationships are more stable when partners trust each other. Trust makes us feel secure, and that makes us feel good about our partner and believe our relationship has long-term potential. These positive thoughts work to keep our emotions on an even keel. When emotions are under control, they don't get the better of us. So we're able to discuss problems openly and with little or no hostility, and have an easier time coming to solutions. We're also able to keep many conflicts in perspective and not use any single event to judge the overall quality of our relationship. Additionally, it's easier to forgive most indiscretions because we don't take them personally and we don't believe our partner would intentionally hurt us.[7]

Jeff and Kathy had trouble discussing almost any issue. Even minor disagreements would include a lot of arguing, yelling, and accusations. As background, Jeff was mostly a likeable and calm person. However, when it came to Kathy, he seemed to have no patience at all. With her he had a very quick temper, and whenever she questioned him about something, he found it impossible to keep his cool and instead would lash out at her.

When asked about Jeff's behavior, Kathy said she felt like he hated her, but she also felt that his reactions during an argument suggested he was hiding things from her. Jeff's response was that she always thought he was hiding something, and she didn't trust anyone. He said that no matter what they were arguing about, she would look at him suspiciously and would keep questioning him to see if he might reveal a lie. He added that, even when she seemed to believe him, he felt that she was judging him. In fact, he said that sometimes he wasn't totally forthcoming, usually about minor things, because he thought she would overreact or be extremely critical of him.

At first Kathy's behavior made Jeff very uncomfortable. He said that at times he would even come to question himself, and began to wonder if there was something wrong with him. After a while, however, he could not help but react intensely whenever she wanted to talk about something. Her lack of trust and criticisms had gotten to be unbearable. He had grown tired of constantly having to defend himself and would become hostile right from the start of a conversation because he knew the direction it would take.

Kathy's issue with trust was a problem, but it was made worse by her tendency to be judgmental. That made him leery about being totally forthcoming with her, which reinforced Kathy's belief that Jeff was untrustworthy and led her to scrutinize what he had to say. Because Kathy couldn't trust Jeff's intentions and Jeff reacted with anger in anticipation of being criticized and regarded as untrustworthy, it was difficult for them to avoid feeling hostile toward each other.

As important as trust is, it's also extremely fragile, and it can dissolve quickly from a single indiscretion. If that event is extreme, such as infidelity, it can be almost impossible to reestablish and will undermine other aspects of a marriage. One of the main casualties is communication. Because we can't trust what our partners are saying, we can have trouble talking to each other. We might avoid discussing problems because we worry that such discussions will lead to bigger battles. For some, they will only take on contentious issues after they've become so emotionally charged that they can only react with anger and hostility. They might also feel they have to be very careful in choosing their words, because they can't be sure how their partner might react to what they say. Or they may feel they can only communicate indirectly through jokes or off-hand remarks, because they don't think they can broach certain topics head on. Under such conditions, it's not surprising that these couples argue much more frequently, and their disagreements have a more negative tone and rarely lead to resolutions. [8]

Partners who don't trust can't feel secure with each other, so their relationship will cycle through frequent emotional highs and lows. That happens because a mistrusting partner's insecurity leads them to try to find out whether the relationship can work. They will closely scrutinize their untrustworthy partner to understand their motives. When their words or actions seem trustworthy or positive, the questioning partner feels happy and has hope for the relationship. But when some untrustworthy or negative event happens, it's used as evidence that the relationship has problems. When we don't trust our partner, we're prone to exaggerate their negative behavior and discount their positive behavior. So because the positives have much less weight than the negatives, we're likely to constantly question the goodness of the relationship. [9]

Sometimes a breakdown in trust is a result of actual indiscretions by one or both spouses. But that's not always the case. Some people, for various reasons, have trouble trusting anyone, and they may not trust their partner regardless of whether or not that person is trustworthy. Those with trust issues often have a few other patterns of thinking and acting that make it difficult for them to have any type of relationship. They tend to be critical of others, interpret situations in a cynical or negative light, and are less willing to give people the benefit of the doubt. Interestingly, low-trust people are themselves more prone to lie and cheat than are trusting people. It's possible they justify such behavior because they believe others are doing the same thing to them.

Low-trust people bring to their marriage the same problems that are found among couples in which one partner truly can't be trusted. They have trouble communicating, constantly question their partner's motives, and allow their feelings of mistrust to cloud their overall perceptions of their partner and their marriage. Furthermore, because they tend to be highly critical, they will look upon what their partners say and do with much less tolerance than would a trusting person. They might also regard their partner's questionable words and deeds as personally threatening, and that can cause them to overreact to minor indiscretions. As a consequence, small problems can have a bigger impact than they normally should.

Someone who's married to a low-trust person will also face problems. They might feel there's constant pressure to make sure they come across as honest and trustworthy. Such scrutiny can mean they have to spend more effort than should be necessary justifying themselves. They might also think there's a "Kafkaesque" quality to their relationship. They feel punished or criticized for no reason, and yet guilty and helpless to fix a problem that really doesn't exist. Along with feeling frustrated and possibly resentful, they're likely to feel insecure about themselves and their relationship. As a result, they're likely to find it difficult to stay personally committed to their partner.[10]

Unfortunately, there's not much advice to be offered if your partner truly can't be trusted. You can try to discuss the issue, but that's not likely to lead to a meaningful solution. If they're really untrustworthy, how can you believe their promise not to be? The hard truth is a relationship without trust cannot flourish long term. It's extremely difficult to disregard or de-emphasize such a flaw in your partner, because its existence will leave you feeling insecure about your relationship, and that in turn makes it hard to feel emotionally connected.

However, if your mistrust is more perceived than real, or is based upon very minor transgressions (e.g., little white lies), then the issue comes down to your perspective, and that's something that can be fixed. If you believe all or most people are untrustworthy or dishonest, or you often feel suspicious about other people's motives, then you might want to consider that your inability to trust your partner stems from your personal issues. Individual therapy can be very effective in developing strategies that will help you cope with mistrust. Keep in mind that learning to trust is certainly worth the effort. Not only will it improve a marriage, but it will help you in other relationships and can improve your overall psychological well-being.

FIDELITY

Having a partner who is faithful is an entitlement of marriage. Fidelity on its own won't necessarily guarantee a marriage will remain intact, but infidelity can surely end one. In fact, it's one of the greatest threats to marital stability. It is a betrayal of one's partner and the marriage vows, and it is a primary reason why couples get divorced in our society. Nothing breaks down trust and commitment more, and there's no violation harder to overcome than cheating.

Some marriages can withstand an affair, and for a few, the outcome might even be positive. Partners might be forced to deal with problems they weren't aware of and as a result have a chance to develop a closer and more honest relationship. More typically, however, the impact is traumatic. A betrayed partner might experience weakened self-confidence and may develop trust or commitment issues that will affect their current marriage, and may carry over into their future relationships.

The taboo against cheating is so strong that even most of those who have done it still regard it as wrong. While their beliefs are inconsistent with their actions, they get around that with some rationalizing. In principle they agree infidelity is bad, but they can excuse their own as a special case. It's because of flaws in their marriage or in their own personalities. They also believe that, taken on a case-by-case basis, others who have cheated probably also had good reasons, so at least they're not hypocritical.[11]

It's difficult to pinpoint how many couples have affairs because most people aren't forthcoming about such things. Surveys indicate that as many as 35 percent of men and 20 percent of women have done so, but our guess is the percentages are higher than that, and the incidence among women may be particularly underreported. Cheating tends to be seen as more offensive when it's done by women than by men, so women may be even less likely to admit to it. Furthermore, while men from past generations were more likely to have affairs, the greater equality between the genders today might lead women to behave more like men.

There's another reason why infidelity rates among both genders may be higher than reported. Couples have more threats to fidelity than prior generations. With the increase of women in the labor force, men and women today share an environment where close relationships can easily develop. Consequently, they have more opportunities to meet members of the opposite sex with whom they have similar interests and goals. [12]

Jim and Lucy came to therapy to fix what they thought was an impossibly damaged marriage. Their decision was triggered by Lucy having discovered that Jim had an affair. This was a one-night stand with a person to whom Jim had no emotional connection at all. Through trying to discover what led to his affair, it came out that they had not had sex in more than two years. In fact, most nights Lucy would go to bed and Jim would fall asleep on the couch and spend the night there. They also had few interactions on other levels. They talked only about issues they couldn't avoid and did not look to each other for emotional support.

That's not to say that they didn't try to improve their marriage. At times Lucy would demand that they discuss their problems, but Jim typically had little to offer and instead would withdraw. Lucy would then react angrily, thinking Jim either didn't care about their marriage or wasn't emotionally mature enough to work on their problems.

Jim's inability to express himself emotionally exhausted Lucy's patience, and that affected how she acted. She treated him with disdain and with little respect, and in fact regarded him as childish, and these feelings diminished her interest in sex. Jim seemed to ignore how she treated him, or at least would not confront her about it. However, while he was mostly an easy-going person, he would often get extremely angry over minor problems in the household or with the children. These inappropriate outbursts may have been triggered by how Lucy treated him. But because he couldn't confront Lucy directly, he took it out in other ways. These outbursts only made Lucy feel worse about Jim.

Lucy certainly couldn't accept that Jim cheated on her, nor could she understand that, when asked to discuss their problems, he would have nothing to contribute. It's true that Jim was not in touch with his emotions and was not very good at expressing himself. However, Lucy also wouldn't accept the idea that her treatment of him worsened his emotional withdrawal and ultimately led to his affair. In the end, she was shocked and angry when, after twenty-five years of marriage, Jim asked for a divorce. I think her surprise came from her belief that she, not Jim, should have been the one to ask for a divorce. Regardless, the reality is Lucy's need for an emotionally expressive partner and Jim's inability to get there suggests their marriage could never have been a happy one.

There are lots of reasons why people have affairs. They may do it out of curiosity, a desire for something new and exciting, to boost their ego, because of an emotional or intellectual connection with another person, or because of a disconnection with a spouse. Some may do it to advance their careers, while others to get revenge on their spouse for some wrongdoing. For some men, there's also a sense of entitlement; they regard cheating as culturally acceptable for their gender, so they're predisposed to it.

There are also different kinds of affairs. Some are purely physical, some purely emotional, and some are a combination of the two. Men and women differ in terms of which ones they tend to experience. Men mostly take part in the purely physical, while affairs for women usually include at least some emotional connection. Affairs that include emotions tend to be more damaging, because they often include a corresponding emotional breakdown with one's spouse. So while women may cheat less, when they do, it's at much greater risk to the marriage.

Emotional affairs start out differently than strictly physical ones. Physical affairs are often spontaneous and based on mutual attraction and availability, and love has nothing to do with it. Those that include emotions, on the other hand, take time to develop and aren't typically planned or actively sought. They might happen as two people get to know each other, and their relationship often begins innocently as a friendship. While initially they may not look on each other as potential love interests, sex happens as they get closer to each other and develop a stronger connection.

Generally speaking, extramarital affairs don't just happen by chance, even those that start out innocently or have an emotional side. There's usually something wrong with the marriage. If partners feel there's a lot of hostility, or if they feel marginalized, unappreciated, or disrespected, or the relationship is unequal in terms of giving and receiving, the stage is set for them to look elsewhere for attention and affection. Such problems make partners feel badly, and they use affairs to make themselves feel better. Again, men and women often differ in how they define a marital problem. Women tend to have an affair if they're unhappy with the overall relationship, whereas men are more likely to do it if they're unhappy with the frequency or quality of their sex lives. It's also worth noting that while a man won't necessarily have an affair because he's dissatisfied with his marriage, he might use that as an excuse. In other words, he might fool around regardless of whether he sees his marriage as good or bad, but if he thinks it's bad, then he can feel justified. [13]

It's not just hostility or unfairness that makes a marriage unhappy; sometimes it's ambivalence. Marriages that have partners who are emotionally disconnected and uninvolved in each other's lives are just as vulnerable. Additionally, there's a greater risk of infidelity if one partner feels the other is not fully committed. Both may cheat in this scenario: the more committed partner to protect themselves, and the less committed partner because their low commitment makes them more likely to consider alternatives. A partner might have personal issues that make them more prone to consider an affair, regardless of how they feel about their marriage. One such issue is attachment style. This refers to the kind of bonds we make with other people. We can have either secure or insecure attachment styles, and it's the insecure kinds that are problematic.

As we mentioned earlier, some people have trouble making an intimate connection to others. These people tend to develop an avoidance-attachment style, which means they maintain an emotional distance in all of their relationships. Because they keep themselves detached, they can't build a strong personal commitment to their partner. At the same time, because they're married, they know they can't build an emotional attachment to another person. Affairs can actually work quite well for those with avoidance-attachment styles. Their personal issues allow them to carry on emotionally disconnected relationships with both a spouse and a lover.

Another that's conducive to having affairs is an anxiety-attachment style. Those with an anxiety-attachment style worry about abandonment. They typically doubt their partner's feelings about them and their commitment to the relationship. As a result, they don't feel as connected as they'd like to their spouse. That makes them look for a stronger connection with someone else, and they use their worries about their spouse's intentions as justification. Establishing bonds to others is essential for their self-esteem, and that's what an affair can provide. And because self-esteem and fear of abandonment are the primary motivators, the affair is usually not just physical. It's the emotional connection that they want, not just sex.[14]

However they get there, partners usually cheat to make themselves feel better. Unfortunately, that's not how things often work out. Most people experience guilt, and some suffer bouts of depression, and virtually all will spend their lives in fear of the consequences if their partner should find out. Emotional affairs are not always quite as problematic as purely physical ones. There tends to be less remorse, possibly because the emotional connection helps to justify their actions, and that's especially so if the cheating partner is emotionally unfulfilled at home. However, regardless of whether the affair is physical or emotional, no one gets off completely from feeling bad after the fact. The truth is if people could keep in mind the discomfort they will likely experience, they might conclude that an affair is not worth the effort.[15]

Given how damaging infidelity is to a marriage, should a cheating spouse confess? While honesty may be the best policy in most situations, we're not so sure that rule applies here. There might be some benefits to owning up: it alleviates guilt, provides couples a chance for a higher level of honesty, and focuses partners' attentions on the cause of their problems. But the downside is much more extreme. A partner's infidelity can hang over the marriage like a dark cloud for the rest of their time together (which will probably be brief after the admission). More importantly, it can scar the faithful partner emotionally and psychologically, and at the same time it won't provide directions for fixing the problem that caused it. On the other hand, letting the episode pass unannounced, while seemingly sleazy, may be the best chance a couple has to move forward together, if they can keep in mind that there's a still a problem to be fixed.

If you discover your partner has been unfaithful, you can either try to come to terms with it or end the marriage. While your first inclination will be the latter, avoid making a hasty decision, as difficult as that might be. If you decide to try and get past it, focus on the issue that led to the affair and avoid ruminating, that is, reliving the event over and over in your mind. Remember that infidelity is usually a symptom of other problems, so the best you and your partner can do for your future is to try to uncover the underlying issues.

From the opposite perspective, if you're considering an affair, you'd be better off in the long run trying to understand why you feel that way rather than looking for a willing prospect. Use those feelings as the basis for a discussion with your partner. Sometimes the issue is clear, such as you don't respect me or we don't have sex often enough, and the conversation is easy, or at least has a specific direction. Sometimes they can be difficult because the issues that lead to such desires can be complex and not always obvious. However, even if it's hard to figure out the reasons, you should still take this path, because you might find that an affair will make you feel worse, not better, and the problem that led you in that direction will still be there.

EMOTIONAL SUPPORT

In a successful marriage, we see our partner as the go-to person for issues we face inside and outside of our relationship, and we look to them in our time of need. Couples regard supportiveness as a purer form of love and caring, because the one giving support does it for their partner and not for themselves. When we're supportive, we take on ownership of our partner's problem, and that makes us both feel more connected to each other. When we are supported, we believe we have more control over our problems, and that makes us feel like we're better equipped to handle them. Support can also contribute to mental and physical health. It does this by reducing stress levels and providing protection from emotional problems, such as depression.

A spouse is the most important provider of support. We might confide in friends and family members, but we won't do it to the same extent as with our spouse, nor do we want to. It's only when we feel we can't rely on our spouse do we look to outsiders, but even in such circumstances it's mostly women who will do that. Women have closer relationships with other people and find it easier to talk about personal issues. Most men, on the other hand, have fewer people they're willing to confide in. Furthermore, they will only reach out to their friends as a last resort. Needing to go to others for help means they have to admit that they're not in complete control of a situation. Having to acknowledge that fact can make them feel inadequate and think of themselves as failures. [16]

Cathy had come to feel that Joe wasn't there for her when she needed him. She said that it wasn't always like that. When they were first married, she would come to him with her problems and they would talk about them as long as she wanted to. Over the past few years, however, he had come to avoid these conversations, and Cathy interpreted this as a sign that Joe no longer cared about her. That had led her to change how she felt and acted toward Joe, and that has caused both of them to pull back emotionally from each other.

Joe explained that his feelings for Cathy hadn't changed at all, but he found that trying to help her was very difficult. When he tried in the past, they would end up fighting, and these arguments had nothing to do with her problem. She would bring up an issue, and he would offer suggestions, but his advice would usually make her upset. She would get angry and tell him that he was absolutely no help to her. After a while, Joe was afraid to offer any opinions because he knew she would react badly to whatever he said. Gradually, Joe would withdraw whenever he was pulled into these discussions.

Cathy's frustration often resulted from the kind of advice that Joe gave. Some men operate from a very practical problem-solution perspective; if you have a problem, here's how to fix it, and don't think about how you feel about it. But women often take a more emotional perspective. For example, Cathy would tell Joe she was upset by something a friend said or did. His response might be to avoid seeing that friend or to say that what that friend said or did wasn't important. He might ask her why she would ever care about what happened or would tell her to forget about it. However, she was not interested in avoiding this friend, nor could she not worry about the issue because she felt it interfered with their friendship.

At these times all she really wanted from Joe was a sympathetic ear. Providing the kinds of solutions he thought made sense was useless to Cathy, and that made her feel frustrated and unsupported. Furthermore, by saying to "forget about it" made her problem appear trivial, and Cathy considered that belittling and insulting. Considering their different perspectives and Joe's approach to his own relationships, he would have been better off just listening to Cathy and providing a sympathetic shoulder rather than telling her how to fix her problems.

There are a lot of ways partners can be supportive. It can be through finances, companionship, and help around the house. All of these are important, but it's emotional support that really affects how partners feel about each other. From time to time each of us will be caught in difficult situations, or we might run into problems with friends, family members, and other acquaintances. Knowing that we can rely on our partner for comfort, security, and possibly advice makes us feel like our problems are important and we're not facing them alone, and that enhances the value of our relationship.

Partners in good marriages also tend to support each other on their individual interests and goals. Supporting our partner's goals shows that we care about their needs outside of the marriage. We also validate the importance of these goals, and when we do that, we validate them as people and help them to stay motivated to pursue these goals. On the other hand, if we don't care about our partner's interests, they might also come to see them as not worth pursuing. In effect, we've rained on their parade. This in itself is hurtful; but worse than that, when we reject what's important to our partner, they can take that as a personal rejection, and that's something they might hold against us. In other words, by devaluing their interests, we devalue them, and they in turn can come to devalue their relationship with us.

Men and women can have very different perspectives regarding emotional support. As we said, women are much more comfortable giving and receiving it, and it's easier for them to identify and relate to other people's problems. In marriage, they're more likely to be on the lookout for difficulties faced by their husbands and are better at reading when their husbands are distressed. Consequently, they're in a better position to step in without being asked. Women also value support more, and the extent to which they receive it has a lot to do with how they feel about their marriage. Unfortunately, many men value it less, and they don't seem to be quite as helpful, or at least that's how many wives see it. However, it's not that they're less involved or don't care. Some husbands might not be able to identify when their wives are having problems because they don't pay enough attention to their cry for help.

What makes this a particular issue is that when wives have problems, they often communicate them indirectly. They will talk about a problem without openly asking for help, or she might use emotional messages, such as moods, rather than words. That leaves it to her spouse to pick up on her need for help, and he's not likely to be very good at that. Furthermore, if he fails to read her subtle or nonverbal cues, she might use that as an indication that he just doesn't care enough about her.

Some husbands might also trivialize their wives' issues. He may feel her problem is not as big as she's made it out to be. He might then choose to ignore her distress, or worse, he might ridicule her or behave impatiently when she tries to explain what's wrong. Such reactions can undermine her ability to cope with the problem, but also gives her an added problem—her husband can't understand or won't support her.

Some husbands may not provide the kind of support their wives are looking for. Men typically approach problems from a concrete perspective. They give instrumental support—that is, they try to provide specific advice as to how to fix a problem. Women, on the other hand, give more emotional support—that is, empathy and sympathy—and very often that is the kind of support they want for themselves. When husbands are posing solutions, sometimes in a dictatorial style (e.g., this is what you should do), their wives might instead really want understanding and a discussion of options. Even if his solution is a good one, she may interpret it as unhelpful because it doesn't take into account her feelings. If her reactions then suggest he's not helping, a husband may come to approach such discussions with dread because he expects to fail. He may then withdraw, become impatient, or change the subject when confronted. However, his wife's take on this behavior is that he can't be depended on when she needs him.[17]

How partners interact day to day is another form of emotional support. Here we are talking about treating each other with respect, kindness, and affection as a normal routine and not just when we want something or we're in the right mood. When we treat each other well, our partner feels liked, respected, and valued. Being nice produces feelings of pleasure for both the giver and recipient, and that makes partners feel good about themselves, their marriage, and each other. Certainly there will be bad times, such as when there are disappointments or conflicts. However, if the style of interacting typically includes tenderness, affection, humor, and just plain interest and concern, that tone helps to neutralize the negatives that emerge on ugly relationship days.

Problem marriages have a lot more negative interactions, and these are truly damaging. The fact is relationships are actually hurt a lot more by bad treatment than they are made better by good treatment. That may be because we expect to be treated well, so when we are, that's what we deserve and there's no cause for celebration. When we're not treated well, we can become upset and angry because we don't believe we deserve to be treated that way.

One obvious form of negative interaction is outright hostility, including insults, a nasty tone of voice, sarcasm, and the like. However, another form is disinterest and ambivalence, and it's just as damaging. While couples who divorce after brief marriages have a lot of conflict and hostility, those who divorce after a long marriage point to a lack of emotional connection. If a relationship lacks affection, consideration, respect, and attentiveness, there doesn't seem to be a reason to stay. These partners aren't driven apart by angry words (although that won't help) as much as they are by a lack of rewards. This kind of negativity can be harder to identify than overt hostility, which may be why ambivalent marriages don't end quickly. These might go ten years or more before they finally throw in the towel.

As with most things, men and women define bad treatment differently. If their wives are not attentive or affectionate, many men consider that negative or hostile. Women, on the other hand, see actual hostile behavior as negative and the absence of hostility as a sign that the relationship is good. Men and women also react differently to how they're treated. Wives have a much harder time ignoring bad treatment from their husbands and tend to be more reactive when it happens. Many husbands, on the other hand, seem to be less put off by their wives' hostility. They will either ignore or hold back their anger for quite a long time when they receive negative treatment from their wives. [18]

When relationships lack something on the emotional side, partners can feel more connected by learning to be supportive. As one concrete step, avoid relying on outside people for help, since that eliminates the need to rely on each other. Then set aside time at the end of each day to discuss the issues each of you had to deal with, regardless of whether or not they were a problem, but make sure you talk about the emotions you experienced with each issue. You will eventually get into the habit of talking about your issues, and might come to look to each other as a sounding board and a source of help.

Keep in mind that husbands are less prone to talk about their own problems, because many are just not comfortable with such discussions. If that describes your husband, don't take offense. He's probably not closing you out; he just doesn't think his problems need to be discussed, nor does he like to admit he needs help. That means it's up to his wife to get these conversations started. Of course, a wife can still discuss her issues even if her husband chooses not to talk about his own, and he can learn to listen and empathize.

Men do well to acknowledge that wives take very seriously the support they receive from their husbands. His involvement implies that he cares about her and that makes her feel better about him. While he might consider some of her issues unimportant, note that her emotional ties to others run deeper than his and she is more likely to notice there are problems in relationships that he would probably miss. Trivializing or ignoring her problems serves no good purpose whatsoever, and can lead to quite a few negative emotions about him.

Supportiveness includes the right emotional tonality. Some men may believe that certain characteristics demonstrate their manliness, and that's what women really want in a man. However, this idea is not supported by the evidence. Conventional masculine traits such as assertiveness, forcefulness, leadership, dominance, and aggressiveness are not what many women prefer in men. In fact, both men and women want their mate to be affectionate, cheerful, sympathetic, compassionate, warm, sensitive, and gentle. While some men may feel such traits are feminine, they make a wife feel that she is supported and that her relationship is warm and loving. Of course, we're not suggesting that a man has to turn himself into a woman or that he can't express these traits in other situations. We are proposing that he consider toning them down when he's playing a supportive role with his wife.

In coping with problems, remember that men and women often use different strategies. Men tend to take more of a problem-solution approach. They will try to change their work patterns if they feel overloaded on their jobs; or if they dislike someone, they will avoid that person. Women rely more on emotion-based strategies. They will try to change how they feel and adopt a positive attitude. Women may also look for help from others, while men try to maintain their independence and accomplish things on their own. That may be one reason why men are reluctant to ask for directions when they're lost, and their wives keep insisting that they ask someone for help.

The issue with having different strategies is that some men may look to apply a practical, results-oriented approach when their wives really just want empathy. When your wife approaches you with an issue, sometimes she needs guidance for decisions, and sometimes she just wants a sympathetic shoulder or a sounding board. Learn to identify what she is looking for and avoid thinking there is only one right way to deal with problems. Knowing the difference and responding in the right way is the difference between appearing supportive and not. If you're not sure how to respond, empathy and sympathy are usually the best starting points. These are more likely to lead to a continued discussion of the problem until the two of you can come to a solution.

Some wives might believe their husbands aren't supportive because they're oblivious to their call for help. That might be the case, but it's not necessarily because he doesn't care. Some men are just not that tuned into other people's distress. Additionally, some wives try to convey their problems indirectly through moods or other forms of emotional expression. However, he might not be able to pick up her subtle cues. The simplest solution is to tell him directly that she wants to discuss an issue, rather than wait for him to figure it out. The husband would probably be relieved to find out that her problem isn't about him and so would be happy to talk about it with her.

Remember that supportiveness in all its forms is reciprocal. If the relationship is even-handed, the amount you give is roughly equal to what you get back. Partners tend to mirror each other, so how one partner acts and feels causes the other to act and feel the same way. If you're there to help when it's needed, that will be repaid to you in your time of need. Furthermore, marriage is a partnership, and as a partnership each person has a responsibility for his or her partner's well-being. Thinking of your relationship from that perspective suggests you really have no choice but to be a caretaker for your partner when needed. You have a right to expect that from your partner, and they have every right to expect that from you.

5

SEX AND INTIMACY

Sex is one of life's most pleasurable experiences. We think about it a lot of the time, play out fantasies in our minds, and for a few it can become a preoccupation. With so much going for it, whether or not to engage in sex when we have the opportunity should be a no-brainer. However, it's not quite that easy when it comes to marriage. Depending on whom you talk to, sex is one of the more enjoyable or one of the more difficult aspects of their relationship. Certainly, many couples are sexually active throughout their marriages and happy about that. But for some, sex can be a major source of conflict, right up there with money, children, and other causes of stress, and it can remain so for the life of their relationship.[1]

Larry and Angela have been married about twenty years. Throughout most of their marriage they had an active and what seemed to be satisfying sex life. However, over the past few years, their activity had declined to a level that Larry found unacceptable. He complained that Angela never seems interested anymore. Whenever he asked her, she would either just say no or would come up with excuses why she couldn't.

At first, Larry felt hurt and rejected. More recently, however, it affected how he acted toward Angela. When she would refuse his advances, he would become angry and resentful, and stay that way for quite some time. He would express these feelings through sarcasm, nasty comments, and other forms of hostile communication. Larry's behavior led Angela to react with the same kinds of emotions, and their mutual negativity affected all the other parts of their relationship.

Angela mentioned that because of what's happened to their relationship, intimacy was the farthest thing from her mind. When asked how her sex life used to be before things went downhill, she said it was okay. She was asked to explain what "okay" meant. She thought Larry was selfish and didn't seem interested in whether or not she enjoyed it. There wasn't a lot of foreplay, the act itself was always the same, and it usually was over pretty quickly. There was no experimenting, and she almost never achieved orgasm. Larry became angry and responded to her comments with "You never had any complaints!" implying that she acted like she enjoyed it.

Angela had tolerated the lack of enjoyment when they were younger, but no longer wanted to. Larry and Angela never had an honest discussion about sex, what each likes and doesn't like, and how it could have been more enjoyable for both. Angela never confronted Larry because she was embarrassed and afraid she would hurt his feelings or make him angry. Larry was also not able to pick up cues, and that was in part because Angela hid how she actually felt about their sex, again because she didn't want to make him feel bad. Consequently, Larry couldn't know how to make sex more enjoyable for Angela. If they had spoken openly and truthfully about their likes and dislikes, Angela might have been a more willing sexual partner, and they could have easily avoided a lot of unnecessary negative emotions.

Looked at objectively, it's perplexing that sex can be so contentious in marriage. It is, after all, an excellent way for two people to spend private time together. Also, in one sense, marriage can be looked at as a sex contract. If it weren't for sex, a marriage wouldn't be much different from other types of personal relationships. While it's not part of the vows, implicit in the marriage agreement is that the two partners will have sex only with each other. Monogamy means that two people have no outside options for sex. Consequently, it can be argued that we have the obligation to meet the reasonable sexual needs of our partner.

Whether or not we agree with that point, it's clear that it's a good idea anyway if only for the health benefits. There are countless magazine articles, websites, and other information sources that list the psychological and physiological benefits of an active sex life. Here is a summary of what researchers from the various health fields have discovered:

- It improves self-esteem, helps to relieve stress, and improves coping with stressful situations.
- It improves immunity to some kinds of illnesses. Sex once or twice per week allows the body to produce antibodies that help protect from colds and other types of infections. Sexual excitement increases production of the hormone DHEA, which boosts the immune system, repairs tissue, improves cognition, and keeps skin healthy.
- It's a great form of exercise. Every thirty minutes of sexual activity burns roughly 85 to 150 calories, resulting in the loss of about a pound for every forty-two occasions.
- It can lower diastolic blood pressure and cut in half the risk of suffering a fatal heart attack among men.
- It makes you feel better about your relationship. Sex helps us to produce oxytocin, the love-related hormone, which enhances trust, nurturance, and bonding between partners. The release of oxytocin also helps to promote better sleep, which is linked to better health and weight loss.
- Endorphins, which closely resemble morphine, are also released during sex, helping to reduce physical pain.
- Sex can lower the odds of suffering prostate cancer among men. Men who have had frequent ejaculations while in their twenties (an average of five or more per week) were less likely to have prostate cancer when they got older. For women, those who do pelvic muscle exercises (Kegels) during sex not only have more pleasure but also lower the odds of suffering incontinence (loss of bladder control) later on.
- It increases production of both testosterone and estrogen. Testosterone helps fortify bones and muscles, and it keeps your heart in good working condition. In women, estrogen also protects against heart disease.

An active sex life also enhances each partner's sense of security. In the previous chapter, we brought up attachment styles, which have to do with how people think, feel, and behave in intimate relationships. Some people are able to connect emotionally and trust their partners and so have secure attachment styles. Others, however, can have insecure styles, which they express either through anxiety (e.g., fear of abandonment) or avoidance (e.g., don't get close to others). Insecure styles make partners feel uncertain about their relationship, and uncertainty brings along negative emotions and behaviors. By strengthening their emotional bonds, an active sex life can actually shut down insecure attachment styles and let couples feel more secure about their marriage. [2]

Sexual activity is a very good indicator of a happy marriage. Because they receive all the benefits that we cited above, couples feel good about their relationship and each other. Just as importantly, an active sex life implies that partners have a lot of positive fundamentals and constructive experiences in their relationship, so they want to be intimate with each other. Most couples seem to be aware of its importance to a marriage. Virtually all husbands and wives believe that a regular pattern of sex adds to a marriage. While it's not clear whether frequent sex creates a happy marriage or a happy marriage results in more sex, still the two ideas tend to go hand in hand and are probably reciprocal—that is, each improves the other. [3]

Despite all this, sex in marriage can be very complicated. It's not just a physical act that occurs between a husband and wife; it's wrapped up within the context of all the other aspects of their relationship. In fact, we can argue that sex is only a purely physical act when it's between two consenting strangers. That's because there's no underlying emotions, outside responsibilities, disappointments, or resentments that get in the way. But for a marriage, the list of issues is a long one, and on any given day there may be reasons to have or not have sex, and it's usually the decision not to that can lead to problems.

A major issue, and what might be at the root of a lot of sexual problems in marriage, is that men and women approach sex differently. Their differences are due in large part to how they're raised. Men live in a more sexual world. Sex is one way they express their masculinity and feel validated as men. Through their socialization they learn to value performance and to be the aggressor, and emotions aren't a necessary component. Women, on the other hand, are taught to be chaste, passive, and to put their own sexual needs below that of their partners, and emotions are considered essential for intimacy.

Men are also socialized to suppress emotions, so they're often unwilling to express much of their innermost thoughts and feelings. Sex provides a socially acceptable way of emotionally bonding to their wives. In other words, many men find emotional closeness to be an important end product of sex. Unfortunately, many wives see things the other way around—that is, sex is the end product. Women attach emotional significance to all their relationships, and especially to their marriage, and feeling emotionally close to their husband is a prerequisite for sex. Once they feel connected, sex is something that flows directly from, and is a by-product of, their emotional connection.[4]

With such opposing views, it's easy to see why men and women can have a hard time matching up sexually. Each believes their way of thinking is more appropriate and natural, and should be the one adopted by their partner. The reality is, however, that neither is inclined to give up their gender-driven perspectives. To quote psychologist Dr. Cheryl Rampage on the perceptions of wives, "Women have been acculturated to expect men to approach intimacy like women. Romance novels, television soap operas . . . have promoted a mythology about men that vastly overstates the actual level of comfort or interest that most men feel about engaging in discussions about their (or anyone else's) feelings. Yet, for many women, such conversations are the sine qua non of intimate encounters."[5]

Husbands and wives can also differ on when to have sex. Men rarely see impediments to lovemaking. Most think sex is a good idea at almost any time, regardless of whose idea it is. While some men might be put off if their wives initiate sex, particularly if it's more often than they do, that's not typical. From most men's point of view, the more the better, regardless of whose idea it is. In fact, many husbands will gauge the quality of their marriage and the quality of their sex lives by frequency. The condition of their marriage doesn't interfere, nor do other aspects of their lives, even if they're facing outside problems. That's possibly because men tend to be good at compartmentalizing. They store various life elements in different mental categories, and the circumstances in one category won't necessarily spill over into the other categories. So if they're in the middle of financial problems, are having difficulties on their jobs, or are angry at their wives, sex can still be a very viable option.

Many wives don't wish to have sex as often as their husbands, even on their best days. Furthermore, her interest can be affected by the various situations and conditions of her life outside the bedroom. One might be how she feels about her husband and their marriage. If a wife feels emotionally distanced from her husband, is insecure about their future together, or believes there are unresolved problems in their relationship, it's difficult for her to put them aside. There can also be other things she's dealing with that have nothing to do with her spouse or her marriage. If she is having emotional problems in other relationships, these could also interfere with her interest in intimacy.

Beyond emotional issues, wives are often a lot busier than their husbands. Much more of their time is consumed by home and family commitments. Children, housework, social responsibilities, and, for many, full-time jobs not only cut into the amount of alone time that's available for her and her husband, they also drain her energy. When wives feel pressure from these outside demands, they're likely to put sex on the back burner, even if she would prefer not to and the relationship is in a good place emotionally.

Unfortunately, a back-burner priority doesn't play very well for many husbands, and that can create problems for wives. Tension can surface from both sides as each partner tries to accommodate the other's needs. Wives are trying to be more willing, and husbands are trying to be more patient. If wives feel pressure to be more sexually responsive, sex may become more of a responsibility than a source of pleasure for them, and thus a cause for resentment.

At the same time, men with overworked wives might feel pressured to reduce their requests, and some might find that difficult, frustrating, and possibly incomprehensible. Furthermore, if their wives treat sex as a chore, men may resent their lack of enthusiasm, spontaneity, and authenticity, which they might regard as important for good sex. Trying to maintain a balance between each partner's views of too little and too much might leave some couples feeling like they're occasionally walking a tightrope.[6]

Debbie was just not that interested in sex. She didn't know why she felt that way, and all she could say was that she was just never really into it. Her husband Jack had a very different perspective. He fully enjoyed sex and would like to have it with Debbie as often as she would allow. Debbie felt that all Jack ever wanted to do was have sex, and she thought he was extremely demanding of her. In reality, from the beginning of their fifteen-year marriage, they only had sex about once per week, and while Jack said he would like it more, he didn't find their schedule too hard to handle. Because Jack seemed okay with things, Debbie didn't think they had a problem. Therapy was Jack's idea. He was hoping they could find a way for Debbie to enjoy sex more.

Both agreed that Jack's performance wasn't an issue. Instead, the problem seemed to stem from Debbie's attitude about sex. "Sex was something that was never, ever talked about in our house. I always had the feeling there was something dirty about it. I remember there were girls in high school that had sex, and we all thought they were sluts." When asked whether there was any specific things that she liked to do, she said she never really thought about it. In fact, Debbie said she never had sexual fantasies of any kind, even when she was younger, and she never masturbated. Debbie learned to think about sex as distasteful rather than as a natural and healthy activity between a husband and wife. Because she avoided the subject, even in her own mind, she never explored her own sexuality, never discovered that sex can be a source of pleasure, and as a result never developed that aspect of her life.

The fact that women's social learning is different from men's can cause sexual problems in some marriages. Some women may have learned to suppress their sexual desires, or have developed inhibitions that interfere with their enjoyment. It's estimated that 10 percent are unable to experience an orgasm, and 40 percent to 50 percent have difficulty reaching orgasm during intercourse. In the extreme, some may suffer from Inhibited Sexual Desire (ISD) or Hypoactive Sexual Desire Disorder (HSD). Women with these conditions haven't internalized the benefits of marital sex, such that it enhances personal well-being and emotional bonding. Because sex isn't very satisfying to them, it's not hard to understand why they're not very interested. However, their passivity and sublimated desires work against their personal needs, and it runs counter to the sexual realities of marriage.

Of course, a woman's lack of satisfaction isn't always because of physical or psychological dysfunctions. There are a lot of other factors that have to be considered. As we mentioned earlier, these can include how they feel about their partner and their marriage, fatigue, and outside sources of stress. We can also add her own self-esteem and, last but not least, her partner's willingness and ability to satisfy her. In some marriages, husbands may be too focused on their own physical needs and not enough on the needs of their partners. So, taken as a whole, while some women may believe there's something wrong with them if they're not interested in sex, it may instead be the case that there's something wrong in their world or with their partner.[7]

For some wives, their lack of interest may also be tied to body image. Women place a premium on physical attractiveness. From a young age, a girl's self-image is tied to her appearance, and especially her shape. As adults, if their body image is poor, the effect can be lowered self-esteem, even depression. They're not likely to feel sexy and may prefer to avoid sex to avoid a situation that leaves them open to ridicule.

A woman's concern with her appearance isn't necessarily her own fault but may derive from cultural realities. We're all taught to regard beauty highly, and those who have it receive a lot of rewards. In comparison to unattractive people, they're more likely to be seen as persuasive, intelligent, successful, trustworthy, and even taller. They may also be nicer people. Because they're treated better by others, they treat others better in return. With more confidence and greater social acceptance, they behave in ways that make them popular. Furthermore, probably because they're more likeable, they tend to get better jobs and higher salaries. Finally, with less stress in their lives, they also tend to have better physical and mental health.

We should point out that our preoccupation with beauty may go beyond just social learning or esthetics. Once again our brains play a role. An attractive person activates the same sections of the brain that are activated when we fall in love or are sexually aroused. That might be why the thought "I'm in love" can pop into our heads when we see a beautiful person. But in the same way that we cannot immediately assess the character of a person we're in love with, a beautiful face can interfere with our judgments of that person. That's why we tend to regard them favorably before we actually get to know them.

Wives' concerns with their bodies can also come from their husbands. Men consider it important that their wives are attractive and will actually link it to their own marital happiness. In their defense, men have their reasons for valuing their wives' appearance, and it comes down to status. An attractive wife enhances a man's social standing and affects how the couple is treated by others. Men with beautiful wives are actually believed to be more successful and have better jobs than those with less attractive wives. Note that a husband's appearance doesn't have the same impact on their status. If a wife is unattractive, that's the image of the couple, regardless of what the husband looks like.

How a wife looks can also affect how partners treat each other. Because he can receive a boost to his status, a husband is apt to treat an attractive wife better. These wives are then likely to react in kind, so the couple has the potential for a happier relationship. Unfortunately, the reverse can also happen, especially if a husband feels he looks better than his wife. He may treat her with less respect and give her less attention, which she then repays to him with the same treatment, causing a more contentious marriage.

The aging process certainly won't help the situation. Appearance can continue to be an issue for wives in longer-term marriages. Even if she was beautiful when she was younger, if a husband thinks his wife's looks have declined, especially if more than his own, he tends to be less attracted to her. That's why it's not uncommon for some men to look for a younger, more attractive partner when they get older. Many wives are aware of this, so whether or not they're happy with their shapes really doesn't matter. They have to worry about their husbands' opinions.

However, this way of thinking doesn't describe all husbands. The reality is many wives are more critical of how they look than are their husbands. Wives will often get it wrong as to what their husbands find attractive and would be surprised to find that their husbands are actually happy with their figures. The problem is that her misconceptions can diminish her feelings of sexiness and can lead to a weaker sex drive. Taken a step further, her lack of interest can then be misinterpreted by her husband as a lack of interest in him, and that can affect how he feels about her.[8]

Couples may also lose interest in sex even if the relationship is fine in other respects. Here we are talking about diminishing returns; sex becomes boring and less pleasurable as a result of repetition and predictability. Sometimes this can happen because couples keep to the same routine in their lovemaking. While all couples are susceptible to boredom, more often than not this is a particular problem faced by older couples, and again, it's more pronounced among women. Men may have physiological issues as they age that prevent them from having sex, but those who have normal functioning usually don't lose enjoyment or interest. For many women, on the other hand, their interest can decline with age. We should also mention that many younger women might lose their sexual appetite after giving birth, although this is usually temporary and their drive returns within a few months.

Besides boredom, problems for older women can be due to hormonal fluctuations. With declines in both estrogen and testosterone, along with physical changes to the vagina and vulva, penetration can be less pleasurable, even painful. There may also be less sensitivity in the genital area as a result of decreased blood flow, making it difficult for some women to become aroused and achieve orgasm. Of course, the hot flashes that are experienced by some women in menopause can be another reason for reduced enjoyment.

It's not that older women prefer to avoid physical contact altogether. In fact, they're very interested in nongenital contact, such as hugging, kissing, and other forms of noncoital fondling. Most also don't regard these forms of affection as a replacement for intercourse. Instead, because of physiological changes, repetitiveness, or other reasons, some women might have a greater need for foreplay, and they may also need to feel more emotionally connected to their partner to become aroused. [9]

There can be other reasons why couples end up in a sexless marriage, and these may have nothing to do with anything we've already discussed. They can get there by accident. It can happen slowly because schedules are too busy or they don't coincide, partners are physically tired, or they're just not aware or had forgotten how much sex can add to feeling connected to each other. If such a pattern continues for too long, partners can lose interest and motivation, and no sex can then become a habit.

Some couples might find that sex is enjoyable, but getting there requires too much work. We are referring to how partners communicate their desire for sex. They might use an indirect approach, because direct language can be embarrassing or they're afraid of being rejected. Ambiguous messages are easier because they make us feel less vulnerable, but they can be misinterpreted or not taken seriously. When that happens, we can misinterpret our partner's lack of response as rejection. Rejection can cause a lot of negative emotions, but it can also make us reluctant to make sexual advances in the future. So, our needs can go unfulfilled, and for that we blame our partners, but in reality it's our own fault for not stating our wishes clearly.

Ambiguity can also occur when it comes to knowing our partner's preferences. Couples have a better sex life if they know what each likes and doesn't like. Such information gives them a better chance of fulfilling each other's desires, so satisfaction increases, and usually so will frequency. When couples don't know each other's preferences, they might have to rely on stereotypes (e.g., men want sex all the time and women never do, or women like this and don't like that). Sometimes these stereotypes are wrong, and can lead partners to think they're more different from each other than they really are. When we exaggerate our differences, we can have a harder time relating sexually to our partner. We might, for example, conclude that we're just not able to satisfy our partner's needs, so why bother trying. The point here is sex is a lot less complicated when partners believe they like the same things and they know what those things are. [10]

As we mentioned at the start, the list of sex problems is lengthy. Yet if a marriage has no major flaws, many of these problems can be resolved. Of course, fixing them may not be easy or fast, because they often become habits. Some amount of patience, understanding, sacrifice, adjustment, and compromise may be required. While this might sound like work, it's probably a lot less work, and certainly less stressful, than fighting about sex.

It's a good idea to keep in mind that an active sex life is essential to a good marriage and a physical need for both men and women. Its benefits are important enough to rank sex high on the list of priorities for couples. There are times when you'll be overworked or overscheduled, the pressures of day-to-day living will inhibit desires, or you'll feel emotionally distanced from each other. Yet it's precisely at times such as these that sex can be particularly helpful. So put in the effort to have your alone time; you'll feel more connected with your partner and probably less stressed afterward. Remember, most people feel better after sex, not worse.

It's also useful to keep in mind that just as a good sex life can improve a marriage, the lack of one can make a marriage unstable. When there's little or no sex, the odds go up that partners will look to someone else to fill that need, even if that's not what they want to do. Furthermore, inadequate sex has some detrimental physical and psychological side effects. Some men can become more aggressive, and the hostility that results can carry over into other parts of the relationship. There can also be disrupted sleep patterns due to feeling restless and being unable to relax. Furthermore, someone who is regularly rejected by a partner might feel unloved, insulted, and humiliated, and that can then lead to problems with their self-esteem and in the relationship as a whole. [11]

Some couples might have to acknowledge that male and female differences in how often they want sex is normal and not uncommon. If that describes your relationship, it's best to discuss what each of you thinks is appropriate so that you can come up with an acceptable schedule. Getting to some middle ground you can both live with is better than uncertainty. It helps you manage your expectations so that you won't have to wonder if you're ever going to have sex again.

Husbands and wives might also appear to differ in what they want from sex, but very often they're looking for the same thing—emotional closeness. They just strive for that goal from opposite directions. For wives, that means accepting that their husbands might not need an emotional connection before having sex. So don't think he's crazy if on a day you're separated, literally or emotionally, sex strikes him as a good idea. The act itself will make him feel connected to you. For men, they need to understand that women attach emotional significance to all aspects of their marriage, and feeling a bond with her husband is usually a prerequisite for sex. That emotional bond is often best achieved through regular caregiving, mutual respect, and support as she needs it.

However, doing or saying something nice only on days you hope to have sex isn't likely to work very well. Part-time kindnesses and superficial attempts to connect emotionally are pretty transparent. Your wife will probably regard them as insincere and see your ulterior motive. Rather, a pattern of respect, caring, and emotional bonding has to be routine in order for wives to believe such feelings are genuine.

In a similar vein, romantic advances are not romantic if your partner is not free to turn them down. Partners must feel they have control over their own lives and can make their own choices. When they don't, resentment and stress will be the result, usually followed by an argument. It's much more worthwhile in the long term to be understanding and patient, rather than angry, if you're occasionally rejected. Your partner will feel he or she has a choice, feel less pressured about sex, and possibly be more open to future advances.

A healthy and satisfying sexual relationship requires a balance between the physical and the emotional for both men and women. Some wives might consider paying more attention to their own physical needs, learning more about their bodies, and getting in touch with what they find stimulating. Men's weakness tends to be on the emotional side. While some husbands may not be aware of it, greater openness and sharing of feelings will make them feel more connected to their wives and their marriages. At the same time it might make them look sexier to their wives because it plays right into their need for emotional bonding.

Outside responsibilities can certainly limit lovemaking opportunities, especially for younger couples. Most wives have more demanding workloads, and some husbands might find their lack of time and energy hard to tolerate. When that happens, husbands are better off embracing the reality of their wives' situation. Becoming angry or frustrated only makes you dwell on your disappointment. If you're empathetic, you might be able to manage your expectations better and maybe find solutions that meet both of your needs.

One possible solution is a barter system. Sex is something that can be negotiated. For example, you can exchange labor favors, such as housework, for favors in the bedroom. This isn't very sexy or romantic, but it's practical, and it happens in lots of marriages. By taking on some of her burdens, husbands can free up their wives' time and reduce some of her stress, so sex can become more of an option. Along with being a sensible solution, it also has an air of fairness. If a wife is not inclined to have sex as often as her husband, she might become more motivated if she were to receive something that helps her in return. In other words, if she's expected to be like you in the bedroom, then she has a right to expect you to be more like her in other parts of the home.

There wasn't much of a connection between Mark and Judy, and that was apparent from how they acted with each other. Mark's attitude and behavior toward Judy was generally negative. He tended to react to what she said with sarcasm or other hostile remarks, or he would say nothing but look impatient or disinterested. Outwardly, Judy took Mark's behavior in stride. She resisted responding to his hostility with her own, and if he was particularly aggressive, she would withdraw and keep her thoughts to herself. However, it was clear that she didn't like the way he treated her.

When asked how he thought he treated Judy, Mark thought he was good to her, or at least as good as any other husband. When asked about his sarcasm or impatience, he said he "doesn't mean anything by that, but sometimes she says some stupid and annoying things." Judy mentioned that Mark treated all women like that. "He seems to hold all of us in pretty low regard."

Surprisingly, they still had sex regularly, but how they perceived their sex life was very different. From Mark's perspective, their sex life was fine. Judy, however, said she did it out of a sense of duty and not out of enjoyment. When asked how she felt about sex in general, Judy claimed that she always saw herself as a very sexual person. In her previous relationships, and even in her relationship with Mark before getting married, she thoroughly enjoyed it.

However, she came to realize that sex for them was all about Mark getting what he wanted. Her opinion was probably accurate, given the things that Mark believed. To him, sex was primarily for a man's enjoyment, and there was even some indication that he thought a woman's orgasm was a myth. Consequently, he didn't bother to put much effort into making it enjoyable for her. According to Judy, "When we have sex, it's just a physical act. There's no love, no emotions, no tenderness."

His beliefs about sex were an issue, but there were bigger problems. Judy's enjoyment disappeared when Mark "began treating me like a second class citizen." She could not enjoy sex with Mark because he didn't make her feel good about herself, and there was more hostility than affection in their marriage. Judy has been happily divorced from Mark for about ten years as of this writing.

Successful marriages rely on what some counselors refer to as *emotion work.* This is the process of suppressing your own thoughts and feelings so that you behave in a way that makes your partner feel good. Emotion work is not as sinister or manipulative as it sounds. Each of us does it regularly in all of our relationships. Pausing from a busy schedule to do or say something nice to your spouse so that he or she can feel appreciated is an example of emotion work.

Compliments and flattery are important forms of emotion work for husbands. As we've pointed out, women have valid reasons to be concerned about their appearance. Positive comments about how she looks can reassure her that you find her attractive. She is likely to feel more loved and valued, more secure about the marriage, better about herself, better about you, and maybe sexier.

From a wife's perspective, if your husband volunteers that he thinks you're sexy or attractive, you should believe him. He might not say it on his own unless he thought it was true. But even if you think he's not being honest, the real point is he cares enough about you to say things that make you feel good about yourself.

Obviously, negative comments also have an impact. Sarcasm, criticism, and other snide remarks might make your wife feel insecure about her appearance, and that can produce negative thoughts about her own sexuality. While she may not outwardly appear to be affected, she's likely to take your comments to heart, and worse, remember them. They can gradually whittle away at her self-confidence and make her uncomfortable about having sex.

Some women may be so concerned about their appearance that it weakens their interest in sex. In all likelihood, they should realize that their husbands are probably much less critical of their appearance. Overly self-conscious women might be consumed with thoughts about all the things that are wrong with their bodies: This sags, I'm too fat, my hips are too big, and and so on. If you find yourself with these thoughts, be aware that at the same time your husband is consumed with one idea: "Hurray! She's naked!"

While we're on the subject of body image, it's worthwhile for husbands to keep an eye on their own appearance. The efforts that you put forth to look good tell your spouse that you still care about how she thinks of you. Besides, while women may not claim to be as interested in appearance as are men, let's face it, everyone would rather have sex with an attractive person rather than an unattractive one. Staying in shape might make you sexier to your wife, and in marriage every little bit helps.

Frank and honest conversations are important for a good sex life. While talking openly about sex is not easy for many people, try to put your discomfort aside and raise the subject if you think it's worthwhile. Sex chats provide partners with a clear idea of what is liked and not liked, and that can lead both of you to have a more satisfying experience. Besides, an open discussion on the topic offers other benefits. It helps to build trust between you and your partner because you're forced to disclose some very personal thoughts and feelings.

Sex discussions have a few essential elements. First, they should have a positive and constructive tone. Telling your partner when you're angry or frustrated that your sex life is not satisfying will likely make them feel embarrassed and inadequate. Your partner might become defensive and react to what you say with accusations or withdrawal. A more appropriate time might be when both of you are in a comfortable place emotionally.

Additionally you're better off using positive comments rather than criticisms. In other words, suggest ways lovemaking might be made better instead of talking about what you don't like. Again, complaints about your partner's performance are likely to lead to defensiveness rather than to trust and intimacy.

Conversations should also be direct. Indirect communication, such as off-hand remarks, tends to be less effective and can be misinterpreted. Additionally, off-the-cuff comments can either go unnoticed by your partner or not be taken seriously. A direct message about what you like, or just that you'd like to have sex now or very soon, gets right to the point and avoids miscommunication. [12]

While some couples might find sex less pleasurable as they get older, it doesn't have to be that way. Quite a few continue to enjoy sex well into their senior years. These couples rely on their imagination and creativity, and keep in mind that variety is the spice of life. Approach sex with an open mind and consider trying different things. You might consider, for example, trying sex toys. If this idea sounds ridiculous to you, put that thought aside. These can be a perfectly acceptable way for two people to have some fun, and besides, there's nothing inherently evil about a piece of plastic that vibrates. Put aside embarrassment and accept that nothing is taboo behind closed doors. Of course, that's not to say there aren't limits: new ideas about how to behave in the bedroom have to be agreeable to both if they are to be enjoyed as a couple.

If couples have problems with arousal, sometimes it's because partners are not paying enough attention to each other's needs. A greater focus on giving pleasure can mean sex will improve over the years, despite the loss of novelty, and both of you will stay interested. If you or your partner are having trouble getting aroused, spend as much time as you need in foreplay. Also, try using your thought processes. Sexual fantasies and mental imagery are often recommended by sex therapists to help patients who are having a difficult time becoming or staying aroused. Here we are referring to imagining the act happening in your mind, with particular focus on the things you enjoy. You can use these thoughts before having sex as a way of getting you warmed up, or during it if you find the act itself isn't sufficient on its own. [13]

We've made a lot of recommendations for improving the intimate side of your relationship. However, we must stress that we're not sex therapists. In fact, most of our ideas for improving your sex life relate to how the features of your relationship can affect your sex life, rather than what to do about the actual sex act. If you feel your problems haven't been addressed through what we talked about, we suggest that you meet with a specialist who is more qualified to help you. We should also stress that it would be a mistake not to take this step if you need to, because your sex life is too important to the stability of your marriage to not give it serious attention.

As one more extremely important note, our discussion about sex starts from the premise that your marriage is sound in other respects. None of these recommendations will be effective for marriages that are not. If there are things in your relationship that inhibit emotional bonding, violate the cornerstones of marriage, or provoke discord and negative emotions, there's not much you can do to make your sex life better without first addressing these underlying problems. Many of these are covered in the upcoming chapters.

6

PARTNERS, FAMILIES, AND FRIENDS

Much of what determines the goodness of a marriage has to do with the characteristics of each partner and the dynamics of their one-on-one relationship. We're referring to how partners interact and communicate with each other, as well as their personal traits, beliefs, and expectations. However, every couple is also a member of a larger world made up of friends, acquaintances, and family members, and each partner brings their folks to their marriage. These outsiders have a lot to do with shaping and maintaining a marriage.

Feeling socially connected is essential to mental health. In fact, some argue that there should be advertising to educate people about the importance of building and maintaining ties to family and friends, just as antismoking campaigns have made people more aware of the dangers of smoking. Our social circle feeds our self-esteem, makes us feel we belong to something meaningful, and forms the basis for our personal identities. Additionally, social events such as meetings, functions, and other gatherings provide us with routines and schedules, and these add structure and purpose to our lives.

Friends and family members also serve as our guardians, helping us to stay on the straight and narrow. They make sure we have medical checkups, don't get too far out of shape, and stay reasonably inside the bounds of a healthy lifestyle. When they provide emotional support and comfort in our time of need, they make it easier to handle problems and keep us from over-reacting to difficult situations. Our friends and family members can actually provide some protection from the physically damaging effects of stress.

In contrast, social isolation can have serious consequences. With little or no ties with other people, we can come to feel alienated. Our self-esteem can be weakened, and we might experience bouts of depression. We can also become cynical and develop a sense of helplessness because we don't feel in control of our lives. Social isolation also increases our chances of suffering from heart disease, cancer, respiratory ailments, and gastrointestinal illnesses. These problems may be brought on by the stress of feeling isolated, but they may also occur because we don't have anyone making sure we follow good health practices.

Many of the benefits we receive from friends and family are also provided by marriage. The relationship we have with our partner really is a social circle of two. As a member of this mini-circle, we receive many of the physical and emotional rewards that we just talked about. Provided the relationship is not abusive, contentious, or demoralizing, married couples have readily available companions, and each partner has a source of emotional support that protects them from isolation and depression. Still, having other people in our lives is important, because our partner cannot satisfy all of our social and emotional needs. [1]

As we mentioned, when we develop an intimate relationship, we bring along our network of friends and family members, and so does our partner. That means our social circle will become wider because we'll merge the two groups into one. However, before that merger begins, the couple typically withdraws from their personal circles to spend time alone with each other. They're in love, and the only objective of each partner is to get as much attention from the other as possible. It's also a time to learn about one another and to determine if the relationship has long-term potential. If it does, each partner begins introducing the other to their family and friends.

Tom did not like Mary's family. This was a well-kept secret; he would not let his feelings get in the way of how he treated them. Mary only became aware of Tom's feelings from an off-hand comment he made about her father. Mary had an extremely close relationship with her parents, so when she discovered how Tom felt, she became angry. She told Tom that his feelings were completely unjustified; her parents always treated Tom well and liked him. Furthermore, she was completely accept-

ing of his family and felt he should do the same for her family. Tom hid his feelings about Mary's family because he knew how close she was to them, and he also knew just how she would react.

However, Tom's feelings were not without some justification, not because of how her parents treated him, but how Mary behaved with her parents. Mary was very dependent on her parents, and when there were decisions to be made regarding her home and family, she would discuss these issues first with her father, and he would tell her what to do. She would usually follow her father's advice, regardless of Tom's opinions, and at times wouldn't even discuss the issue with Tom. As a result, he came to feel that Mary didn't respect him or trust his judgment, and that she had more faith in her father than in him. Consequently, he came to resent how Mary treated him and for what he thought was her opinion of him, and he came to resent her father because he believed he interfered in their lives.

As we get comfortable with our partner and begin merging our networks, we go through a weeding-out process. While each partner will usually end up with more friends than they had on their own, not all of the friends will be retained. Rather, couples typically cull down their network to a select group. The end result is usually some shrinkage from the total. In a perfect world, about an equal proportion of friends are retained from each partner's circle.

The shrinking process is gradual, but it isn't random or haphazard. Rather, we consciously try to make our network more homogeneous. That is, we focus on building a network of friends whose lifestyles match our own. We might drop some single friends, especially those of the opposite sex who might be a threat to our partner. Instead, we'll look primarily for other married couples.

Proximity plays a role in the friendships we keep and the new ones we develop. Married couples tend to live in the same neighborhoods and belong to the same organizations, so these friendships are more convenient for us. More importantly, however, we lean toward other married couples because they share our issues and concerns, as well as our interests and activities. Note that our social circle might evolve again after we have children. Parents have a lot of restrictions on time and money, and have interests that only other parents can truly appreciate. Consequently, we'll come to spend more time with couples who also have children.

Adopting a homogeneous social circle is good for our relationship. If we have too many friends whose lifestyles differ from our own, we can feel out of place and uncomfortable in our marriage, and that can disrupt the bond with our partner. On the other hand, friends who are similar to ourselves validate our lifestyle and make us feel secure in our married role. They also strengthen our identity as a couple, leading us to move away from seeing ourselves as two individuals. Married friends also help to keep a marriage intact. They have a vested interest that a couple stays together because their lives are intertwined and each couple validates the lifestyles of every other couple.[2]

Our married friends and acquaintances also provide another, although unintended, benefit. They give us something to compare our own relationship to. We gauge the quality of our own marriage by observing other couples. With an idea as to where we stand versus the rest of the world, we can identify things we do well and areas where we could use improvement. We have another motive for making these comparisons. We want to make ourselves feel good, and we can do that when we're able to say to ourselves that "my marriage is at least as good, if not better, and maybe much better, than yours."

In order for us to make this claim, we tend to go for downward comparisons. We'll focus more on couples that just don't seem very happy or appear to have problems. We try to avoid making upward comparisons because they're risky. It can be hard to feel good about our partner and stay committed if we focus on a marriage that we think is better than our own. Instead, if we compare our relationship to those we think are inferior, we have a better chance of feeling good about our marriage. Downward comparisons are especially useful when our marriage has problems and we can't easily come up with solutions. We can feel better and more secure if we believe that other relationships have as many or more difficulties. It's not that we're happy that other couples aren't doing well, but when we feel badly, it helps to believe that we're not alone or things could be worse.[3]

As our networks merge, partners come to share their friends with each other. We establish relationships with the people introduced to us by our partner, and some might even make it into our own personal inner circle. Sharing of friends sometimes is a result of competition for time. As there are only a limited number of hours per week for socializing, and much of that time is taken up by our partner, it becomes easier and more efficient to combine friend time with spouse time.

Stable marriages have a lot of sharing of friends. In fact, the more sharing that goes on, the better the marriage. When we accept our partner's friends as our own, they believe we've accepted them, and they take it as a sign of our commitment. Our partners also feel more secure because they believe we want the same things out of our social lives, and we're more bonded because our friendships further intertwine our lives. Of course, it also means that splitting up can become more complicated because we might have to give up some friends along with a spouse.[4]

Obviously, the way we go about combining our friendship pools doesn't apply to family members. There usually isn't any shrinkage. We don't choose our family members; we just have to accept them, and we expect our partner will also accept our family without any restrictions. When partners are willing to do that, they get the same benefits of bonding and security as they get from merging networks and sharing their friends.

For many couples, merging and sharing of networks goes smoothly. The majority of the people that matter to one partner are accepted by the other. Even if there are a few who don't make it into our hearts, we can usually tolerate putting up with them. However, if we decide to reject our partner's friends, especially those who are highly valued, that can become a source of friction. If our partner doesn't like who or what is important to us, we might think that says something about how they feel about us. We're also likely to feel anxious when we get together with friends or family our partner doesn't like, and we can come to resent our partner for making us feel that way.

In some marriages, dismissal of a partner's network might in fact be an act of passive-aggression. This can happen when a couple has underlying problems in their relationship. For example, let's say we resent the way our partner treats us, but we're uncomfortable with confronting them directly about this problem. We want to do something hurtful to them in retaliation, but we have to find an indirect way to do it. That indirect way might be through rejecting our partner's family and friends. The thing about such behavior is that it has everything to do with the underlying relationship problem and nothing to do with the people we're claiming to reject. Passive-aggressive rejection occurs more frequently than we might realize, and not just over social networks. We might reject our partner's personal interests, belittle their careers, or denigrate other things they say or do. When we do it without having a rational reason, it might be a passive-aggressive attack.

George liked just about all of Judy's friends and family. From when he was first introduced, he treated them like they were his own, and he enjoyed their company. Not so with Judy; she had never really taken to George's group. In fact, whenever they were making plans, Judy would push to visit her family and friends and not the people from George's side. On those occasions when they did go out with George's friends, Judy wasn't engaging; she usually sat quietly and would rarely start a conversation. According to George, Judy would constantly be checking the time to see when it would be okay to leave. George said that the way she acted was embarrassing and made him uncomfortable, and he never enjoyed the time they spent with his friends. Eventually he got to the point where he would avoid making plans with them and felt that his relationships had suffered as a result. Not surprisingly, George also came to believe that his family and friends weren't very fond of Judy.

When confronted, Judy said that George had the wrong impression. She claimed that she didn't dislike them; on the contrary, she regarded them as nice people. Then she added that the problem was she didn't think she had much in common with them. That led her to admit that she thought they were a little beneath her. Of course, George didn't take well to that comment, and so he challenged her. He compared her friends and family to his own on their accomplishments, education, status, and any other factor he could think of, and Judy had to agree that his group really wasn't that different from her own.

The real issue came down to this: George's group just wasn't her group. She saw them as outsiders and never tried to get to know them. The truth is Judy found meeting people to be extremely intimidating, in large part because she feared being rejected. She tended to withdraw or would have a negative attitude when introduced, and that first impression was hard for her to overcome. Rather than confront her feelings of insecurity, it was easier for her to say to herself that these new people weren't good enough for her. Unfortunately, her inability to deal with her problem was affecting how George felt about her and their relationship.

Adopting our partner's group is one side of the story. There's also how our family and friends react to our partner. Feelings that partners have for each other can be strongly influenced by the opinions of the people in their networks. When our friends and family like our partner, we feel good about the relationship. However, if they dislike or are ambivalent to our new person, it can cause a rift in our relationship. Note that friends and family can be particularly disruptive for women. Because they place more importance on their relationships with friends and parents, women can be more affected by their opinions.

There are a few reasons why feelings for a partner are affected by our social circles. When a partner is liked by our friends and family, we have less second-guessing about our selection and believe we're accepted by and still a member of our network. Keep in mind that we value being a member of a group, and if we continue to belong after becoming a couple, we can actually feel more attracted to our partner. There's also the principle of transitivity, which suggests that if we like our friends, and they like our partner, then we should also like our partner. Another relates to building our identity as a couple. If we are considered to be a good match by people who are important to us, then we're also likely to label ourselves as a good match.

We're aware of how our family and peers can affect our feelings. That's why we're likely to be nervous when we have to introduce a partner into our social circle. We might even put it off for a while just to make sure things are going well in the relationship and our new partner won't give us a reason to be embarrassed. When the meeting occurs, we will do whatever we can to make sure our partner leaves a good impression. If it doesn't turn out that way, we'll then talk our partner up in the hopes of convincing our group that they should approve.

Popular folklore suggests that the opinions of our network can also produce the opposite result. This is the so-called Romeo and Juliet effect, where the disapproval of our network leads to stronger feelings of love between two partners. While there's a romantic quality to this idea, such relationships really don't have much of a chance, especially in the long term. The stress brought on by the rejection of others can eventually cause problems. Typically, these couples come to be less trusting and more critical of each other, will argue frequently, and might experience more intense disappointments when one partner doesn't meet the other's expectations. In other words, we'll keep looking for reasons why our group doesn't like our partner until we find them, and if we can't find them, we might make them up.[5]

Romeo and Juliet relationships aren't typical, and usually they'll end of their own accord. Nor is it typical that our partner will be rejected outright by our social circle. That's because we have a good idea that he or she will be accepted before we bring them around, or we wouldn't do it. What is more typical is that our partner will be highly regarded by our network. That's a good situation as long as the couple is happy. However, their positive feelings can actually get in the way if the relationship is not working. It may be difficult to end it because family and friends can pressure the couple to stay together, but they may not be fully aware of the problems the couple is dealing with. From what they can see, the relationship appears good enough, and good enough is fine with them because they want the couple to stay in their network. Of course, they probably won't force partners to stay together forever, but they may end up staying with each other longer than they should have because of outside pressure.

Friends and family can also get in the way when marriages are having problems, even though that's not their intention. Very often they can end up adding fuel to the conflict and further dividing the couple. Sometimes we're to blame because of whom we choose from our network to help us when we have problems. We're trying to feel better, so we pick friends who are most likely to support our point of view. These people might even go so far as to give us reasons why we shouldn't be happy about our partner or our marriage. We might not go to people who would be objective, because sometimes objectivity is not what we're looking for.

Outsiders might also offer opinions about our problems that are misguided or inappropriate. They probably will only know one side of the story, and their advice won't take into account our partner's perspective. For example, telling a friend our partner always yells at us might lead that friend to give one piece of advice, but probably very different advice if they find out we do the yelling first. As the biggest concern, when friends and family insert themselves into our conflicts, we can become too reliant on them for guidance, and we might then avoid talking our problems out with our partner.

That's not to say that we should never discuss problems with others. Friends and family can provide valuable emotional support when times are bad. They are a counterbalance to the negativity we're dealing with at home, just as our spouse might be when we're coping with problems with friends, coworkers, or family members. However, confiding in a friend or family member cannot be much help in fixing a difficult marriage. Our friends can only give us moral support, but our marital issues won't get resolved until we work through them with our partner—without the assistance of outsiders.[6]

Another part of the socializing puzzle has to do with the amount of time couples spend with friends and family and with each other's network. Each of us has a social activity ideal, that is, an amount of social interaction we need to feel comfortable emotionally. Some prefer to spend a good deal of time with other people, while some prefer less social involvement and more solitude. Marriages work better when partners are matched on how often they want to attend social events or visit friends and family, but can face difficulties when they don't see eye to eye in this regard.

Men and women often have different ideas as to how much socializing is enough. In many marriages, wives prefer to see their friends and family more often than their husbands. As we've mentioned earlier, women have closer social ties and put in more time and effort to maintain their relationships. Most men, on the other hand, don't work as hard at their friendships. It's not that all men are socially detached; surely there are some who are more social than their wives, but that's not the rule.

Part of the reason might have to do with how men regard their relationships. They tend to focus more on tangible and practical benefits. For example, they might have friends who can get them a great price on appliances, let them know about job opportunities, know a good mechanic or handyman, and the like. Men actually have more people they can go to for practical help than do women. Unfortunately, their relationships also tend to be more superficial and lack the emotional investment usually found in women's relationships. Relatively few men confide in their friends or even make plans to get together. Instead, they typically look to their wives to help them with their social lives. It's because wives keep their husbands socially connected that marriage is more beneficial, and being single can be more damaging to men than to women.[7]

Rich and Deb had very different views about their social life. Deb liked to go out with other couples and visit their families fairly often, and she worked hard at keeping these relationships strong and connected.

Rich, on the other hand, preferred to stay home more or just do things alone with Deb. Rich actually liked their friends and enjoyed their social events, but it was more important that he and Deb spend time together. Rich was also somewhat of a loner who didn't have a lot of close friendships; instead, he really enjoyed spending time alone pursuing his own hobbies.

It became difficult for them to strike a balance between social time and time alone. Deb would get angry with Rich because she felt he didn't understand her social needs. Rich would get upset because he believed Deb was much less interested in him than her friends. It got to the point where being alone or with other people was not satisfying to either one. Deb was uncomfortable when they were with other people because she knew Rich didn't want to be there. Rich felt stressed when they stayed home because he knew Deb would rather go out. Both believed that the other didn't really understand or care about what they wanted, and that left them feeling distanced from each other.

Obviously, part of the solution required compromise, but it wasn't just their behaviors they had to change. They had to adjust how they thought about each other's socializing preferences. They had to learn that both had important and legitimate social needs, and the needs of both have to be respected and satisfied. That meant they had to acknowledge that, when they stayed home, it wasn't about punishing Deb or denying her social needs, and going out was not a denial of Rich's needs. Instead, they had to focus on the idea that doing what their partner wanted was a way to meet their needs and make each other feel good. Finally, they had to understand that, to truly meet their partner's needs, both would have to live with what they decided to do on a particular evening. Being angry or unhappy about staying home or going out would mean they hadn't solved their problem.

When partners differ on their social needs, they must find a mutually agreeable solution if they're going to avoid problems. Couples have to decide how often and which social gatherings they will attend so that both feel their needs are met. They must adopt the right attitude. Negotiated solutions are only that when they're made in good faith, that is, with total acceptance of the final decision by both partners. If we behave badly at a social gathering we don't want to attend, that's not a negotiated solution. Our partner won't feel comfortable; he or she may regret having attended at all and will resent us for making them feel that way. Similarly, a partner who wants a lot of social involvement cannot become angry or resentful when they're asked to skip some activities that their partner doesn't want to attend.

As another form of negotiated solution, we might decide to attend some events without our partner. This can be a good solution if partners are so far apart in their socializing preferences that choosing to go to some events and not others just won't make either one happy. However, we should point out that, even if this approach is acceptable to both partners, it may not be the best solution. We might get too comfortable going alone to events. If it becomes a habit, we've basically adopted the lifestyle of a single person. In other words, we might come to see ourselves less as a member of a couple, and we might come to feel less connected and committed to our relationship.

Along with couple friendships, each partner may have some friends that they see on their own. Having separate friends is healthy for a marriage and each partner. They allow us to maintain some of our individuality and personal identities, and let us satisfy certain needs that are not met by our spouse. If we like to go to the movies or to sporting events, we should not have to give these up if our partner doesn't enjoy them and won't go with us. Separate friends also keep us from becoming overly dependent on our partners and help keep our self-esteem strong. They also allow each partner time away from each other, and that can keep a relationship more engaging.

Couples are happiest when they spend about equal time with shared and individual friends. If a relationship is too lopsided in favor of couple friends, partners have little time for their own interests, or they may end up losing friendships that they value. Too much time spent with single friends, on the other hand, can leave each partner feeling uninvolved or alienated from the other's life. If separate-friend bonds overpower the bond between the couple, that can leave the relationship vulnerable because partners are less absorbed in a married lifestyle.

To summarize what makes for a successful social life for a married couple, it really comes down to balance and fairness. We need a variety of people to satisfy all of our emotional and social needs, and the larger and more diverse our network, the better. With a large circle of friends that are separate and shared, we're less dependent on specific friendships and on our partner, and so we feel more in control of our lives. Furthermore, unless a couple prefers one group over the other, time should be split between each partner's family and friends. Splitting time equally between the two groups makes both partners feel their relationship has some fairness to it, and it allows each to stay connected to people who are important to them. [8]

George and Linda both had a lot of outside interests, but they rarely did things together. The problem seemed to stem from Linda; she wasn't interested in doing anything that George liked doing. George said that when they were first married, they did a lot of things together, but that stopped a few years ago. Now, they both either have activities they do on their own or have things they do with their separate friends. This has led to some emotional distancing and some questions about the future of their relationship. From George's perspective, he began to wonder how they could stay married if they couldn't enjoy doing things together.

George said that every time he asked Linda to join him, she always came up with an excuse, so he stopped asking her. When asked to respond, Linda became angry. "Whenever he asks me to go to the movies, it's always something he wanted to see; if I tried to do something with him that I've never done before, say like playing golf or dance lessons, he would make fun of me because I wasn't very good at it. If I recommended we do something or go somewhere on vacation, he never wanted to do that, or if we did do it, he'd complain the entire time. I've learned that he's a control freak. If we're not doing what he wants, it's not good enough, and when we're doing what he wants, I'm not good enough. He has taken all the fun out of doing things together."

More than taking the fun out, Linda really came to hate how George treated her whenever they did things together. George didn't realize that every time he criticized her choice of activities, he wasn't just putting down the activity, he was also putting down Linda, and she was angry with him for that. Linda was finally convinced to give George a second chance, but he had to do some penance. For the immediate future, they could only do things of her choosing, and when they did them, he was not allowed to complain. George was going to have a hard time keeping his side of the bargain.

Another aspect of balance that makes for a successful marriage has to do with the amount of time couples spend doing things with each other without other couples. Partners who do things together become more closely connected and come to enjoy each other's company. That's because shared experiences give partners something in common and that gives them a reason to like each other. For couples who have established a habit of doing things together, they actually come to enjoy these activities more than those performed either on their own or with other people.

We should point out that it's not clear whether spending more time together leads to a happier marriage, or couples who are happy just spend more time together. This is an important distinction, because the former implies that an unhappy marriage can be made better if partners participate in more joint activities. That certainly may be the case for some, but it would seem just as likely that added time together means more opportunities for conflict for couples who aren't getting along well.

Nevertheless, the evidence suggests that the two are reciprocal—that is, a good marriage leads to more joint activities, and joint activities improve a bad marriage. That's why therapists will look at how much time couples with chronic problems spend together and will suggest they do more things as a couple as a way to improve their relationship. Starting this process can be difficult, particularly if these couples have a lot of bad feelings for each other or are not used to doing things together. More time with each other can spell more occasions for negativity. Nevertheless, if couples can be patient and accumulate some good experiences, they'll come to feel better and closer to each other. Positive time together can actually lead to better ways of communicating, and that can help partners become better at handling other issues. [9]

It's not just the amount of time together that matters; just as important is how that time is used. For joint activities to be beneficial, they have to meet a few criteria. First, they have to lead partners to interact with each other in a positive way. Even simple chores, such as grocery shopping or gardening, can add to a relationship if partners are engaged while they're doing it. If our activities don't provide opportunities for us to talk or joke around with our partner, they may not be very useful.

Some of the best activities are those that neither partner has tried before. What makes a new activity so beneficial is that it's owned by the couple and not one partner. It's something that is specific to their relationship. Additionally, when we're involved in something new, we have to work our way through it together with our partner, and that can make us feel more bonded. Besides, doing something you haven't done before not only can add to personal growth, the awkwardness that's often associated with learning new things can be amusing, and laughing with and at each other can definitely make you feel more connected.

Secondly, joint activities have to be enjoyable to both partners. Some couples have at least a few similar interests, so they shouldn't have much trouble coming up with things they can do together. Having similar interests is just as important as having the same values and beliefs when it comes to two people liking each other. If they don't have things they both enjoy or can't find something new, they can take turns participating in each other's activities. Again, fairness and balance are essential. Partners should have an equal say in selecting activities, and equal time should be dedicated to each partner's interests. If we only choose to do something we like, our partner will probably get tired of that arrangement, and our time together may then become more damaging than enhancing to our relationship.

Just as important as fairness is commitment. This is the same point we made earlier about accepting a partner's social circle or balancing the time we socialize with each network. If we agree to participate in our partner's activity, we have to do so willingly and give the impression that we're interested. This is another form of emotion work, the art of presenting ourselves as attentive even though we might not be, because we have the goal of making our partner happy. If we act bored, impatient, or disinterested with a partner's activity, we not only take away their enjoyment, but that same attitude is likely to be reciprocated when it's our turn to pick an activity. [10]

Marriages also benefit when spouses have time for themselves, either to pursue their own interests or just to relax. Personal leisure time is good for each partner's psychological well-being. As with separate friends, it allows us to maintain our individual identities, provides opportunities to do things we like to do, and lets us feel like we have some control over our lives. It's generally acknowledged by marriage counselors that alone time is important because it helps to keep a relationship fresh and less stressful.

How much personal time is optimal varies from couple to couple. What's most important is that spouses agree on how much time they want together and apart. In marriages where personal time is handled correctly, neither partner feels neglected and both think they're getting their fair share. In this regard, perceptions are more important than the actual number of hours. Even if couples spend very little time together or apart, the relationship is fine if that's what they both want. If each partner has different perspectives, however, the amount of time together and apart can be a source of conflict. For some partners, too much together time can be suffocating, while for others too little can make them feel insecure and isolated.

Again, husbands and wives tend to have different ideas as to the value of their time together, and how much time should be dedicated to the couple and the individual. Wives tend to want more couple time, usually because they regard it as important for bolstering a marriage and making sure there's solidarity as a couple. Many husbands, on the other hand, tend to prefer less time with their wives and like more time for themselves.

That's not to say men aren't that interested in spending time with their wives. Rather, it may stem from the fact that men have more and better quality leisure time than women. As we brought up in a previous chapter, men are pretty good at compartmentalizing, so issues they're dealing with in one part of their lives don't interfere with the other parts. That makes it easier for them to put their work and home responsibilities aside and enjoy whatever else they're doing. Perhaps more importantly, many husbands expect their wives to take care of their home and family. Consequently, they don't feel as much pressure to sacrifice their personal time as their wives might. Furthermore, it's our guess that the activities men engage in are not only enjoyable; it may be their way of staying emotionally and socially connected to other men. The tactics that women use to feel connected with their friends, such as heart-to-heart conversations about their issues and concerns, are not available to most men. However, men can satisfy their need to connect by doing something they're pretty good at—playing with other men.

Women's responsibilities make their leisure time problematic. Their concerns about child care and maintaining their homes are always on their minds, even when they're supposed to be taking time off. While some may be good at balancing their various roles as spouse, worker, and home maintainer, many are unable to switch off these roles and relax enough to get absorbed in their personal activities. The result is to make their personal time more fragmented, stressful, and much less enjoyable. Additionally, despite all their responsibilities, many women don't feel as entitled to free time as do men. They might feel guilty when they take time for themselves, and that can take a toll on them. It's likely that work overload and their inability to take time off may be why women are more prone to suffer from anxiety and depression, and get sick more often than men (even though they outlive them).

Taking a break is important for the mental health of each partner and the well-being of the marriage. For wives who find it difficult to take personal breaks or who constantly sublimate their own needs to those of her family, husbands might want to encourage them to pursue their own interests. However, in order for her to enjoy such activities, he will have to assure her that her home and family will be fine, and a big part of that assurance includes taking on the responsibilities she's trying to let go of. Husbands might want to keep in mind that this is not entirely altruistic, but rather is in their best interests. A break away from responsibilities will make wives happier, and when wives are happy, husbands generally feel the same way.

As we've referenced throughout, balance and compromise are the essential points to remember when it comes to using time. A mix of time with friends and family, time together as a couple, and separate time for each partner, add to marital quality. An equal split between our circle and activities and those of our partner is not only fair, it's also healthy for the relationship. We should also mention that a couple's leisure time should be split between spouses-only versus time spent with children. While men will tend to lump the two together, possibly so they can kill two birds with one stone, wives will generally differentiate between the two, and will require time with her husband, both with and without children. Women are with their children quite often, and time with just her husband breaks up her workload and helps her feel she has a balanced lifestyle, along with her sanity. [11]

If balance is missing, it's wise to have a straightforward discussion with your partner and work out the necessary compromises to get to a better place. Such discussions should focus not only on the practical aspects of time allocation, but also on the reasons for the imbalance. For example, if your spouse avoids joint activities with you, find out if it's the activities themselves or some other reason. Your partner may have issues about how you act when doing your activities or how you react to his or her activities. While you might not like the answer, at least you'll learn something about your relationship, and you can then work on that. Putting such discussions off or dismissing this issue as unimportant is wrong-headed. The negative emotions that result from how you use time as a couple could affect other parts of your relationship. Besides, if your problem is truly time allocation, this is one that is easy to fix, so it's best to eliminate it and have one less thing to worry about.

Keep in mind that partners have psychological needs filled by people outside of their marriage who are important to them. When we reject the people from their social circle, we not only deny our partner the opportunity to connect with them, we also deny them the ability to have those needs satisfied. If we find it hard to accept our partner's network, it's good to acknowledge that each of us has friends and family members who are a bit strange or difficult, and yet we keep them in our own circle. If we can show the same tolerance to our spouse's group, he or she will feel better about us and more committed to our relationship, and at the same time we've eliminated a source of conflict. Besides, expanding our circle to include people who are different from what we're used to can add to our own personal growth and well-being.

As a final point, when your marriage is in a difficult phase, do yourself and your spouse a favor and keep family and friends out of it. While you might want to seek comfort from those close to you, they're likely to be more of a problem than an aid in the long run. Because they will hear only one side of the story, their advice may not be accurate and therefore not particularly helpful. More importantly, they will come to know your secrets. These they will not forget, nor will you; so going forward, your private life will become part of the relationship you have with them, long after your marriage problems have been resolved. Besides, when you go outside the relationship, you lose opportunities to learn how to solve your problems together. That skill is important; you not only can fix what's wrong, but working through them together actually builds the connection between partners.

7

OUR PERSONAL BAGGAGE

In the previous chapter we talked about how outsiders, such as friends and families, can affect the course and quality of a marriage. There are other outside forces, such as children and money, which can work for or against a marriage because they can affect how partners treat each other. Yet more impactful than these external factors are the things that are inside each of us and define who we are.

Each partner brings along personal baggage to their relationship. These are the things that are stored inside our heads that we've learned and experienced since we were children; they form the bases for our thoughts, emotions, and behaviors. They affect how we interpret situations, the kinds of emotions we experience, and the behaviors we display to the outside world. How we turn out as adults has a lot to do with how we interact with our partner; and how we interact with our partner has everything to do with the goodness of our marriage.

Some of our baggage is good and some not so good. The good stuff makes it easy for us to have close relationships. It gets others to like us and allow us to develop strong emotional connections. It also gives us the tools we need to overcome problems that emerge in all marriages. The bad stuff can be destructive. It makes it difficult for us to connect with other people and causes us to have relationships that are contentious and unfulfilling. When one or both partners possess such traits, the marriage can become unstable and very often this is the reason for its failure.

Our personalities are one form of baggage. When we talk about personality, we mean the characteristics that make us unique individuals.

Personality begins to form from the moment of birth—and possibly from the moment of conception. Many social scientists argue that some parts of our personalities are inherited, that is to say, genetic. It is well known, for example, that mental illness and certain types of mood disorders run in families. There's also evidence that the way newborns respond emotionally to their environment is pretty much how they will do so as adults. Calm newborns become calm adults, and excitable ones become excitable adults. Some researchers even propose that if we inherit characteristics that affect our ability to have close relationships, then by logical extension, some of us might be preprogrammed for divorce.

Whether and to what extent our inherited characteristics emerge depends on our environment. Said another way, we're born with a certain amount of potential, that is, talents and predispositions. Our environment and experiences determine to what degree we reach our full potential. For example, we could have the talent to become a great musician. If we're never given the opportunity to play an instrument, then that potential will never be realized. That's a reason why two people with the same talents can become very different people if they're exposed to different environments. Likewise, because people have different potentials and talents, they will still develop into very different people even though they grow up in the same environment.[1] Regardless of whether it's genetics, the environment, or both, our personality traits are firmly embedded in us. The fact that our traits are permanent is a good thing. They make us act consistently in similar situations, and that makes us predictable. Predictability of behavior patterns, attitudes, and beliefs makes it possible to have close relationships with other people. If people weren't consistent, our interactions with them would be difficult because we couldn't trust how they would react to something we say or do. They would seem to be completely different people each time we dealt with them.

Nevertheless, people won't always behave the same in all situations. Our personalities are actually multidimensional—that is, each of us possesses many traits to one degree or another. We have some traits that are strong, some that are moderate, and some that are weak or submissive. Some traits may be dominant in certain situations, while others may be stronger in other situations. That's why a person who is shy in social settings can be very assertive in business settings. Consequently, while most people have behavior patterns, thoughts, and beliefs that are predictable and that consistently define who they are, no person is perfectly consistent or predictable all the time. It can depend on the situation and the people they're interacting with.

There's also fluidity to our personalities. We might be very agreeable and easy-going under normal circumstances but act neurotically or become very difficult in extreme situations. We can also change how we act, think, and feel—that is, we can change the way we express our personalities. We can learn mental strategies that allow us to act or think in a way that runs counter to what our personalities incline us to. If that weren't possible, psychological counseling would have no purpose.

Julie wasn't the type of person who was afraid of confrontation. She had no problem discussing issues that bothered her with friends and family. However, she had a much harder time expressing herself when it came to her marriage. She tended to avoid confrontation with her husband, Mitch, and when that wasn't possible, she would remain quiet while he did most of the talking. Mitch, on the other hand, was very outspoken during conflicts, and he found it troublesome that Julie wouldn't engage with him when they had something to deal with.

Julie claimed she hated arguing with Mitch because she always felt belittled afterward. He became emotionally intense and would do a lot of shouting, and she found his behavior and his words intimidating. When confronted with Julie's opinion, he became defensive and claimed he didn't mean anything by it. "I am naturally excitable. When people in my family get angry or frustrated, we always yell and scream. It's just my nature to be like that and not something I can control, so you have to find a way to put up with it."

Mitch believed the things he learned from his family justified how he behaved as an adult. He found it hard to accept that his behavior was inappropriate, and that as an adult he could not use that as an excuse to act that way. He wasn't aware that while he might have picked up such traits as a child, it was in his power to change how he expressed himself, even if he still felt a tendency to behave that way.

Our marriage can also determine which traits are dominant and submissive. We can behave one way if we feel good about our marriage and another if we don't like the way we're treated. If we're in an abusive relationship, we're likely to become more anxious and alienated. If we're constantly under financial pressure, we might become more impatient and aggressive. As a key point to keep in mind, marriage is a dynamic situation with forever-changing circumstances, and these changing circumstances can change us. How we change actually reflects our need to adjust to the demands of our changing environment.

As we mentioned, personality traits are beneath the thoughts and emotions we experience. Some traits produce negative thoughts and emotions, while others incline us to positive thoughts and emotions. Our thoughts and emotions become the triggers for our behaviors. We do and say things that are consistent with the thoughts and emotions we're experiencing. For example, when we have problems trusting people, we might react to whatever they say or do by making cynical or sarcastic comments. We might also keep an emotional distance from others, causing us to appear aloof and disinterested.[2]

Because personality traits drive thoughts and emotions, and thoughts and emotions trigger a corresponding set of words and deeds, it's clear that our personalities can affect our marriage. The behaviors and attitudes that spring from our emotions are what we express to our partners, and these can influence their mood and emotional state. When they react to whatever we've said or done, that can cause us to reciprocate; then they do the same to us, and so on. An overly aggressive husband might cause his wife to give him the silent treatment, which then might make him feel isolated and depressed. A wife who makes condescending remarks might knock down the self-esteem of her husband, causing him to be resentful, which in turn makes her angry. Our point is that some of the ways partners react to each other may be triggered by a specific event, but it can be made worse or better depending on the personality traits of each partner.

We're very much aware that we can be affected by other's personalities. We like to be around some people and not so much around others, and it's because of their traits, or rather, what these traits lead them to say or do. We actually use that awareness when we select a mate. We'll take a careful look at a person's behavioral and emotional patterns, because that's how we can discern their personality. What we often say we're looking for is someone who is nice. In actuality, we gravitate to others whose personalities are like our own. We might do so because we personally believe we're also nice, but more likely we do it because it's easier to relate to someone who's like ourselves. The fact is marriage is a lot easier when partners share many of the same personality traits. Similarity doesn't necessarily guarantee we'll be happy, nor is it the case that if our personalities are different we'll never be happy, but similarity makes it easier to get along.

So when we say we want someone who is nice, we actually mean compatible to us. Such a person may not possess the finest qualities, but he or she may have traits we also possess or ones that fill our needs. So in that sense they're perfect for us. When personalities are well-matched, partners often interpret events in the same way, and have similar expectations, psychological needs, and goals. Because our traits are linked to thoughts and emotions, we also have the same emotional reactions to various experiences. Consequently, we have an easier time understanding our partner's intentions and motivations. When partners understand each other, it's easier for them to feel emotionally connected. Being understood also makes us feel good about ourselves because it validates who we are and our perspective on the world. [3]

While we strive for similarity, sometimes we end up with a person whose personality is different from our own. However, even if couples don't share many traits initially, they tend to become more similar the longer they're together. Remember, we possess a variety of traits, and these can be dominant or submissive depending on circumstances. When we adopt some of our partner's traits and they take some of ours, we mean certain traits we already possess will become more dominant. Converging of personalities can actually be looked at as a form of adapting to our environment. Usually it's the submissive partner who does the changing, becoming more like the dominant partner. High-powered individuals have the capacity to influence others in a variety of contexts—and that includes in their marriage.

Partners won't only adopt each other's traits; they can also take on their social skills, eating and drinking habits, how they view others, as well as their cognitive skills, such as inductive reasoning, word fluency, and intellectual aptitude. Put another way, who we choose to marry can affect our mental capabilities. A higher-functioning partner may bring up the skills of a lower-functioning one; but the opposite can also occur. It is possible for the higher-functioning spouse to be brought down to the level of the lower-functioning partner. For example, we might alter our speech patterns to include more profanity if we're married to someone who expresses themselves in that way.

Even if partners don't become similar, they will think they are. They will see similarities where they don't exist. We tend to take an egocentric view of the world, which is to say we project our own values, traits, beliefs, and even day-to-day feelings onto others. When we do that with our partner, it makes us feel more connected. Sometimes we can't see the similarities our partner sees, but that's okay. Just the fact that he or she thinks we're the same is likely to make us feel good about our relationship.[4]

Starting out with similar personality styles, developing similar styles over time, and perceiving similarities that aren't there are typical of successful marriages. It's one of the many ways two people can believe they're compatible. However, in unhappy marriages, partners are either very different from the outset and never move closer, or come to be less similar, or at least think they're less similar, as their relationship progresses. These real or imagined differences make the marriage contentious. Because they interpret events differently and have different emotional reactions to the same situations, they find a lot of reasons to argue. As these marriages deteriorate further, partners focus more and more on their personal differences and will come to believe they've either grown apart or were incompatible to begin with.

It actually makes sense that couples in bad marriages adopt this way of thinking. Partners can use their personal differences to justify their negative feelings about their marriage. As these beliefs take hold, their emotional distance widens, and as they move further apart, they give themselves more justification for their negative feelings. Unfortunately, as they adopt this perspective, it can also become much harder for them to get back together.[5]

Nick believed he was easy to get along with. He saw himself as social; he claimed he had quite a few friends and enjoyed being with other people. However, his relationships tended to be superficial. He just didn't connect emotionally with others, nor did he want to, and he wasn't much better at connecting with his wife, Marisa.

With the right kind of person, he might have made an acceptable partner. Nick might have learned from that person how to get in touch with his emotions and be more willing to express his feelings. A more secure person might also have been more comfortable with how Nick behaved in his relationships. Unfortunately, his wife, Marissa, was not that kind of person. Marissa had a tendency to feel insecure in her relationships. When she felt things were not right, she could spend a good deal of time worrying about what was wrong or what she did wrong, and she sometimes needed to be reassured that she was still liked.

About five years into their marriage, it reached a low point. They were fighting quite a bit and neither felt there was much of a marriage between them. Nick claimed that their fighting was always caused by Marisa: "No matter what we argue about, she gets nasty and acts irrationally, and it always comes down to there being something wrong with me."

Marisa disagreed completely. She said that while she was the one to bring up issues, it was how he acted when they discussed something that would make her so angry. She felt the real problem was that she couldn't get through to Nick. "When we argue, he just sits there and says nothing, or at least nothing of any value. And the more I try to reach him, the less I feel I am." She never knew what he was thinking, and she believed he didn't care about her. As a result, she was in a bad mood all the time and thought her marriage was falling apart. For that she blamed Nick, and she treated him accordingly.

Nick didn't realize that his inability to express himself made Marisa feel insecure about their relationship. What Marisa didn't realize was that when she pushed Nick to connect with her emotionally, he would withdraw even further. The more she pushed, the more he withdrew, and the less secure she would feel. And the more insecure she felt, the harder she would push, and the angrier she would become when he wouldn't respond. His tendency to avoid emotional connections and her need to be connected and reassured meant the two were caught in a negative pattern that was going to be hard to break out of.

For some couples who are mismatched, it may be a result of not knowing what they should have been looking for in a mate. It can be difficult to be aware of the traits that mesh well with our own personalities and truly understand which ones we can live with. We may think we can tolerate certain traits, but instead they turn out to be detrimental for a relationship, or they might negatively affect how we think and act. Unfortunately for some, they may not come to understand that a partner has destructive or incompatible traits until after they've tied the knot.[6]

That brings us to the issue of which traits are linked to successful relationships. Psychologists break down personality into what they call the Big Five. These include agreeableness, extroversion, conscientiousness, emotional stability, and open-mindedness Each trait has a polar opposite, so emotional stability has emotionally stable at one end of the scale and unstable at the other end. Each of us falls somewhere on the scale between the two extremes on all traits. Where we fall dictates how we interact with others and interpret events as well as how we are viewed by other people.

AGREEABLENESS

Agreeableness relates to our ability to get along with others. People who are agreeable are trusting and trustworthy, and even-handed in their relationships. They're typically positive, altruistic, and obliging, rather than antagonistic, egotistical, and competitive. In marriage, agreeable partners are less likely to provoke conflicts and are better at handling them when they arise. They're open to compromise and are willing to sacrifice their own personal needs to accommodate the wishes of their partners. Because they're more trusting, they're less prone to question the motives and intentions of their partners.

At the opposite end, spouses who are disagreeable tend to stir up conflicts with their partners. Their arguments are often accompanied by yelling, insulting, criticizing, and other forms of verbal abuse. Disagreeable individuals place their personal needs and interests above getting along, so they can be insensitive and inconsiderate. Sometimes their skepticism about their partner's motives causes them to be suspicious, unfriendly, and uncooperative.

EXTROVERSION

Extroverts love to engage with other people and don't get much enjoyment out of alone time. They tend to be enthusiastic, action-oriented individuals who are up-beat, assertive, and have a positive attitude. Introverts, on the other hand, tend to be less socially engaged and have lower energy levels. They tend to require less stimulation than extroverts, and while they might be perfectly comfortable in social situations, they prefer instead time to themselves to pursue their own interests.

This is the only grouping that doesn't seem to affect the success or failure of a marriage. There's no evidence that you're better off being married to an extrovert or an introvert. On the one hand, extroverts are very good at establishing emotional connections with others—and that includes their partners. On the other, their need for social involvement and stimulation can put pressure on a marriage, especially if their partner prefers less social stimulation and more downtime. Still, one style is not necessarily better than the other, and it really depends on how one partner feels about the extroverted or introverted tendencies of the other.

CONSCIENTIOUSNESS

Conscientiousness refers to being goal oriented and having a need to achieve. Highly conscientious people tend to be reliable, self-disciplined, and well organized. They're likely to be reasonable and considerate of their partners, and are prone to putting effort into making their marriages work. Their sense of responsibility, willingness to work at their relationship, and need to make it succeed makes them much less argumentative and antagonistic.

In contrast, those who are not conscientious are more self-involved and less considerate of others. Because they tend to be less motivated, they might not work as hard at their marriage, nor are they likely to put in their fair share when it comes to household chores. They've also been found to have weaker impulse control and so may be more prone to act without thinking, make off-the-cuff negative comments, or have extramarital affairs.

EMOTIONAL STABILITY

Emotional stability may be the most important trait for marriage. Emotionally stable individuals tend to be secure, confident, and even-tempered. They're not overreactive and generally maintain a positive demeanor. In short, they take things in stride and are effective in getting along with others, even those whom others might find difficult.

In contrast, people who are emotionally unstable are highly anxious and tend to be absorbed with negative emotions. They suffer from chronic bad moods, and these affect how they interact with people. They're also more prone to irrational thoughts and misinterpretation of events. They may, for example, interpret an off-hand remark or joke as a personal affront or as a sign that there are problems in the marriage. Because of how they can interpret situations, they're usually unhappy in their relationships and hold negative feelings about their partners, and these feelings come out in how they treat them.

Highly anxious people are often argumentative and are likely to overreact during conflicts, expressing themselves through complaints, criticisms, contempt, defensiveness, and loudness. They also tend to believe they're not listened to during an argument, which provokes them to even more anger. Additionally, they can be self-absorbed, demanding, jealous, and possessive. In short, their partners have to work hard to keep their relationship on an even keel.

OPEN-MINDEDNESS

Open-minded people generally have liberal attitudes, are intellectually curious, creative, adventurous, and like new experiences. They're prone to hold unconventional opinions and beliefs, and tend to be more in touch with their feelings. Because they're empathetic, their partners see them as caring, sensitive, understanding, and concerned about their needs. Additionally, their ability to be flexible means they can take a proactive and thoughtful approach to disagreements. They are very good at handling conflicts with others but are in fact less likely to have them in the first place.

Those who are closed-minded have more conventional and traditional interests. They prefer the familiar, are more conservative, and are generally uncomfortable with change. While such attitudes are not necessarily problematic for a relationship, closed-minded people tend to lack the positive traits associated with open-mindedness, such as flexibility and empathy. Instead, their rigidity can make them appear self-absorbed, neglectful, and inconsiderate, particularly when presented with new ideas by their partners.[7]

People who lean toward the positive end of the scale on agreeableness, conscientiousness, open-mindedness, and emotional stability have the potential to be excellent partners. However, very few people have all the positive traits. As we've mentioned, each of us possesses all traits to one extent or another, and most of us are positive on some and negative on others. There are highly conscientious people who are weak on emotional stability or highly agreeable people who are closed-minded.

Whatever personality weaknesses we have, we tend to compensate for them with our strengths. Take a person who is disagreeable but also highly conscientious. While he or she might be prone to instigate arguments, at the same time they might work extra hard meeting their partner's needs so that their relationships can stay intact. It's the balance of our good and bad traits, with the good helping to cancel out the bad, that makes us tolerable to others. It's often those who are at the extreme negative end on certain dimensions, such as emotional stability, who are likely to have chronic marital problems that spring specifically from their personalities.

However, even if we have a good balance of strengths and weaknesses, there can still be personality issues in a marriage. For example, a moderately disagreeable partner who conscientiously tries to fix the conflicts they start can be a constant source of anxiety to someone who doesn't like confrontation at all. Another who believes success is most important might find a partner who's only moderately conscientious to be unworthy of their love and respect, even though that partner may possess other good traits. An extroverted person might find the solitude that's preferred by their introverted partner to be boring.

Furthermore, even if partners' personalities are in sync, the conditions of the marriage can upset that balance. Again, personalities have some fluidity, and environmental conditions can affect how we think and act. An open-minded person may become frustrated and develop a pattern of combativeness if married to a close-minded individual. If a partner is uncommitted or untrustworthy, an emotionally stable person can come to act chronically anxious and angry. A person who is easy-going may gradually become more aggressive and less agreeable if they are under constant stress or have to cope with chronic negative events, such as financial problems.

Phil was a highly conscientious guy who was extremely dedicated to his career. In other aspects of his life, he had a very casual live-and-let-live attitude and didn't put many restrictions on himself. Barbara tended to be little more rigid; she liked things organized and had strong opinions about how her marriage should play out. They came to counseling be-

cause they were disillusioned with their marriage. More to the point, they were disillusioned with each other.

According to Barbara, "You're just not the person I thought I married. When we were dating, you were patient, kind, and easy-going. That was the type of person I wanted to marry. Now you have no patience for me, and you always seem on edge. It takes almost nothing for you to lose your temper. I'm at the point where I'm afraid to bring up things that are bothering me because I know you'll get crazy. Even when we make up after a fight, I just can't get out of my head how nasty you can be to me."

Phil responded, "Well, you're not the person I thought I married either. When we were dating, you didn't worry about anything. But after we got married, you had all these rules as to how I should act and what I'm supposed to do. I'm really not that much into the rules, and I don't like being told what to do. And when I don't do exactly what you want, I get the silent treatment. I'm always looking over my shoulder waiting to be criticized for one thing or another."

Barbara and Phil changed how they treated each other because the rules of their relationship had changed. Barbara's concerns about "doing the right thing" played against Phil's open, laissez-faire style. He felt frustrated and angry much of the time, and he took it out on Barbara. He was also having a hard time dealing with the stress of his career.

Phil's preoccupation with his career made Barbara feel insecure, which she expressed by forcing Phil to pay more attention to their relationship. The truth is they both had certain traits that they normally kept under control, but changing circumstances had caused these to come to the surface. Phil had a tendency to become aggressive and disagreeable when he felt out of control, and that's how he felt because of the stress of his job and the pressure he was feeling from Barbara. Barbara tended toward insecurity when she felt Phil was not as interested in things that were important to her. The changes in their lifestyle had caused them to behave like very different people as compared to when their living conditions were less taxing.

Beyond our individual personality traits, we bring other types of baggage to our marriage. These are probably best described as behavioral styles, and they may derive from how certain personality traits work in combination with each other. One of these is expressivity. This is usually a problem for men, or more precisely, a problem that women have about men, and includes being in touch with one's emotions and being able to express them. When couples are emotionally expressive, each partner believes the other is actively and emotionally engaged, and that helps them feel close to each other. There's also greater clarity in communication, and that makes it easier for them to work through their problems. When we know our partner's thoughts and feelings, we can understand their needs and be more effective in meeting those needs.

At the opposite end is ambivalence, the inability to make our true feelings known. Emotional inexpressiveness suggests a lack of trust and/ or commitment, or at least that's how partners are likely to interpret such behavior. If our partners cannot express themselves, we're never really sure of their thoughts and intensions, and that makes it almost impossible to discuss problems. Furthermore, inexpressiveness may actually cause broader problems. When we're uncertain what our partners are thinking or feeling, we can develop a more generalized and extensive sense of insecurity. We might question how our partner feels about us and where our relationship stands overall. When we're not sure where we stand, we're prone to distance ourselves emotionally in an effort to protect ourselves.

Constraint is another behavioral trait, and it relates to our ability to control our impulses. Constraint is much more than just being able to avoid extramarital affairs; it relates to how we conduct ourselves on a day-to-day basis. It's what keeps us from overreacting to all kinds of situations. The underlying dynamic to constraint is commitment. We're best at controlling our impulses when we're committed to our spouse and our marriage. Commitment makes us feel there's nothing more important than keeping our relationship happy, so we're careful about what we do and say.

Relationships sometimes run into problems because partners are hurtful to each other, and that's especially likely to happen with a low-constraint partner. If we lack constraint, we might make a sarcastic comment or give our partners a hostile glance for something they've said or done, even if it's harmless or silly. We tend to be impulsive and cannot disengage emotionally. So, during conflicts, we're prone to lose our patience, surrender rational thinking, and let our emotions get the better of us. We might say things that we shouldn't or that convey a negative attitude through our tone of voice or body language. Consequently, our arguments are likely to be intense and will usually move off the issue, and that means we'll have a hard time finding solutions.

Another behavioral style is narcissism. Although we've touched on this in a previous chapter, it's worth revisiting here because it's believed to be more prevalent today. To review, narcissistic individuals focus primarily on their own personal needs and interests. They have a few positive qualities (e.g., high self-esteem), but their negative traits really can't make up for their positives when it comes to intimate relationships. Narcissists typically lack empathy, have difficulty making emotional connections, and tend to exploit the people around them.

In marriage, narcissists tend to put their own needs ahead of those of their relationship and their partner. They're less inclined to compromise and can act aggressively when criticized, when they believe their personal interests are threatened, or when they feel rejected. A disagreement with a narcissist often ends with a "my way or the highway" attitude, so we're not likely to have many of our own needs satisfied. We're also likely to resent their unwillingness to bend and their desire for us to be subservient. If we then show our resentment, they're apt to interpret it as a signal that they're not loved, or at least not loved as they want to be, so the relationship becomes less important to them. [8]

Another topic we've already touched on is attachment styles. To reiterate, attachment styles have to do with the way we connect with other people. They're a set of beliefs that we learn from how we were treated in past relationships, and we use them as guidelines when we get older. If, for example, when we were young and felt upset, someone made us feel better, we come to expect the same from our adult partners, and we're prone to see relationships as a source of comfort and security. But if we felt abandoned or neglected in the past, then we might feel insecure and anxious in our future relationships. Attachment styles can have a profound effect on how we interact with our partners.

People typically have one of three attachment styles. We're not usually completely one or another; rather, we tend to lean toward one style to varying degrees. However, the more entrenched we are in one camp, the greater is the impact on our relationship skills. Additionally, each partner has their own attachment style, so these have to be considered in combination because some pairings might work better than others.

Of the three, a secure attachment style is the healthiest. Securely attached individuals enjoy their relationships and make intimate and close bonds to others. They're more likely to treat their partners well because they don't feel threatened, and their partners tend to treat them better in return. When there are disagreements, they tend to stick to the topic and don't exaggerate the importance of what they're fighting about. Consequently, disagreements are less likely to escalate or degenerate into something ugly. Even when times are tough, they can feel good about their partner because they don't overanalyze their relationship.

More troublesome is avoidance attachment. These individuals tend to be uncomfortable with intimacy and keep an emotional distance in their relationships. At the heart of avoidance attachment is a lack of trust and a fear of separation. If we're married to someone who has an avoidance attachment style, we're not likely to feel they're emotionally connected or committed to us, and that makes it hard for us to stay committed to them. They can be particularly tough to deal with when there are conflicts because they tend to withdraw into a shell. That's because avoidance attached people feel most threatened during difficult times or when confronted.

The third and possibly most destructive style is anxiety attachment. This is defined by insecurity driven by worries over rejection or abandonment. Those who have an anxious style are hypervigilant in their relationships. They watch their partners closely and suspiciously, looking for evidence that justifies their insecurity. Their worries lead them to instigate conflicts, and these can be emotionally charged. Not surprisingly, anxiety attached people are generally unhappy in their relationships and pessimistic about their future. They also presume their partners feel the same way, which increases their fear of being abandoned. Through their own actions, anxiety attached individuals unwittingly produce the result they fear most—a damaged and uncertain relationship.

It doesn't take much to imagine that certain pairings might work better than others. Combining anxiety and avoidance styles could be a nightmare. The emotional detachment of avoidance individuals would play directly into the abandonment fears of their anxiety attached partners. On the other hand, it's possible that two avoidance styles might work out. These partners are likely to have a peaceful coexistence, although there's not likely to be much emotional bonding. It's also possible that two anxiety styles can work. Although each is likely to drive the other crazy, they probably understand each other's issues. Consequently, they might be in a good position to reassure each other that they want to stay together. Of course, a person with a secure style would make a good partner in all relationships. Although being paired with an anxiety or avoidance partner is likely to try their patience, a securely attached partner may provide enough stability to the relationship to make their partners feel secure.

While attachment styles are somewhat resistant to change, they're not completely so. In fact, attachment styles actually play a much larger role early on in a relationship, when partners are learning about each other. Through the course of a marriage, all partners tend to move toward a more secure style, regardless of where they started out. Those who are already secure become more so, while those with insecure styles may improve as the relationship becomes more stable.

However, whether or not partners come to feel more secure depends on other dynamics of the relationship. If our partner is supportive and committed, any fears we have of rejection or abandonment should subside over time. But if we continue to feel vulnerable or uncertain about our partner, we'll probably end up holding onto our insecure styles. In fact, if we started out with a secure style, a relationship that makes us feel vulnerable or threatened can actually cause us to develop more of an insecure style.[9]

There's one more pattern that falls into the category of personal baggage. These are the behaviors and attitudes that we have picked up from our parents. They apply specifically to intimate relationships such as marriage, and may not necessarily be the same ones we use in other kinds of relationships. They can't be completely separated from our personality traits or attachment styles; they are part of our belief systems and are unique to marriage.

According to psychologist Albert Bandura, many of our thought patterns, beliefs, and behaviors are learned through watching and imitating the influential people around us—and most influential of all are our parents. They serve as role models and affect our social and interpersonal competence, that is, our ability to maintain positive relationships. How much of our thinking and behavior is affected by our parents depends on how well we remember our experiences as a child. The more negative the experiences and the greater the recollections, the greater the difficulty in overcoming their impact.

As a critical piece of learning, we tend to mimic their communication and interaction styles. For example, if parents bicker or use sarcasm, or do a lot of yelling when they argue, their children are likely to use them in their own relationships. If they tend to deny problems or avoid dealing with them head on, their children may have difficulty confronting their own problems as adults. Worst of all is the tendency for children coming from physically abusive and violent households to copy these patterns. For men, they're more likely to be the perpetrators of spousal abuse, while women are more likely to end up as victims. The difference between men and women seems to stem from the tendency for children to pick up the behavior of their same-sex parents. Boys learn to be abusers and girls to be victims, because those are the typical roles that their fathers and mothers played.

Whether or not we believe our parents were happy can influence our overall perspective on marriage. We see marriage as good or bad, depending on what it was like in our home, and we use that attitude to guide how we think about our own marriage. Children growing up with happily married parents regard marriage favorably and won't consider divorce as their first option. Starting out with such a positive attitude also has the benefit of being self-fulfilling. If we think something will succeed, odds are it will because we try to make it successful.

On the other hand, if we hold a negative attitude and expect our marriage to fail, we're less committed and more open to alternative lifestyles and alternative relationships. That's the risk faced by children who come from divorced households. They're more likely to run into relationship problems and end up divorced themselves, especially if their parents split up when they were twelve years of age or younger. In fact, even if their own marriage seems to be working, divorce is always something they will consider, and becomes foremost in their minds in the midst of hard times.

Along with their openness to divorce, these children often learn other behaviors that are detrimental to intimate relationships. These can include jealousy born out of insecurity, inappropriate emotional patterns, and infidelity. They may also have difficulty trusting others or have problems making a commitment. As we've pointed out, these are fundamental cornerstones of a successful marriage, and without them it's extremely difficult to have a meaningful and emotionally connected relationship.

Certainly not everyone who grew up with divorced parents will end up divorced. Some adopt attitudes and behaviors as adults that allow them to be successful in all kinds of relationships, including marriage. Nor are we necessarily a slave to every emotional slight we suffered as children. We can learn more effective ways of thinking from other relationships and experiences outside those with our parents. We can learn not to dwell on past events, and we can identify things we should try to keep out of our own relationships. In other words, we're not carbon copies of our parents, and what we have learned we can unlearn.

Throughout this chapter we've stressed a few key points. First, for couples with chronic problems, be it constant fighting or feeling disconnected, sometimes they stem from our idiosyncrasies, personality traits, or past experiences. Events may serve as triggers, but it may be how we think and act in response to events, rather than the events themselves, that are at the root of a conflict. More to the point, it's how we express who we are—the emotions, attitudes, and behaviors we display to our partner—that might be the real problem. For example, in marriages where a partner is untrustworthy or uncommitted, anxiety and avoidance attachment styles might be justified. However, if our partner is committed and trustworthy, our attachment style may be the underlying problem, not our spouse's behavior.

Determining whether chronic problems are brought on by outside situations or from our personal characteristics requires self-examination. Only by understanding what's truly at the heart of our issues can we know what to focus on to improve our relationship. It also requires that we acknowledge our personal flaws, those things that prevent us from having a satisfying relationship. Coming to terms with our personal issues will make us a better person; ignoring them won't make them go away, and they may continue to wreak havoc on our marriage.

If we have certain traits that get in the way of our relationships, we can change the way these traits manifest themselves. We can change our behaviors and the way we think, so we are not controlled by irrational beliefs and non-adaptive emotions. It is possible to learn to be more open-minded and flexible in our thinking. We can learn to put negative thoughts aside so that we can interpret events more realistically and alter the ways we express our emotions. If we respond with anger every time we're frustrated, we can learn to monitor our anger, change our thinking about frustration, and thereby learn to control our anger.

Some of the things we want to change may be hard to accomplish on our own. Such patterns as narcissism, inexpressiveness, and low constraint can be the basis for chronic discord in a marriage, but they're well embedded in us and may have their own underlying causes. Yet these are precisely the kinds of problems that are the bread and butter of counselors and therapists. In other words, they're very treatable, but they require the right kind of help.

As we mentioned before, keep in mind that you can't change your partner's personality. Trying to make your partner a different person will only lead to frustration and disappointment. On the other hand, asking yourself or others to change their behavior has a better chance of succeeding. It is better to ask your spouse to change how they express anger (yelling, throwing things, name calling) than it is to ask them not to get angry. Similarly, excusing your behavior because that's "who you are" is nonsense. Screaming and yelling is a behavior, an expression of your anger, and that can be changed. So don't let yourself or others use innate nature or childhood experiences as an excuse for not learning to act in more appropriate ways.

We have to be careful when we conclude that a partner's personal flaw is what's wrong with our marriage. First, if that's so, we need to recognize that it's their choice to change, not ours. In fact, they might not regard the characteristic we're pointing to as a flaw and don't want or feel a need to act or think differently. If that's the case, we really don't have much choice but to adjust our thinking and accept them as they are. However, we ought to consider that it might be our own flaws, or our beliefs and expectations, that lead us to blame our partner. Who we are and how we think might lead us to misinterpret situations. So while we'd like to believe the fault lies with our partner, it might in fact lie within ourselves.

That's the problem with relying on self-diagnosis and treatment for such complex issues. You can get it wrong and do it badly. For example, an extremely conscientious person may have little patience for those who lack this trait, and as a result may appear argumentative or condescending in some situations. While a lay person may consider such a person as disagreeable, their real problem may be overconscientiousness. The point is you might find it much more fruitful to work out many of the problems we've discussed in this chapter through marriage counseling or one-on-one therapy.

8

COMMUNICATION AND CONFLICT

Larry and Maria were angry at each other. The problem was Larry had to leave work early to pick up Maria, and she kept him waiting fifteen minutes because something came up as she was about to walk out the door. When they were asked to describe why they were angry, Larry turned to Maria and said, "You think I have nothing better to do but sit in the car and wait for you. You always do that, and you don't see how inconsiderate you are. It doesn't even occur to you that having to leave work just to pick you up was a major imposition."

Maria then responded, "You think I was just fooling around and taking my time to get you angry. It never occurs to you that I couldn't help it. You never give me the benefit of the doubt." Maria then continued: "Besides, no matter what I ask you to do, it's always a major imposition. You can't stand to do even the smallest favor for me."

Then it was Larry's turn: "What do you mean? I'm always doing things for you! I spend half my life helping you out in one way or another."

Maria came back with "Really? I can't remember the last time you did something nice for me that didn't make me feel guilty for doing it. I swear you're more considerate of the dog than of me."

Larry was not to be outdone. He retorted with a list of things he had done for Maria, and then said, "I do a lot more for you than you ever do for me."

Maria then went through her own list of things, including cooking and cleaning and taking care of the children, to which she then added, "Besides, if I didn't do this stuff, it wouldn't get done. You just can't wait to go out and play golf when you're not working."Larry replied, "When's the last time I played golf? I haven't played in three weeks. You can't even give me a few minutes to relax when I'm not killing myself at that job."

This continued along the same path for quite a while. The argument was supposed to be about Maria being fifteen minutes late, but they never discussed that, and so they never had an opportunity to come to an understanding about it. Instead they covered a lot of things they disliked in their marriage and that caused them to resent each other. In reality, their argument was never about the fifteen minutes, but everything else that made each of them unhappy.

In the simplest of terms, communication is the means by which we exchange information with other people. While such a definition is accurate, it belies the fact that communication is a complicated process. There are volumes written on the nuances of how people transfer information between each other, and it's impossible to do justice to the topic in one brief chapter. Consequently, we've decided to focus our discussion of communication just as it relates specifically to the ways couples communicate during conflicts. Our skills in this area govern how effective we are at solving problems, and solving problems is essential for maintaining a harmonious relationship. It's easy for couples to talk when things are going well, but it's during conflicts that the darker side of the marriage can emerge.

As anyone who's been married for more than a few days knows, conflicts between spouses are unavoidable. They can crop up for any number of reasons, but very often it's because of some perceived inequity in the relationship. Why inequities can cause conflicts is best explained through what is known as Social Exchange Theory. According to this theory, marriage can be looked at as a barter system. Each of us strives to get certain benefits from our partner. We also understand there are things of similar value we have to give if we're to receive these benefits. Said another way, most of what partners will do for each other have strings attached.

Couples make all sorts of exchanges to keep the relationship equitable. The income one partner brings into the home might be counterbalanced by the amount of household chores done by the other. We may make certain personal sacrifices for our relationship and expect the same or similar kinds of sacrifices from our partner. When there is balance—that is, the amount we give is equal to what we receive—our relationship feels right. However, when one partner gives more than is received, the perceived imbalance becomes a concern for the shorted partner, and that becomes a reason for a confrontation.

Looked at from this perspective, arguments are actually good for a marriage. They are the primary vehicle for improving our relationship. If we're unhappy with something our partner does or doesn't do, only by confronting them can we give ourselves a chance to make our needs understood. Partners can then make the appropriate adjustments so that these needs can be fulfilled. Arguments also make partners come together to fix their problems as a couple, and if they're successful at it, can actually make them feel more bonded to each other.

Of course, it's not always easy to see the benefits of fighting. Marriages can go through times when partners feel like they just can't get along with each other. Dealing with crisis situations or entering into a new life stage, such as starting a family, can make life stressful. Some couples might come to believe that their marriage is damaged beyond repair, or they're no longer in love or compatible with each other. We might think other couples don't argue as much, or with such intense hostility, or they're just better at handling their problems than we are. However, going through periods of high conflict is completely normal. It happens to virtually all married couples, and we're probably no worse or better than others in this regard. In fact, although we never really know what goes on behind closed doors, there's an excellent chance that the couples in our social circle argue as often and as intensely as we do, and maybe even more.

The reality is couples who don't have at least the occasional battle might have bigger problems than those who argue regularly. They may have issues with trust and honesty, or they keep their interactions at superficial levels. Or they may avoid conflicts because they believe their issues cannot be resolved, or their communication styles may be so dysfunctional that even minor confrontations turn into major fights. Other couples, such as those who have traditional views of husband and wife roles, may avoid certain issues because they're considered to be closed to discussion. Whatever the reason, when a couple dismisses issues to avoid conflicts, any aspect of their relationship that causes discontent will remain unresolved. Consequently, an unhappy partner doesn't feel they have the power to make his or her marriage better.[1]

That's not to suggest that how often we argue doesn't matter at all. If partners are constantly at odds with each other, or virtually any situation leads to an argument, the marriage probably has unresolved issues. There actually is a relationship between how much fighting goes on and the psychological health of the marriage and its partners. When arguing is excessive, especially if these arguments never result in solved problems or end on a positive note, there's a good chance the marriage will end in divorce.

So how do couples know if there's too much fighting? That depends entirely on the couple. Some people have a high tolerance for confrontation. Others are uncomfortable with any amount of arguing, so even a moderately disagreeable partner can be difficult for them to live with. For most of us, we're probably within acceptable limits if we're able to keep our disagreements in perspective. We don't allow them to interfere with other aspects of our relationship. Our overall thoughts about our marriage stay positive, we don't harbor bad feelings long afterward, and we enjoy our partner's company during times of peace. Additionally, if we're able to hammer out workable solutions as a result of our arguments, then we're probably fighting as often as we need to.

More important than how often couples argue is how they behave toward each other when they do. Their interactions determine whether or not their communication is effective, and by that we mean it achieves the straightforward objectives of solving a problem and doing it efficiently. We're efficient when our disagreements are not drawn out longer than necessary, don't move on to topics that have nothing to do with the original problem, don't escalate to personal attacks or a rehashing of past disappointments and resentments, and leave partners feeling better about each other when they've ended.

Effective communication comes down to style, and by that we mean the way we express ourselves. The impact of how we express ourselves is so powerful that it's extremely difficult for unhappy couples to improve their relationship without changing their communication styles. It is one of the primary areas therapists will focus on when treating marriages that have chronic problems.

Broadly speaking, communication styles are either positive or negative. Positive styles allow couples to find solutions to their problems, but they can also have other benefits for the marriage. We believe our partners are approachable and care about our issues, and we don't have to avoid conflicts, because we believe they're constructive. When a disagreement ends, emotions de-escalate and partners come to an understanding they both can live with. On the opposite side, negative styles do not yield solutions. Instead, they often cause an argument to escalate and get out of control. Both partners usually feel less satisfied after an argument because they haven't made any progress, and so they feel more distanced from each other. [2]

The specific words we use when we argue are one way to determine whether our communication styles are positive or negative. Words are a measurable quantity, and so it is possible to evaluate communication style by counting the number of positive and negative messages partners send to each other. Couples with good styles have as many as five times more positive to negative comments passed back and forth, or negative comments will usually be counterbalanced by jokes, laughter, and other forms of positive interaction. In contrast, the ratio of negative to positive messages may be as high as three to one in favor of the negative among couples who have ineffective styles. Of course, each of us will express some aggression or hostility during a fight because we can't always control our emotions. Most marriages can withstand that. However, if there are consistently much fewer positives to offset the negatives, and if negative feelings persist afterward, we probably have communication problems. [3]

A major distinction between positive and negative styles is the kinds of emotions each produces. When we argue, we present our case in a few statements, but at the same time we're also letting our partner know how we think about the issue. The words we choose can be more or less emotionally charged. Along with our words, we send out a lot of emotional information non-verbally, through our posture, facial expressions, tone of voice, eye contact, and various gestures. The emotions we send out through our body language and our words are as important as the statements themselves, and have as much, if not more, to do with how our message is interpreted and reacted to by our partner.

When we use a negative style, we convey negative emotions along with information. Additionally, we may inadvertently communicate more than our feelings about the problem we're talking about. We may also convey how we feel about our partner. We may not intend to communicate these broader feelings, but that's how our partner is likely to interpret what we're saying. How they take our words can then affect our partner's feelings about us.

That's why negatively styled arguments tend to escalate into bigger fights. The negative emotions that we send out provoke negative emotions as a response from our partner. The words we say and the emotions we express can make our partner feel hurt and humiliated. The emotions they then experience will lead them to say and do things that will make us feel just as badly. If our tone is condescending or sarcastic, there's a good chance our partner will give that back in return. Unfortunately, it usually doesn't end there, because the negativity we receive often leads us to retaliate with more negative messages. Many issues that could be resolved won't be because our communication style prevents us from having a meaningful dialogue.

Styles can also be habit forming. The one we adopt is often dictated by our past experiences. We remember the prevailing attitude and tone of our prior conflicts, and we assume that our future arguments will follow the same path. Partners can become conditioned to expect each other to behave negatively, and these expectations can cause conversations to start contentiously. If we believe that disagreements will deteriorate, we're ready to approach them with a negative attitude. So, bad fighting tends to get worse over time.

Because our styles can become habits, they can broadly affect our marriage. When we use a negative style, the bad things that we say are remembered by our partner, and that's long after we've forgotten what was originally argued about. These memories can then carry over into other parts of the relationship. Partners may prefer to avoid each other's company, may lose interest in being intimate, or may take on negative attitudes even when they're not arguing. This hurts the relationship beyond and out of proportion to a specific problem.[4]

Sometimes our expectations regarding the direction an argument will take can cause us to misinterpret what our partner is trying to communicate. When someone is speaking to us, we don't just receive information, we process it. We transform the information we receive so that it conforms to our experiences, motives, and expectations. In other words, we often see what we expect or want to see. If we're anticipating negativity, comments made by our partner can be taken as worse than they were intended. In fact, we can be so predisposed to negativity that we can be the ones who initiate it, and we do so for no reason that is apparent to our partner. We're focused only on receiving hostility and we're only thinking about our counterattack, so even the slightest provocation may be enough to get us going. Note that while this is going on, we're not really listening to the content of our partner's message and consequently we're not thinking about solutions.

With such underlying dynamics as reciprocity, clouded perceptions, ingoing expectations, and the bad feelings these provoke, it's easy to see that negative styles prevent effective communication. Many couples in this predicament may come to think they cannot approach each other on any issue, and conflict discussions are just not worth the trouble. The result is usually some emotional distancing between partners, and from there the relationship has a very good chance of spiraling downward as they drift further and further apart.

Margie had just returned home from shopping and put her purchases on the table. Her husband Jack took a look inside the bag and pulled out the receipt. He became angry and confronted Margie, "I can't believe you spent all this money!" She said she knew she went a little over her budget, but these were things she had to buy. "What you do mean you had to buy? You always seem to need stuff." Margie then said, "What are you saying? That I spend too much? When was the last time I spent any money on me? But we're always spending money on things you want."

"That's total nonsense" Jack said, "You don't give a damn that we're on a budget. You're unbelievably selfish. You only think about yourself. Now you can just go back to the store and return all this junk. Sometimes you act like a child. You're a real idiot!"

Margie responded, "I'm an idiot? Yeah, well, you're a real genius. You do more stupid things than anyone I know!" She then went on to list all the questionable decisions Jack had made over the years. "And what about all that stuff you bought that's in the garage?"

"Yeah, but I'm the one out there earning the money!"

Margie then said to Jack, "You know, I'm just sick and tired of the way you treat me!" With that, she stormed out.

After she left, Jack took a look at the items Margie bought, and found that more than half were for him, including clothes, a pair of shoes he wanted, and the like. Of course, he felt badly about what had happened. He had completely misinterpreted the situation and had said things that were meanspirited and hurtful. Moreover, they could easily afford the purchases Margie made. It seems Margie's on a budget but Jack's not.

Despite the fact that it was a complete misunderstanding and Jack wanted to apologize, Margie wasn't about to forgive him. That had nothing to do with the money she spent and everything to do with his abusive language. However, Margie's not completely blameless. She could have mentioned that some of the purchases were for him right at the beginning and avoided an argument. But instead she baited him to make him look foolish, and she might have done so because she resented his control over their money, or because his immediate attack just set her off and made her go on the offensive. Whatever her reason, we can't discount the possibility that she did it just to stick it to her husband. In other words, their relationship had a lot of underlying hostility.

There are a number of ways we can express a negative communication style. As we mentioned, one of the more obvious is our choice of words. In positive styles, partners use words that are non-abusive and non-threatening. In negative styles, language is often peppered with defensiveness, sarcasm, accusations, ridicule, insults, demands, and the like. All forms of abusive language can be taken as expressions of contempt. They will immediately provoke one's partner to anger and lead to hostile comebacks.

Sometimes it's the attitude rather than the words that are abusive. We can make seemingly innocuous statements that are offensive because our tone of voice and/or body language conveys a negative attitude or a lack of respect. To reiterate, we convey a lot of emotions when we communicate, and these are picked up by our partner. In fact, they tend to pay more attention to our attitude and tone of voice than to the words we are saying during a confrontation.

We might also be ineffective communicators because we're not accurate. We are referring to stating our problem clearly so it's understood, but also to avoiding hyperbole and exaggeration. A partner who begins an argument with "You always . . ." is essentially begging for a hostile response. Forgiving our overstatement for the moment, nobody does all things right or wrong. When confronted with "always," our partner is required to point out the occasions when he or she did not do or say what we claim. That can move the argument into a historical review of the good and bad in the relationship, but also gets the escalation process going by coercing a defensive reaction. Additionally, exaggerated statements are likely to leave partners feeling incompetent and without any direction as to how they should proceed. How do we make improvements when we "always" do or say the wrong things?

We might have stylistic problems because of our choice of pronouns. "I," "we," and "you" convey very different messages to a listener. They also suggest very different ideas about what is really at the center of our thinking. The first person plural pronoun, "we," implies partners have their identities defined by their relationship rather than as individuals. During a conflict, "we" also suggests that a problem is owned together and both partners are responsible for coming up with a solution. When we say to our partner, "We have to stop treating each other like that," we're actually saying that neither is at fault alone, that we're at fault together. Shared ownership reinforces our sense of connectedness and makes it easier to come to a mutually agreeable solution. Neither party has to defend themselves, so escalation is kept to a minimum. Of course, all this is true provided that both partners actually are equally to blame for the problem and both can admit to that.

Using first person singular pronouns such as "I" or "my" may also be effective during conflicts. When "I" is used, partners provide information as to how they feel as they present their point of view. Self-disclosure can be an important step toward working through a problem. The information we provide to our partners about our personal thoughts and feelings gives them something to think about and react to, and are less inclined to make them feel attacked. They have a better idea where we're coming from and can offer ways to clear up misunderstandings and disagreements.

However, there are conditions where "I" may not be the best way to initiate a conversation. That's when it's linked to a negative idea, such as when sentences begin with "I don't like when you . . ." As its major drawback, a negatively worded statement doesn't necessarily provide clear direction as to what we want from our partner. We are telling them what not to do but not what they should do instead. It can also be interpreted as a complaint and can provoke a hostile or defensive response. On the other hand, setting up the statement in the positive, such as, "I would prefer that you . . ." provides your partner with direction as to the specific changes you would like.

"You" is the problem pronoun during arguments. It is often used to make an accusation, as one partner attempts to place blame on the other (e.g., "you do or don't do this"). It can also be attributional, and by that we mean one partner claims to know the innermost thoughts and feelings of the other (e.g., "you think this" or "you believe that"). Accusations produce negative reactions because the accused has to provide a defense for his or her actions, or for the sake of balance, he or she might respond with their own accusations. Attributions leave us in the uncomfortable and frustrating position of persuading our partner that we really don't think or feel a certain way. Sentences that begin with "you" can easily cause an argument to escalate and digress from the original problem.[5]

There are a few other stylistic characteristics that affect how well we communicate during conflicts. Some of these are tied more to the attitude we bring to a confrontation. One is accommodation: the willingness to bend and negotiate. We've talked about accommodation as a personality trait, but it can also be looked at as a communication style. Communication can't really be separated from our traits because, as we discussed, words spring from our thoughts and emotions, and these flow from our belief systems and our personal traits.

When we adopt an accommodating style, we approach conflicts with a mind toward reconciliation. From that perspective, we're willing to make sacrifices and negotiate trade-offs so that both partners' needs are met. Typically, those who are accommodating treat their partner's issues seriously, make an effort to understand their concerns, and have little difficulty admitting when they're at fault. In short, they try to sublimate their personal needs to that of the couple so that conflicts with their partner can be fairly and quickly resolved.

Those who are accommodating tend to have other characteristics that help them communicate effectively. They're empathetic, meaning they can relate to their partner's point of view and consider their opinions and feelings to be valid. They also approach conversations with an open mind. When we approach disagreements with an open mind, we're not limited in our expectations as to the outcomes. We're able to consider alternatives, and that includes our partner's way of thinking, so we're not as likely to launch into a counterattack when our partner tells us they have a problem with something we've said or done.

On the opposing side is a non-accommodating style. This is where we focus on our personal needs and interests rather than those of the partnership, and compromise is not first and foremost in our minds. We might try to browbeat our partner until they give in to our demands or accept our point of view. However, we should point out that getting our partner to scream uncle typically comes with a price. Partners on the receiving end of such intimidation tactics walk away from conflicts feeling humiliated by their partner and negative about their relationship, not to mention that they don't get their own needs considered or satisfied. [6]

Effective communication also includes listening. When we listen, we don't just think about the points we want to make; we try to grasp our partner's message. Careful listening allows us to keep the discussion on target and moving toward solutions. We have to keep in mind that communication during a conflict is two-sided. We give information to our partner, who then gives information back to us. It is the give and take, with each person responding and reacting to words and gestures of the other, which makes for a meaningful conversation and true communication. When we don't listen, there is no give and take of information.

It's easy to grasp the idea that listening to our partner is important. However, it can be much harder to put that into practice when in a confrontation. We can be so preoccupied with our own arguments that we forget there's another side to the story. Or, out of frustration or anger, we dismiss what our partner has to say as not worth listening to. It's obvious when couples have a listening problem, because they tend to talk *at* each other instead of *to* each other. In other words, they have a mutual monologue. Mutual monologues are what occur in a political debate, in which candidates are only interested in what they want to say and not interacting and sharing ideas with each other. When couples aren't listening to each other, they can't negotiate or compromise to a solution because they're not taking into account each other's point of view.

As we alluded to, one of the more common disruptive communication patterns is reciprocation. We've talked about reciprocation as something that can occasionally occur between all couples during the heat of an argument, but some of us might use it as part of our normal style. When we respond to a partner's complaint, for example, "You do this," with our own complaint, "Well you do that," we move a disagreement off the original topic and away from finding a solution. Furthermore, such confrontations can be expected to escalate, and intensely so, as partners present each other's shortcomings and mistakes, sometimes going as far back in their relationship as they can remember.

Going blow for blow is an easy trap to fall into. We store a lot of wrongs done by our partners in our minds and use them as ammunition when they bring up something negative that we've said or done. Howev-

er, when we reciprocate, we have essentially decided that solving a problem isn't entirely what we're looking to do. We want to prove that we're
at least as good to our partners as they are to us. It's only after partners
step away from each other for a while and calm down that they might be
able to tackle the original cause of their argument.

For some couples, communication problems have less to do with
what's said than with what's not said. We are referring to the tendency
for a partner to withdraw when faced with confrontations. Sometimes a
partner might do that because the same problem is raised over and over;
since it never gets resolved, they see no point in rehashing the issue, and
that's understandable. Others, however, are just unable or unwilling to
present their own thoughts and feelings when confronted. Conflict makes
them anxious, and avoiding conflict is a way to not feel anxious. This is
another of those patterns that we talked about earlier, one that is used by
avoidance-attached individuals. However, some people who are emotionally secure in other ways might still withdraw from an argument because
they have a hard time with confrontation.

When one partner is a withdrawer, the other has to take on the role of
demander, because someone has to be responsible for the health of the
relationship. More often than not, men are usually the withdrawers and
women the demanders. That's because these roles line up better with their
nature and social learning, not because wives are more demanding than
their husbands. Because women are more emotionally expressive and
look to be connected in their relationships, they work harder to keep a
bond with their husbands. For many men, emotional connectedness takes
a backseat to independence and a display of strength.

There's also some evidence that men feel stress more so than women.
If that's the case, they're more likely to try to avoid conflicts so that they
won't have to experience the discomfort that comes along with them.
While women also feel stressed by a confrontation, their interest in keeping the relationship healthy may override any feelings of discomfort, and
that would especially be the case if stress is easier for them to handle.

Another explanation revolves around the relative position of men versus women. Fair or not, men generally have higher status and receive
more benefits from marriage than do their wives. Consequently, it's in
their interests to preserve the status quo, and they can do that by avoiding
confrontations that may require them to change. Many women, on the
other hand, want their relationship to move toward greater equality, and

they can achieve that goal by removing the obstacles that prevent them from getting there.

Regardless of which partner holds which role, the demand-withdrawal pattern is just as destructive as other types of ineffective communication styles and can be frustrating for both partners. The demander can feel insecure because a withdrawer refuses to engage. Just like being married to an avoidance-attached person, we might interpret our partner's lack of a response as a lack of interest. In fact, we may actually prefer that our partner use a negative communication style over withdrawal. While negativity certainly isn't pleasant, at least we get some feedback, and we can believe our partner is as emotionally involved with the issue as we are.

For withdrawers, there is the pressure to respond, and that may not only make them feel anxious, they may feel their personal space is being invaded. Depending on what's being asked, the withdrawer can feel they're being forced to adopt a new way of thinking and behaving. Additionally, as the demander seeks a stronger connection, they're likely to ratchet up the pressure on the withdrawer, who then seeks to protect himself through further emotional distancing. That can lead to even more pressure, and then more distancing, which continues until one or the other gives up.[7]

Another fairly common communication problem, although it's not a stylistic one, is misinterpretation. Sometimes couples can have difficulty communicating because they can't pick up the exact meaning of each other's messages. While we generally become pretty good at reading even the most subtle messages of our partners, miscommunication can still occur in any conversation. That's especially true during an argument, when we're emotionally upset and we're not thinking as clearly as we can.

Occasional misunderstandings aren't really surprising, considering that communication requires us to process and interpret a lot of information very quickly. On top of that, it seems that many of us overestimate our communication skills. We might think we've made a point clearly or we know precisely what's said to us, but we will make mistakes. For example, we might think our partner's facial grimace during a conflict reflects anger or disappointment targeted to us, but it might in fact just be a reaction to another thought that occurred to them, or even to something they ate. The obvious problem with misinterpretation: it can lead partners to think the conversation is taking one direction when in fact it's taking an entirely different one.

Miscommunication would seem to be an easy problem to avoid. We only need to check with our partner by requesting clarification, or we can play back what we think they meant. Unfortunately, we're not always aware that we've misinterpreted our partner's message or that we haven't presented our own thoughts and feelings clearly. We might assume one thought was communicated, and because we're already reacting to that thought, we've taken the argument down the wrong road. Because we don't know the problem has occurred, we can actually cause other problems.[8]

As we implied throughout this discussion, negative communication styles are ineffective because they lead to negative outcomes. They prevent us from reaching solutions, prolong arguments by swaying us off the target issue and degenerating into personal attacks, and usually cause arguments to escalate into something more. Partners will often be provoked into saying things they don't mean or that are better left unsaid, and usually will feel worse, not better, afterward. It's usually only after both partners can remove themselves from the situation that a meaningful dialogue can take place, one in which more effective strategies can be used.

Unfortunately, couples with communication problems may not realize that they have negative styles. For some, their patterns are learned from their parents and past experiences, and so they use them unconsciously or out of habit. For others, they might develop negative styles as a result of the stresses and strains of marriage. Partners may harbor disappointments and resentments, and the anger that's retained from these experiences can emerge in how they communicate during conflicts. Eventually, such styles can come to be accepted as the normal way of confronting each other.

Nevertheless, it's certainly possible to develop better styles, with and without outside professional help. Remember, our communication styles are behaviors, and it is possible to change how we behave. Couples can learn how to work through their problems together and reduce negative interactions. Through the right training, many have found they have fewer arguments that get out of control, have faster paths to solutions, and feel more connected and supported by each other.

We might even find it's not that difficult to change bad patterns. That's because we already possess what we need for effective communication. We have a variety of styles in our arsenal, and we use different ones depending on with whom we're speaking. We might use a more formal style at work or with acquaintances and a more casual one with friends and family members. When we interact with those outside our marriage, we pay more attention to how we communicate. We're prone to think before we speak because we understand there are consequences to the words we choose. We won't blurt out every thought or express every emotion for fear of our listener's reaction. If we apply the rules we use with others—that is, be controlled and thoughtful with our words—we will have made an important step toward more effective communication with our partner.

That's not to say that changing how we communicate is without its challenges. As we said, a negative style often develops into a habit that can be hard to break at first. We may have a tendency to fall back into old patterns when in the middle of a heated confrontation and our emotions are out of control. Additionally, because styles feed on themselves, if one partner moves to the dark side, the overwhelming urge will be for the other to do the same.

So the real struggle comes down to fighting your urges. Focus your attention on the issue at hand, keep your cool, and avoid escalation. In other words, don't use a specific issue as a starting point to go through every other thing that you dislike about your partner or your relationship. Try to avoid ingoing expectations about how you're partner will react to something you say. Just as negative styles provoke negative reactions, positive ones can produce positive reactions. If one partner can break the cycle of negativity, the other might follow that lead and learn to approach confrontations with a more positive style.

There are a few other thoughts to keep in mind for couples who have difficulty communicating. First and foremost, the fundamentals of any relationship, trust and commitment, are at the heart of effective communication. Trusting our partner means we allow ourselves to be vulnerable, and we're not afraid to reveal our true thoughts and feelings. Self-disclosure allows our partner to know what we're thinking, and gives our partner permission to reveal his or her own true feelings. When we're committed, we approach conflicts with the interests of the marriage in mind rather than from the perspective of our own personal needs, so we tend to be more accommodating and better listeners.

This is an important point, because only if there's trust and commitment can there be honesty and mutual respect, and these are essential for effective communication. Partners who communicate well do so on an equal footing—that is, each respects the opinions and feelings of the other. Both are more likely to listen and less likely to make hurtful or insulting comments. Furthermore, when equality and respect are lacking, we're more prone to regard our own perspective as more important and not pay much attention to our partner's feelings and opinions, or to what they're saying to us.

Openly expressing our thoughts and feelings can go a long way to getting our partner to empathize with us when we're arguing. But that's only if we express ourselves appropriately. Communicating our emotions with yelling or other abusive language will produce the opposite effect. When we're upset, we may believe that such behavior is an honest expression of what we think and feel, and we have a right to behave that way. The truth is we might be expressing hostility rather than honesty. Let's say our partner makes a joke at our expense that we don't find funny. At the right moment we scream at them, "I hate when you make fun of me like that!" Certainly that's an honest reaction, but it really doesn't get to the heart of what's bothering us. We may actually feel hurt or insecure by what was said, but rather than admit to feeling hurt or insecure, we instead lash out in anger. The truly honest discussion of our emotions should focus on the real problem, which is feeling hurt or insecure. When we take that approach, our partner has a better chance of understanding where we're coming from and might feel badly about being hurtful.

It's also important to choose the right time for confrontation. While we might think it best to take on an issue as soon as it arises, sometimes we might be too emotionally upset to handle it well. There is a relationship between how we feel and how well we can interpret things happening around us. When we're angry, our perceptual skills tend to narrow; by that we mean it's harder to take in all the information presented to us and process it accurately. So, it's possible we won't hear or we might misinterpret important points our partner is trying to communicate. Additionally, when we're extremely upset, we may have trouble expressing ourselves clearly, or we may say things that only intensify the argument.

Instead, there's a better chance you will communicate effectively if you wait for your emotions to subside. If it's reasonable to do so, set aside time for both of you to discuss the problem, using direct conversations that are devoid of hostile language, threats, and accusations. Frank and honest discussions convey the seriousness of the issue and will get your partner's attention, so you and your partner can work toward a solution together.

To that point, sometimes to soften the blow, partners will try to present a problem indirectly by making jokes or off-the-cuff comments. However, when you sugarcoat issues or try to present them too delicately, your partner may not take them seriously or may not pay attention to them at all. So while remarks made in passing may allow you to sidestep a difficult confrontation, they may not get your partner to recognize that an issue is real and important to you.

Unfortunately, an honest and straightforward approach won't mean confrontations will always be calm or that your partner will be open or happy to hear about a complaint. So it's best to be prepared for a back-lash. A confrontation might be construed as a personal attack, or your partner might feel inadequate because he or she isn't living up to your expectations or meeting your needs. If your partner reacts defensively and turns the conversation negative, the trick is to not rise to the bait. Try to remain calm and supportive, and empathetic to how they are feeling. This can help to limit the intensity of their reactions.

Sometimes it's the message itself rather than your style that can cause problems. You might behave perfectly, and yet your message is still received with anger or resentment. Your partner may regard the issue as particularly irksome, or may consider your request to be above and be-yond what's reasonable. Under these circumstances, it might be helpful to use a quid pro quo strategy. In other words, if you have a request of your partner, be prepared to make an exchange or a concession from your side. As we've discussed in other chapters, it's perfectly reasonable to make exchanges so that both partners get what they want. Exchanges can actu-ally be a good way to moderate conflicts so that they don't get out of hand. Rather than get angry at a request, your partner can justify giving in because he or she is also getting something out of it.

Note that a frank conversation does not mean using honesty as a weapon. Communication problems can crop up when we disregard our partner's feelings and present an issue in a way that is hurtful, embarrassing, or humiliating. Our comments may be honest, but brutal honesty is essentially beating up on your partner, and that's destructive to a relationship. Being sensitive to our partner's feelings, on the other hand, just as effectively gets the point across, but with less risk of a counterattack. If we keep in mind that the words we choose and the attitude we convey affect our partner's feelings for us, that might provide some motivation for us to be honest, but to do it in a thoughtful and considerate manner.

It's a good idea to pay attention to our spouse's reactions as we present our side of the story. If we watch their body language and listen to their words, we can gauge their emotional reaction and determine whether our message is understood and not taken as a personal attack. We can sense that a person is paying attention by their eye contact, and we can tell by certain facial expressions how they feel about our message. From their feedback, we can make real-time adjustments to what we're saying and how we're saying it. If, for example, they appear uncomfortable or are getting angry, we can tone down our own emotional expressiveness or choose softer words. The point is to keep your partner engaged and focused on the issue so that the conversation can move along to its logical conclusion.

The best way to improve communication styles is for partners to work at it together. First, both need to acknowledge they have a problem communicating during conflicts. Once you accept the fact that it is a problem you own together, you can take the time to set up rules of engagement. Using the principles we've outlined in this chapter, it would be worthwhile to review some of your past disagreements to discover where your communication problems lie. Start with your most recent conflict and think about the words and body language that were used, and how each of you reacted to what the other said. Examine whether either of you resorted to any of the negative elements that we've talked about, such as accusations, abusive language, reciprocity, withdrawal, lack of listening, miscommunication, and so on. Try to uncover what was really underneath some of the negative things you might have said or done during your argument. Reviewing the stylistic mistakes you've made in the past will make you more aware of your own tendencies, and that can help you focus your attention on what you need to change. This is an exercise you should consider repeating for as many arguments as you can remember, since practice will make you better.

Don't forget that forgiveness is critical to resolving conflicts. If your spouse admits to a wrongdoing and apologizes, accept the apology, and if not, offer to forgive it nonetheless. If you plan to stay in the relationship, there's no value whatsoever in holding onto anger or other bad feelings once you and your partner have resolved a conflict. Of course, if it's the same problem that keeps coming up, an apology from your partner is meaningless. You have never really solved the problem, so it might not be an issue of communication style. However, barring repeated offenses, you will do a lot of good for your marriage by letting bygones be bygones. Holding onto disappointments and allowing them to cloud how you think about your partner will cause them to haunt your relationship in the future. [9]

On a final note, keep in mind that marital disputes are not about winning a contest of wills. They're about maintaining and improving a relationship. When there's a winner, there's also a loser, and a loser never gets much enjoyment from the experience. Don't look to a victory in an argument as a triumph to be celebrated. Truly effective communication not only leads to resolution and avoids escalation, but, in the end, each partner feels their point of view was heard and understood, they feel good about each other, and the relationship has moved in a positive direction. If that's not the outcome that you're looking to get from your disagreements, then you might want to go back and read this chapter again.

9

PERCEPTIONS AND ATTRIBUTIONS

Each of us holds opinions about the people around us. For those we're especially close to, we have a good idea of their strengths and weaknesses. This person is good at this but not at that, or I like this trait about her but not that one. We try to accept our friends for who they are because these relationships are beneficial for us. We often choose to overlook their faults and focus more on their positives. When a person's strengths outweigh their flaws, we enjoy the relationship and want to keep it together. But when our perspective leans too negative, meaning we see more flaws than strengths, we're less interested in maintaining the relationship and might even consider terminating it.

We develop our opinions of other people from the things we can observe about them. We take into account the way they look and dress, how they speak, and the way they act. As we spend more and more time with them, we also become familiar with their personalities and come to learn what's important to them and what they believe. We also have things we remember from interacting with them. Since we can't recall everything, we generally stick to the most salient memories, the ones that are most noteworthy or that are most personally meaningful to us.

As we accumulate information, we develop what is referred to as a global perspective for each person. This is essentially a mental tally of their various characteristics. While we're aware of their specific strengths and weaknesses, our thoughts about them are in very broad terms. We might classify some people as caring about others, some can't be trusted, that one's a snob, and so forth. Our classification of people is in part affected by our values and belief systems. For example, if we place a lot of importance on a sense of humor, we might like someone because we consider them to be funny, even though they may have other traits that are less likeable.

Global perspectives are a useful way of simplifying our world. We can categorize people according to how we feel about them with just a few summary ideas. But what's most important about global perspectives is how they affect our relationships. They dictate how we think and feel about others, and these thoughts and feelings determine how we treat them. If our global perspective about someone is positive, we're likely to treat that person well. If it tends to be negative, we might act aloof when we're with that person, or we may prefer to keep our interactions to a minimum.

We also use our global perspective to make guesses as to how people act. We make assumptions about what they're capable of doing and saying, and we make predictions as to how they will react to different situations. But we don't only try to predict what they will do or say, we also attribute motivations, intentions, and thoughts that are behind what they do and say. If we think a person is dishonest, he or she might be the first one who comes to mind if something is missing. If we think another person is a liar, we won't take what they have to say without checking the facts. If we believe a person is only out for themselves, we're skeptical that any act of kindness he or she performs really has an ulterior and self-serving motive.

Attributing thoughts and motives to others is unavoidable. We all do it, and we do it because we believe we understand our friends and family. In fact, if we didn't think we could read their intentions or predict their behavior, we would not feel very connected to them. When we can come up with explanations as to why someone has done something, we feel we really know that person. We also feel more in control of our lives because the world around us seems to be predictable, sensible, and orderly. When the intentions we attribute to someone are wrong, we can feel a little disoriented because things aren't as predictable as we need them to be, and we're not sure how to think and feel about that person.

We don't only attribute rationales and motives to people we know, we also do it with strangers. For these people, we rely primarily on what we see, but we also assume that people with certain characteristics will think and behave in a certain way. We will take in a person's attractiveness or size up how they're dressed and try to draw conclusions as to their occupation, personality, and lifestyle. If they're highly attractive or dressed well, we're likely to conclude they're successful, intelligent, or popular. If they're overweight or dressed sloppily, we might regard them as lazy, careless, or dull-witted—and possibly not likeable. Note that attorneys understand the importance of observable characteristics when it comes to evaluating others. They will often instruct their clients to come to court wearing certain types of outfits or hairstyles because juries will use their appearance to make judgments, irrespective of the facts of a case.

Our attributions regarding strangers can often be inaccurate. That's because we have to rely solely on what we see or hear, and appearances can be misleading. However, we can also make errors with those close to us. We tend to rely mostly on what we think of a person globally, that is, how we have classified their personality and character, rather than on the situation they're in when we try to figure out their intentions. If a person who we thought was patient has taken on a stressful job or has just started a family, we may find they're less patient and accommodating than they used to be. We might then conclude that person is different and we no longer understand them. However, we're not interpreting things correctly because our global perspective doesn't take into account a change in circumstances. Relying on our global perspective without fully taking into account situational factors is considered to be one of the fundamental errors people make when attributing motives and thoughts to others.

Sometimes we get it wrong because our global perspective is incorrect, even for people we think we know well. We might have arrived at an overall judgment about someone too quickly or without enough information. Furthermore, people do change, and what might have been true about someone at one point in their life may no longer apply at another point. Most of us have known people who we thought we understood, and then something happens that makes us feel we no longer understand them. They might have changed or their circumstances might have changed, and that causes them to think or behave differently. Because they're no longer who we thought them to be, we might come to feel we can no longer relate to them and so the relationship can break down.

Once a global perspective is formulated, it has a good deal of stability. If we continually misinterpret a person's intentions, we'll adjust our global perspective so that it's more in line with how that person is now. However, changing one's view of another person, or their view of you, comes slowly. This is in part driven by selective attention, which is the tendency to recall things about a person that are consistent with our perspective. Regardless of how a person may behave in the present, our overall opinions are relied upon more to guide our thinking about that person.

We also develop what is known as sentiment override. Essentially, this is a filter we use to interpret events according to the general perspective we've developed. The feelings we have for people affect how we process information about them. If we like a person, we'll cut them some slack when we attribute reasons for their actions, or we'll focus on factors that justify their behavior, even if we disapprove of that behavior. We may look at the circumstances or we may just dismiss it as untrue because we believe that it's just not part of their character.

On the other hand, if our overriding sentiment is negative, we're likely to judge that person's behavior and their motives as negative. We'll look for all sorts of negative reasons for something they might say or do. Even if we would acknowledge that this person has done something good, we're pretty sure they had ulterior motives that aren't so good. Or we might accept what they've done as positive, but still think it's not at all indicative of who they really are. In short, if someone does something that's inconsistent with how we expect them to behave, we try to force fit their behavior into our global perspective of them. They either get or don't get the benefit of the doubt, depending on how we feel about them in general.

Global perspectives have their advantages and disadvantages. They are the means by which we organize our thoughts about other people. They add structure and consistency to our relationships because we can predict how people will behave in different situations. However, they can lead to biases, misinterpretations, and the wrong conclusions. Our judgments about people can be clouded because the intentions and motives we attribute to them is in the direction of how we feel about them. They also make it difficult for us to change our perceptions, because we remember or focus primarily on things that support our ongoing perspective.[1]

John believed that Sarah was bothered by him. According to him, Sarah had a problem with most things he would say or do, and she could fly off the handle at the slightest provocation. If John did something or said something that could be construed in positive or negative ways,

Sarah always took the negative one. When he did something that was considerate or nice, she didn't seem to notice, but if it was something that she didn't like, she might stay angry at him for days.

John was asked privately to describe Sarah's good and bad points. He was able to come up with a pretty long list of about an equal number of strengths and weaknesses. Sarah was then asked about John. On the good side, she said that John was basically a nice guy, but she didn't give many specifics. When it came to his faults, however, she had a fairly lengthy list. She thought he lacked ambition, didn't think things through, had some disgusting habits, was sometimes immature and childish, and so on.

The ease with which Sarah could list John's faults suggested they dominated how she thought about him. The truth is Sarah didn't think highly of John, and she couldn't help but have her thoughts affect how she treated him. It's not that she consciously tried to be mean or disrespectful; in fact, she said she really tried to hide her true feelings. However, very often it was difficult for her to feel close or loving to him, or to be patient when he did something she didn't like.

John had a pretty good idea of how Sarah regarded him, and he resented her for it. While he tried to control his feelings, at times his resentment would sneak up on him, and for no reason that was apparent to Sarah, he would be angry or emotionally distanced. Without knowing exactly why John was upset with her, Sarah would then get angry with him. They could both stay upset with each other for days without ever having had a fight. Sarah didn't seem to realize that John's negative feelings stemmed from his beliefs about her opinion of him. Unless she could improve her views about John, he was not going to feel better about her.

We also develop a global perspective about our spouse, as they do about us. These tend to run deeper than for other relationships because husbands and wives are much more invested in each other. As with other people, they're based upon what we have learned about our partner and what we remember from our experiences together. But we would guess they also include how well partners meet expectations and fit within the belief systems of each other. In other words, we have rules for marriage that don't apply to other relationships, and our global perspective of our spouse probably takes into account how well he or she satisfies these rules.[2]

Global perspectives are important in marriage because they can affect its quality and the path it takes. As we said, global perspectives are often what's behind our thoughts and feelings. These thoughts and feelings in turn determine how we behave, so they affect how we treat our partner. Happy and unhappy couples can be differentiated by how partners think about each other globally and the motives they attribute to their actions. Those in good relationships have a positive bias while those in bad ones have a negative bias.

A positive bias toward our spouse helps a marriage in quite a few ways. We're more prone to attribute good motives and intentions to our partners' actions, even if their actions aren't very good, because we believe they're honorable people and have our best interests in mind. If our partner then does something wrong, we forgive that behavior as an aberration, possibly the result of a bad day. Because we don't take what they say or do as reasons to be angry or disappointed, we're more likely to have a positive attitude when we're together. Conversations tend to be even tempered, and we're more prone to treat our partners with patience, consideration, and affection rather than with hostility or disrespect. When we treat them in a way that makes them feel good, they then adopt a positive attitude toward us and are more disposed to treat us well, and that further reinforces our own positive bias. A negative bias, on the other hand, leads to negative treatment, and that causes our partner to be negative and hostile toward us, which we then repay with more negativity.

Global perceptions can also affect what couples argue about and how well they solve problems. With a positive bias, conflicts tend to be less frequent and less intense. They're also more productive, because partners focus specifically on a problem and look for causes and solutions, and are less likely to include personal attacks. Couples are also more likely to have arguments that are about external factors, such as finances or household chores, rather than personal characteristics. In contrast, couples who hold negative perspectives have more arguments that are really about their views of each other and their personal shortcomings, and less related to a specific situation or event. These arguments don't produce solutions because they're basically about asking our partner to be a different person. Instead, they will typically escalate into something meanspirited and damaging to the relationship.

Minor transgressions are also not as likely to turn into major battles. If, for example, a husband has to be repeatedly asked to take out the garbage, a wife's positive thoughts about him can help her keep such minor problems in perspective. That's because she believes he is good to her in general, even though it may not come across with respect to waste disposal. Her overriding positive sentiment allows her to take a broader view of their relationship, and not get caught up with a slightly annoying situation. We should also point out that a positive bias can help with life stage transitions. It's easier for couples to adjust to such difficult situations as starting a family because they're not dwelling on disappointments and don't see their partner as someone on whom to dump their frustrations.

Finally, a positive bias is self-fulfilling. Because we're less likely to question our partner's character, we won't question ourselves as to whether we've made the right choice in marrying that person. We also give ourselves a reason to trust them, and that means we won't be as full of doubt about the relationship when it's in a downturn. Positive thoughts make us want to stay together because we like our partners, not just love them. Consequently, we're more prone to work at making our relationship better because our partner is worth the effort. The net result is we feel better and more secure about our marriage, and that makes us feel better about ourselves and our futures.[3]

While a positive bias can make a marriage better, a negative bias can bring one down. It's not possible to say whether negativity causes an unhappy marriage, or whether a marriage declines first and that leads to a negative perspective. It can work in either direction, and they can feed on each other. Regardless, when thoughts about our partner are mostly negative, either because we're focused on their personal shortcomings (e.g., impatience, arrogance, unkempt appearance, etc.) or because they fall short of our expectations (e.g., not successful enough, not thin enough, inept, etc.), neither partner is happy. We're not happy because our partner isn't what we want them to be; they're not happy because they know we don't regard them favorably.

That's not to say we can't hold any negative opinions about our partner. We're well aware of their faults, as they are of ours, and there will be times when we can't help but be angry with each other. Being aware of each other's flaws and temporary hostility won't destroy a marriage. It's only if their flaws or the reasons why we feel hostile are mostly on our minds will we put the relationship in jeopardy. There seems to be a threshold for negativity; a level that is too high can make a marriage unstable. When we go above that threshold, we primarily see the dark side to whatever they say or do.[4]

A negative bias leads us to adopt harmful ways of thinking. We'll focus primarily on things we don't like and ignore the positives about our partner. Their bad behaviors are regarded as a true reflection of their character. So even if our partner does or says something good, we're likely to regard that as an aberration, or we'll dismiss it because we believe there is a negative motive behind it. If we regard our partner as self-centered, we may attribute a good deed as just a way for them to get praise and attention from others. Marriage counselors often encounter situations where one partner will claim the nice things said or done by the other is only because they're in therapy, and he or she won't act that way once therapy has ended.

Couples in these marriages also have a harder time forgiving each other. In fact, they tend to go in the opposite direction when something disagreeable happens. They're likely to stay angry longer. A negative sentiment makes us predisposed to getting angry, and bad behavior by our partner adds fuel to the fire because it reinforces and justifies our negative opinion of them. The deep hostile emotions we're experiencing can often cause us to overreact to whatever they've done.

These relationships usually lack trust and commitment—two key ingredients for a successful marriage. How can we be committed to a partner we hold in low esteem, and how can we trust them if we assume the worst of their motives and intentions? We can never be sure they have our interests or the interests of the relationship foremost in mind. Even if they try to explain their actions, we're not likely to believe them, and that's in large part because their explanations are inconsistent with our negative perspective. If we're looked down upon by our partner, we know whatever we say or do is regarded with skepticism and our intentions constantly questioned. We won't feel loved or supported, we're always on the defensive, we can't feel in control of our lives because we can't change our partner's perspective, and our self-esteem is likely to suffer. These are not the feelings or experiences that make us feel good about our partner or make us want to stay in a relationship.[5]

Martin and Lois's marriage was for the most part a good one. The one problem seemed to be that Lois tended at times to be overly dependent, and that drove Martin crazy. He was a highly successful and very well-

educated professional, and he defined himself by his ability to focus on and solve problems. He saw such traits as something to admire in others. Lois had also been successful in her own right before they were married. However, she felt she had become a different person over the years and she wasn't quite sure why.

When asked to describe Martin, Lois had mostly good things to say; she mentioned some flaws, but at least as many strengths. When asked how she thought Martin saw her, Lois believed Martin thought she was an airhead and completely incompetent. She explained that he always had the right answers to their problems and the best way to do things, but she rarely did. She had come to believe that, left to her own devices, nothing would get done right. So she had come to rely on him to make most of their decisions. When asked how he would describe Lois, he also had a lot of nice things to say, but he was really stuck on her inability to make decisions. He said, "If there are two ways to do something, you can count on Lois to pick the wrong way. She could be such a boob, but I love her anyway."

It eventually came out that throughout their marriage Martin had made jokes and other disparaging remarks about Lois's inability to make decisions. Sometimes it came across as playful, but at other times he would get angry and demeaning. His behavior had taken a toll on Lois. She had come to doubt herself and believed she actually was ineffective and incompetent. Martin had gradually whittled away at Lois's self-confidence, eventually causing her to be more dependent on him than either wanted her to be. While it wasn't Martin's intention, he was in part responsible for how Lois had changed. However, Lois had to take some of the responsibility for giving up control of her life. Probably the best solution for her would have been to go back to work so that she could reestablish her skills and break her dependency pattern.

In most marriages, the overriding sentiment leans positive. It's only in the worst relationships or those that are about to end that negative opinions of each other dominate. The truth is many couples start their marriages in the opposite direction, with an overriding sentiment that is too positive. Their partners' negative traits are hardly noticeable, or if noticed, they're either ignored or downplayed. Many will hold onto highly positive illusions throughout the first few years, imagining their partner to be just who they had ever hoped for.

Putting our partners on pedestals when just starting out is understandable and not at all surprising. Our partners are the cause of the euphoric feelings we're experiencing from love, and these feelings lead us to have positive thoughts about them. It would be impossible to work out in our minds that we love someone who we do not regard in the best possible light. Additionally, our partner loves us and wants us to love them back, so they treat us well and give us lots of attention. Because they behave so well and make us feel so good, it's hard to see many of their faults, or for our partner to see our own.

Although not as problematic as a negative perception, an overly positive one can still pose some risks. When we're not cued into our partners' weaknesses, we set ourselves up for disappointment, and the more we idolize them, the greater is the likelihood that our partners won't meet our expectations. Additionally, they can mask problems because it can lead us to deny realities. Some couples who have difficulties getting along before marriage may decide to marry anyway because their feelings of love prevent them from noticing the obstacles that can prevent them from becoming happy companions. Many of these problems will probably be handled eventually, but some may remain as issues throughout the marriage, and some may never get resolved.[6]

Moving beyond the honeymoon period takes some adjusting. As the relationship evolves, so must our perceptions. As partners learn more about each other and their passions soften, a more realistic picture is pretty much forced to emerge. Each partner's various shortcomings, flaws, bad habits, and the like become noticeable and can't be ignored. It's at this point that couples go through a process of fine-tuning their global perspectives so that they include their weaknesses along with their strengths.

Global perceptions can actually fluctuate upward and downward as we get to know our partners better. Even though we generally acknowledge that everyone has weaknesses, we still have to reconcile our feelings for our partner each time we learn new things about them that aren't exactly what we love. The ups and downs occur because we're adjusting how we once thought about our partner and how we have to think about him or her now. Each time we learn something new, we might feel some disappointment because our partner is not exactly what we thought or expected them to be.

This is where an overly positive global perspective can get us into trouble. We're especially prone to be disappointed and have more problems adjusting than do those whose positive bias was a little less extreme. If there are too many disappointments, we can sometimes feel like we're at a crossroad. We have to weigh our partner's good and bad points, and then we have to decide whether or not their good points are good enough and their bad ones aren't too bad. In other words, are we still able to hold a largely positive global perspective of our partner, or are we starting to develop a negative one?

Most couples make the appropriate adjustments, and as they develop a more informed idea of the person they're married to, their perceptions become more stable. We generally end up with a realistic image of our partner that's made up of both their strengths and shortcomings, rather than one that is completely positive or completely negative. In successful marriages, partners learn to tolerate each other's faults and still like each other.

An accurate assessment of our partner is a good thing, and can actually protect us when our marriages hit rough spots. When we know our partner's strengths and weaknesses, it's easier to be supportive of each other. We know what to expect, and we can feel more in control of our relationship because our partner behaves in a predictable way. We also have an easier time recognizing and dealing with problems as they arise. We're just not as surprised or disappointed when they say or do things we don't like as we might be if our perspective is unrealistically positive or negative. Of course, it's still important for the success of a marriage that partners hold onto a globally positive perspective of each other, but reality lets us know exactly what we're in for.[7]

Holding onto a positive global perception about our partner in the light of their faults may require that we reach into our bag of mental tools, especially if they have shortcomings that are really annoying. We might also use the technique discussed briefly in a previous chapter of making comparisons to other married couples to judge the quality of our own partner and our relationship. This tool can be particularly useful when our marriages are on a downturn, helping us to keep things in perspective.

To review, we generally make downward comparisons. We consciously select couples who we think have marriages with more problems than our own. This really isn't so difficult, since most of us are already predisposed to think our relationship is better than that of many of our friends and acquaintances. We'll look at their marriages and attribute negative intentions and motives to what they say or do for each other, even if those things are positive. We might believe a wife treats her husband with kindness because she's afraid of losing him, or a husband does nice things for his wife because she's so demanding, so he's just trying to placate her.

If we have a hard time convincing ourselves that our marriage is as good as or better than others in general, we'll focus on the details. We'll make comparisons to specific aspects of their marriages and think they are not as good as our own, or we'll look at the bad aspects of these relationships as worse than the bad aspects of our own. We'll also place more importance on what we see as the negatives of their marriages and less importance on our own negatives. The point is we do whatever we need to do to reach this conclusion: "Ours is better than yours, and if not yours, certainly theirs, and if not in every way, at least in these ways." And if that doesn't work, we comfort ourselves with, "Well, at least we don't have their problems." Focusing on the specific things we do better as a couple, even if these things are minor, still lets us feel our relationship is a good one. If we can believe that, then we can also believe we have a good partner who deserves to be thought of in nice ways.

If we can't find suitable comparison couples, we can use other strategies to maintain a positive bias. We can make comparisons to past times in our own relationship, and adopt the perspective that things are not as bad as they used to be, or convince ourselves that, while we're not doing well right now, things will eventually improve. In this way couples are able to admit to feeling unhappy, but still feel good about their relationships overall because there's hope for the future.[8]

We also can hold onto a positive perspective through what are called benevolent cognitions. This is a way of thinking that essentially gives our partners the benefit of the doubt. We might look upon less agreeable words and deeds in a positive light or attempt to find explanations for their bad traits so that they're more palatable. We might, for example, justify a partner's road rage as a result of being under pressure at work or because other people are horrible drivers. When we use outside forces as a way of explaining a person's actions, we remove the responsibility from them. We can believe their bad behavior is a result of circumstances, so it has less of an impact on how we feel about them in general.[9]

Benevolent cognitions can also help us cope if we're worried about incompatibility. They provide us with a way of changing our priorities.

Suppose our partner has very different interests from our own and we believe shared interests are important. In order to avoid having this difference become a point of contention, we'll place less importance on shared interests and place more value on other aspects of our relationship. We may not like to do the same things, but we have a great sex life and she sure can cook. Or we might even decide to change our thinking altogether; we can rationalize that our differences in interests are good because it gives us time to be apart and maintain some of our personal independence.

These various mental tools help us maintain a generally positive bias under normal, day-to-day circumstances. Unfortunately, life and marriage don't always run smoothly. Despite their best efforts, most couples will have periods when they'll feel mostly negative about each other. Remember that our opinion of our partner includes both their strengths and weaknesses. We will focus on positive traits at certain periods of our marriage, but the negatives will be more dominant in our minds at other times. While our bias is generally stable, it can still sway in one direction or the other from time to time.

These fluctuations very often are caused by a change in lifestyle or other outside forces. When there's little stress, or partners feel connected and supported, positive perceptions prevail. However, when faced with challenging circumstances, such as stress at work, financial or time pressures, or starting a family, our bias can move toward the negative. The trigger might be such thoughts as our partner doesn't understand what we're going through, he or she isn't helpful enough or is too demanding of our time, among others. Alternatively, there are times when our marriage is just not that fulfilling for a number of reasons, such as boredom, lack of connectedness, or a general feeling of dissatisfaction. At such times we might shift our focus more on our partner's shortcomings, and from there we might interpret their words, deeds, motives, and intentions in a more negative light.

Fluctuations that result from lifestyle changes or outside forces are normal and will occur in even the most successful marriages. When in the middle of a financial problem, we might think that, if he earned more money or she didn't spend so much on silly things, we wouldn't have this problem. In many instances, however, this is not a long-term situation. When the thing that is causing our distress goes away, very often so will the negative bias. Of course, we're assuming that the outside events causing the problem are themselves temporary. If we're faced with issues, such as financial problems, that never go away, there's a very good chance our negative global perspective will stay with us and can cause the relationship to deteriorate.

It's far more damaging when our negative bias is caused by internal factors—by that we mean things that relate specifically to the relationship and not because of outside pressures. In other words, there are just too many things we don't like about our partner. It could be their habits and idiosyncrasies, how they treat us, or how our relationship is structured. One or both partners might think their relationship is one-sided, have unmet expectations and needs, feel insecure or unloved, have unresolved conflicts and festering resentments, feel abused, have to cope with long-term life-changing events such as infidelity. Unfortunately, under these circumstances, partners can't use outside forces as an excuse for how they feel about each other. Instead, they have to struggle with the thought that they don't want to be with each other.

A negative bias is present most of the time in these relationships. As we mentioned earlier, such couples are more prone to be on the lookout for cues that confirm the bad feelings they have for their partners, and to attribute disagreeable motives to whatever they say or do. When they've actually done something wrong, their tendency is to react out of proportion to their wrongdoing, so even minor indiscretions can have a major impact on their relationship. Additionally, remember that actions by one partner are usually reciprocated by the other, so hostility is repaid with hostility. That sets the stage for a negative back and forth that's so typical of distressed relationships.[10]

As a major problem with chronic negative bias, there is the tendency to ruminate. We can become obsessed with the faults we see in our partner to the point of constantly reviewing them in our minds. When we become preoccupied with such thoughts, we can get locked into a cycle of negativity. Ruminating fuels itself, meaning that each negative thought or emotion causes another one to pop up in our minds, and then another, and so on, and that chain reaction of negativity can be hard to break. When we're stuck in this pattern, it can be hard to interpret anything they say or do in a positive light.

In most marriages that stay together, it's rare that negativity is so extreme that couples are only absorbed with each other's shortcomings. However, there are probably a few marriages that suffer from marginal negativity—that is, the perspective of one or the other partner leans a little more negative than positive. It's not always easy to tell whether that's the case. We might believe that our bias is positive, but on closer inspection discover it's not as positive as we think. For example, if our tendency is to respond to something our partner says or does with skepticism, sarcasm, or criticism, or have similarly unpleasant thoughts come into our head that we don't voice, these may be more indicative of how we think about our partner rather than how we're reacting to what they're saying or doing. It's worth the effort to count the kinds of thoughts we have when we think about our partner. If we come up with a lot of faults and not as many strong points, we might need to work on that.

When negative thoughts creep into our minds, we should avoid ruminating. Remember that negativity can be feed on itself; a mental image or thought produces a related emotion, and that emotion produces another like-minded thought, and so on, and before we know it, we can get stuck in a pattern of negativity. However, we can control what we're thinking and can change from one type of thought to another. If we're in a negative cycle, we can replace a negative thought with a positive one, and in so doing, we can start a positive chain reaction instead of a negative one.

As with other destructive patterns that are found in problem marriages, we can actually get into a habit of negativity. It can become our go-to way of thinking about our partner without even realizing it. Yet with any habit, while it can be difficult to break, it's not impossible. Marriage therapists have had a lot of success in training couples to develop more positive perspectives of each other. Again, it requires that partners learn to focus on each other's good points and not dwell on their shortcomings.

Acknowledge that your partner has faults and come to terms with your disappointments, and don't let them drive your overriding opinions of them. Accepting your partner for who they are can eliminate a major source of negative thoughts. Besides, when you focus primarily on their positives, you won't have to ask yourself why you're still with this person.

Of course, partners will become angry with each other when mistakes are made, or they're in the middle of an argument. At times like these, kind and loving thoughts are the furthest things from our minds. However, the point here is to not let negative thoughts linger too long or use them as the way you define your spouse in general. Put your arguments and your various disappointments into the past as soon as they are over.

Holding on to the various ways your partner has disappointed you or has made you angry won't change anything, and can lead you to ruminate about your partner's flaws. Additionally, if you can hold onto a positive bias, you might find you will approach confrontations with an attitude and tone that can make them more productive and less hostile.

It's important to figure out if your negativity stems from things that are wrong with your relationship or from outside factors. If it's the former, then you should try to identify the underlying reasons that are making you think and feel that way, and not just your negativity. For example, if you feel insecure about your relationship, you won't think well of your partner, but the problem really stems from your feelings of insecurity and not your negative bias. Trying to think more positively about your partner without first working on the reasons for your insecurity can be difficult because you haven't eliminated the cause. Nevertheless, you can work on both at the same time. Regardless of the source or reasons, a negative bias is destructive on its own, and eliminating that as an issue might make your relationship better even if other problems, including the ones that cause the bias, are not completely resolved.

For some couples, one partner might have a negative bias that's not deserved. They might have personal issues such as a lack of self-confidence or an anxiety attachment style that prevent them from seeing their partner realistically. Because they have problems with trust, the relationship can have a lot of emotional ups and downs, which can be extremely frustrating for their partner. In such marriages, working on their negativity won't be very helpful. The more effective approach would be for their partner to seek personal counseling. If these kinds of problems are not dealt with, they can remain a defining feature of the marriage and a driving force behind their negativity.

While we're focusing mostly on a negative bias, we should again caution against being overly positive toward our partners. This tends to be a problem for newlyweds, and much less so for those who've been married for many years. For the latter, it's hard to keep our partners on a pedestal after we've been exposed to all of the strange things they do. Nevertheless, if we're too positive, other problems in our relationship can go unnoticed, or we might have difficulty solving some problems because we really don't understand our partner's strengths and shortcomings. Additionally, as we discussed in an earlier chapter, when we're too positive, we might expect more from our partner than they can realistically provide, and that can lead us to be disillusioned and unhappy in our marriage.

As we mentioned many times, the bias you hold toward your partner will affect how they treat you. If it's negative, they'll pick up on it and behave toward you in a similar manner. Or, because they're not sure what's behind your behavior, they might feel insecure about the relationship. Either way, it won't be good for your marriage.

But, as we have also mentioned frequently, global perspectives can change, for the better or worse. If you can think more positively of your partner, he or she is likely to feel and think better about you. However, you should also keep in mind that if your spouse thinks highly of you and your behavior doesn't justify it or your bias is negative, you will eventually be demoted. Bad behaviors and attitudes will be excused once in a while, but not forever.

10

MANAGING THE HOME AND FAMILY

Pete blamed their marital problems on Joyce. He claimed that she was continuously in a bad mood and was cold, and that was making him frustrated and upset. Pete believed he was a good husband and didn't deserve such treatment. When confronted, Joyce said she still loved him and certainly didn't want a divorce, but felt completely unsupported. Pete became defensive, presenting a list of things he does for Joyce, first and foremost of which was to earn money for the family. Joyce became exasperated and pointed out that she also had a job and brought in almost as much money as he did.

Then Joyce came to her point: Pete didn't help around the house at all. She could tolerate that before kids, but afterward the work load was too much to handle. She thought Pete didn't care how hard she had to work. Pete responded by saying, "I never had to do anything like that when I was a kid, and I never saw my father doing it either, and my mother never complained. Besides, when I do something, you're never satisfied."

Joyce then said, "First, your mother always complained to me that she was treated like a servant. Second, everyone knows how to run a vacuum, and if you don't know how to change a baby's diaper or bring dirty clothes to the laundry, I will gladly teach you. Third, yes, I'm not happy how you do things because after you're finished, I have to do them all over again."

It finally came to Pete's real issue with housework: it's a woman's responsibility and not supposed to be done by a man. Pete had to realize that doing housework is something we all have to do, and it doesn't reflect on one's masculinity. But Joyce also had to adjust her thinking. She didn't realize that she contributed to his behavior by criticizing his performance. There appeared to be two potential solutions to reduce her workload: she could adjust her standards and be more accepting of Pete's way of doing things, or she could teach him to do some chores better.

However, there was another way around this issue. Joyce explained that because he didn't help her, she was too worn out to do anything else. Pete then asked, "Are you saying that if I do more work around the house, you'd have more sex with me?" Such a question made Joyce uncomfortable, and when asked why, she said that sex should be romantic and intimate, and treating it that way made it sound cheap and not at all sexy. "Besides, he should be willing to help me just because he loves me."

It was pointed out to her that Pete wasn't likely to link housework with love. On the other hand, here was a very reasonable negotiation, because both get what they wanted. Joyce was told that lots of couples negotiate in this way, and Joyce had to weigh whether changing her views on sex and love was worth the reduced work load. Pete would also have to learn how to do chores better, but now he was an eager student.

In this chapter, we focus on the practical side of living together, including finances, maintaining a home, and raising a family. We deal with these issues every day and spend a lot of time talking about them with our spouse. How partners handle them together can affect how they think and feel about each other, and so can affect all other aspects of their relationship. They're considered by most to be a major cause for marital problems.

Let's begin with housework, something that most people consider to be a real pain in the neck. It's a thankless, repetitive, and boring job that eats up time, yet it can't be ignored, and it won't go away. Most tasks, with the possible exception of cooking, which can allow for some creativity, provide little enjoyment and don't give us reasons to think we're productive or feel good about ourselves. In fact, these kinds of repetitive tasks can leave us feeling depressed, especially when we don't have other more creative and satisfying outlets. [1]

While both partners know housework has to be done, wives are regarded as the ones who are supposed to do most of it, and that's by both men and women. In many marriages, housework for women is assumed, whereas men believe that taking care of their home is optional. When they do something, men see it as helping out their wives and playing the role of good husbands; they don't regard these chores as their actual responsibility. They often expect what they do to be noticed and praiseworthy, and sometimes a point for negotiating for other goods and services from their wives.

The situation has improved for many women, as their home workloads have declined in recent decades. Husbands are more willing to pitch in today, although that's probably not out of choice. By contributing financially, women have raised their value within the household, and so are in a better position to demand assistance. Furthermore, working may have changed how committed some women are to housework. Their jobs allow them fewer hours for doing such chores, so they've been forced to live with a lower standard of everyday tidiness. Couples are also more likely to use cleaning services and eat more takeout meals now, both of which were fairly uncommon not that long ago.

However, while better than it used to be, equality is not the new standard. Taking care of the home is still squarely on the shoulders of wives. Some studies suggest that women have almost three times the workload of their husbands. They average about thirty to thirty-five hours per week doing chores, as compared to about ten to fourteen hours per week for their husbands. Interestingly, these proportions stay about the same regardless of whether the wife works full time and whether or not their husbands have jobs.[2]

This inequity is in part a result of childhood training. We learn from our parents that girls are the home keepers and boys are the breadwinners. We use these roles to define ourselves, and we perceive and interpret events in terms of our self-definitions. We then behave in ways that reinforce our self-definitions. If you see yourself as a nice person, you are nice to others; if you see yourself as a lively person, you behave energetically; if you're a husband and the breadwinner, you're not the housekeeper.

Such role definitions play right into the hands of men, but women also have some responsibility for keeping the stereotype alive. Many women want to control the housework because they see the home as their territory. Some, particularly if they hold onto traditional roles, see housework as a way to confirm their identities as homemakers, and to express love and support for their families. Additionally, because the cleanliness of a home reflects on the wife and not the husband, she may have higher standards on how to do things, even if her standards might have dropped because she's working.

Men also gain some psychological benefits from having their wives maintain their homes. Being cared for reinforces their sense of manliness. However, they might regard the work their wives do as something they've earned. As the protector of the family, he deserves to be compensated. Our guess is he also sees every chore done by his wife as one less thing he'll have to do, and it's probably safe to assume that if his wife thinks he's inadequate as a housekeeper, that's something he can live with.[3]

While neither expects an equal split, how much housework is taken on by each partner can still be a problem. The real issue comes down to perceptions of fairness, but men and women have different ways of defining what's fair. Men look at the total picture. They consider everything they do in their marriage. They throw in the amount of money they make and time spent at their jobs or with their kids. Some add in activities they feel forced to take part in, such as visiting family members or other people they don't like. They add it all up and then calculate how many household chores they still owe. Women tend to focus only on the amount of housework that has to be done, irrespective of everything else they do. They look at how many chores she does and her husband does, and from there she determines if both are doing their fair share.

A more precise way to define fairness is through the idea of balance. We refer again to thinking about marriage in terms of social exchanges. To review, in all relationships we seek to maximize our rewards and minimize our costs. We aim for balance, so that what we put in is equal to what we get out. When there's an imbalance, partners will look to make adjustments so that the relationship is not lopsided against them. When evaluating the rewards and costs for housework, partners take into account what each brings to the table. A husband with a non-working wife expects to do less than one with a working wife, and a working wife expects more help than a wife who is not working.

Translated into actual chores, from a husband's viewpoint, if he has to do half the housework, he considers that to be unfair, regardless of whether or not his wife is working. Women also believe an equal split is unnecessary, even if she is working. They think the situation is unfair only if all, or virtually all, of the workload falls on her. That said, the general consensus on fairness, and that's from both men and women, seems to be about two-thirds for women and one-third for men. In our opinion, that ratio makes sense if a wife isn't working, but not if she holds a full-time job. After all, if a man has a male roommate and both are working, neither one would think the other should have more of the workload. Such perceptions imply that both genders still regard house-work as mostly a woman's responsibility.

Partners will also consider how they expect to be treated. Housework is not just about physical labor. Like everything else in a marriage, it has an emotional component. Many wives regard help from their husbands as a demonstration of love and appreciation. They might look at what other husbands are doing, and if their husband is doing as much or more, they interpret that as being supported and treated well. If he doesn't compare well to others or she feels her workload is unfair, then she's apt to think she's unsupported and paying too a high price for her marriage.

It really comes down to a simple point: when men help around the house, the relationship benefits, but it suffers when either partner sees the split as unfair and unjustified. Overburdened wives may feel abused and taken for granted, and they will be dissatisfied with their marriage. If she's working, she may find it too difficult to balance her work and family life, and that can lead her to feel depressed and demoralized.

Men will also be unhappy when they think they're overburdened. They can feel demoralized, sad, and even anxious, and that can be with only a few chores. However, they differ from their wives in that these feelings won't necessarily carry over into how they rate their marriage overall, nor do these chores affect how they feel about themselves. In-stead, how men feel is tied specifically to the chores they have to do, and when they're completed, the bad feelings go away.[4]

It's not just the amount of work that can get men down; it can also be the types of tasks they're assigned. Many men, particularly those who hold onto traditional gender roles, consider only certain chores to be appropriate for them. Tasks like landscaping and repairs are acceptable because they affirm their manliness and personal identities. Others, such as cooking, cleaning, and laundry are seen as women's work; being asked to do these makes some men uncomfortable. One individual boasted about how much he helps his wife around the house. When asked if he cleaned the bathrooms, and more specifically, the toilets, his response was "absolutely not." That's not something a man should do because it runs counter to his beliefs about men. How cleaning toilets is appropriate for his wife is a mystery, but for his sake he's fortunate that women don't use chores to define their self-image. They simply do what needs to be done.[5]

As we mentioned, housework is not just about keeping a home clean and organized. The specific things that have to be done and who does them are wrapped up in emotions. There are expectations, self-image and role issues, support, status and fairness questions, and possibly feelings of abuse. It's the emotional side that can harm a relationship. While housework may not directly lead to divorce, it still can lead to other problems. When there are bad feelings from any source, and that includes housework, these feelings can spill over into other aspects of a relationship. Resentments that we develop because we feel overburdened will affect how we think and feel about our partner, and that will come across in how we treat them. So it's through a back door that housework can disrupt a marriage.[6]

Fred and Nancy once had all the elements of a happy marriage. Then kids came along and everything changed, and Fred was caught by surprise. While he assumed they would have to budget their time better, still he expected their relationship would stay the same. But Nancy seemed to have little time or interest in him, and that was not something he signed on for.

Nancy said that she did feel differently about her marriage, but she was focused on taking care of their family. However, she did have a problem with the way Fred acted with the children. He'd spend very little time and had no patience for them. Furthermore, she couldn't count on him to help out if she wanted a minute for herself. Fred's reaction was to remind Nancy that he never wanted kids. He reluctantly agreed only after she kept pursuing the issue, but they were going to be mostly her responsibility. He liked his life the way it was, and he didn't want to give up his freedom and the things he liked to do.

While Fred said he didn't want kids, he still agreed to it. Once he did so, he had to accept the responsibilities of a parent and commit to that role. And while he interpreted her treatment of him as justification for not wanting kids, Fred didn't realize that Nancy's behavior had changed because she objected to his lack of involvement. If he had been more committed as a parent, Nancy might have treated him better. However, Nancy didn't realize that how she treated Fred contributed to his lack of involvement with the children. He said, "I'd probably feel better about the kids if I felt better about us." In a nutshell, Fred blamed the children for what had happened to their marriage, but Nancy blamed Fred.

As troublesome as housework can be, circumstances become much more difficult when children come into the home. Again, it's wives who suffer the most because they pick up much of the additional workload. For some reason, couples tend to adopt the more traditional roles of husband as breadwinner and wife as homemaker after having children. Men spend more time working at their paid jobs and doing less housework, while women work fewer hours at their jobs and dedicate more time to taking care of the home. That's regardless of how modern thinking two people are, how housework was divided beforehand, or whether or not the wife is working.[7]

Parenthood is such a radical departure from how couples lived together before that it's almost impossible to be completely prepared for what's ahead. The greatest impact is in the early stages, when new parents are confronted with all the ways their lives are altered. They might think things have taken a turn for the chaotic, and many will feel like they're out of control. As they struggle to adjust, they will be under a great deal of stress, and that means more opportunities for conflicts. Couples are more reactionary and arguments become more intense because they're both overburdened. It's almost unavoidable that marriages will go through a decline after the first child is born.

Actually, how well couples adjust to children can depend on a few factors. These can include the parents' upbringing, financial stability, how well partners cope with stress and change, and the temperament of the child. What seems to be especially important is planning. When a child is planned for, we're emotionally prepared because we've committed to the idea before the process is set in motion. Another is whether both parents are on board with the decision. A partner who isn't sure might have a harder time adopting the right mind-set to deal with the situations and responsibilities of child-rearing. They might find what it entails to be frustrating and difficult, and a reason to resent their partner.

It can also depend upon the quality of the marriage. Couples who have a happy and supportive relationship before kids have an easier time dealing with the added stress. Unfortunately, that's not the case for unhappy ones. While couples with problems might think that having a child will bring them closer together, they're more likely to accelerate the direction the marriage was already heading. The new challenges and demands will cause their ongoing problems to come to the forefront and intensify, worsening their relationship even further.[8]

Regardless of whether the marriage gets worse, stays the same, or in rare cases actually improves, there's no denying it will be different. One major change is how we define ourselves. To fit into our new role as parents, we have to adopt new ways of thinking. As we've discussed, self-definitions are important for our psychological well-being. They connect us to a group or a situation and focus our attention on the issues that pertain to that group or situation. Normally, we don't immediately define ourselves by a new role. We change how we define ourselves gradually as we build some experience and get used to this role.

That's not how role adoption works with parenthood. New roles are thrust upon a couple literally from one day to the next, and they have no choice but to try to adjust. Before children, partners are mostly concerned with each other. However, from birth the child becomes the most important person in their lives. So how they define themselves as a couple moves in the direction of a functional rather than an emotional connection, and they see themselves more as a partnership and less as a romance or friendship. They lose opportunities to be intimate and instead might find at times feeling emotionally distant from each other. So partners not only have to cope with the added responsibilities and workload, but they must also learn how to put their relationship on the back burner.[9]

Adding the parent role and changing the definition of the couple role can be stressful. One way to understand why that happens is through the "scarcity" hypothesis. We have roles to fill, and each time we add a new role, we have less time devoted to our other roles. We run into a problem of role overload or inter-role conflict as we try to balance our time between each role. When we're balancing our time well, we believe things are working out. However, when we feel we're unable to manage all the roles we hold, we don't feel in control of our lives, and without control we have a hard time figuring out how to make our lives better. Importantly, if in trying to fill our non-parent roles we reduce our quality time with the children, we can feel upset and inadequate as parents.[10]

As we mentioned, women experience the greatest change to their life-styles, because they pick up most of the responsibility for the child and still hold onto most of the household chores. With constant demands on them, they often feel rushed and overwhelmed. Since virtually all of their time is dedicated to someone or something else, there's usually very little left over for themselves, and that means they don't have many opportunities to decompress.

Working women seem to have it especially hard. They do a double shift, coming home to care for the home and family after leaving their paying jobs. As they strive to be good in each of their roles, the pressure can be overwhelming to keep things going well at home. If they're too devoted to one role, such as their careers, the others will suffer. Very often, working mothers find their jobs less satisfying because they feel they no longer can be fully invested in their careers. Work comes to be seen as an add-on role rather than their primary one.

That's not to suggest that stay-at-home moms have it easy. While they put in about the same number of hours working at home as their husbands do on their jobs, the kind of work they do is not always satisfying. Interacting with children can be emotionally rewarding, but not all the time, and household chores don't add to one's psychological well-being. In contrast, working mothers get personal rewards from multiple sources (their careers and their families), and have opportunities to do something personally meaningful. Additionally, on their jobs they're with other adults, some of whom are friends, and the time spent in adult conversation reduces the chances of feeling isolated and depressed. And, of course, they actually get a paycheck.

Whether working or not, women with children often feel emotionally and physically drained at the end of the day. They're often deprived of sleep, which when combined with overwhelming responsibilities, can undermine their well-being. Part of it is due to the amount of work they have, but it's also how they view their responsibilities. Women put a lot of pressure on themselves to do their jobs to the maximum. When their stress levels run particularly high, they can experience a whole range of negative feelings, such as frustration, impatience, hostility, and resentment, as well as incompetence if they're not handling all of their jobs to their liking. These emotions will eventually find an outlet, sometimes appropriately, and sometimes not.

We should point out that men might also feel stressed, but not to the same extent as their wives. Many are more concerned about their bread-winner roles and are less worried about how well they do at their home-based responsibilities. When things are overwhelming, they might be concerned, but they're not likely to feel too upset, have their confidence shaken, or think that it reflects on them personally. In fact, some men may actually become more upset about a loss of their personal time rather than lost time with their family.[11]

Part of what affects our ability to adjust to parenthood has to do with expectations. As we mentioned earlier, both husbands and wives may not fully grasp how differently they could act and feel toward each other. They might expect that the emotional parts of their relationship would stay the same. That doesn't happen, and the more partners are off with respect to how they thought it would be, the greater the relationship can be damaged.

Not surprisingly, men and women differ in this regard. For wives, their expectations are straightforward. They presume their husbands will be supportive and take on some of the added responsibilities. As with housework, it doesn't seem to be childcare per se that causes women to be less happy in their marriages, but rather the added work makes the split even more unbalanced. We know this because when wives don't expect much help from their husbands, their relationship is harmed to a much less extent. However, if they expect assistance and don't get it, or if they feel the labor split has become too lopsided, they won't feel good about their husbands and their marriage.

Men's expectations, on the other hand, are that their share of respon-sibilities won't change much. There will be the occasional feeding and diaper change, but it won't be so often as to interfere with their normal routines. They may also expect that their relationship with their wives will pretty much be as it was before the baby. That's not how things typically go, nor is it realistic to think they should. With their time con-straints and pressures, some wives don't have the energy for more inti-mate forms of spousal interaction. Additionally, her priorities have changed from taking care of her husband to taking care of a child. When one of her roles has to be put aside, it's likely to be as caregiver and lover to her husband.

What's often at the heart of marital dissatisfaction for men during the child-rearing stage is the loss of intimacy combined with the increase in responsibilities. Again, if we think in terms of social exchanges, husbands are being asked to live with fewer rewards (less attention and affection) but at the same time they have to absorb greater costs (childcare and more housework). Getting hit with a double whammy might make them feel as though their marriage has shifted out of balance against them.

How partners react to the disappointment of unmet expectations can range from emotional withdrawal to outright hostility. Again, men and women behave differently when their expectations are violated. If a husband feels good about his relationship with his wife, he tends to be more nurturing and involved with his children. However, he can be less so if he doesn't feel his wife is loving and attentive. In fact, how a man feels about his marriage can have more to do with how he acts toward his children than his skills as a parent. That's not how it works with mothers. They tend to treat their children the same regardless of how they feel about their husband or their marriage. Bad days are bad, but they won't take it out on their kids.

Problems can also result from differences in parenting philosophies. In some marriages, one parent may prefer to take a relaxed attitude while the other may want to institute rules for the child to follow. When parents bump heads on how to raise their children, not only do they give themselves reasons to argue, but they also work against the interests of the child. Sometimes in these situations one parent may try to gain the child as an ally against the other parent. The child may then feel forced to take sides with one parent or the other, or become confused as to what they're supposed to do. The parent who loses that power struggle can feel alienated from the family, and may resent their partner or the children.

Parents who are having problems with each other may inadvertently take out their frustrations on their children. They may find the stress of their relationship so emotionally draining that they don't pay enough attention to their children's emotional needs. Others may feel their children are responsible for marital problems. Even if they don't consciously blame their children, parents who are hostile to each other might target their hostility to their children.

Regardless of how marital problems come about, it's not just the parents who suffer. Fighting between husbands and wives can harm the psychological and emotional development of their children. Children can tell when their parents aren't getting along, and they find that environment frightening. There's a chance they will suffer from depression, have problems in school, and even develop some physical health issues. Some might even blame themselves for their parents' problems, and that can leave them feeling vulnerable, fearful, and anxious. As adults, they can end up as more dependent, insecure, and unsociable. They may also learn some inappropriate behaviors. If parents' arguments are hostile and aggressive, their children might use the same style in their own relationships. If they're aloof and emotionally distant from each other, their children might have a hard time making emotional connections to other people. And if the children then develop behavioral problems because of the negativity they're exposed to, these can further fuel problems in the marriage.[12]

Conflicts about housework and childcare, especially if they result from an imbalance of workload, should be avoidable. All that's needed is for both partners to contribute their fair share. However, as we said, there's a strong emotional element to housework. Partners have feelings about the amount and types of tasks each does. Furthermore, because there will always be more to do than we have time or energy for, there is always the potential for stress. Stress can come from how much we have to do, but it can also come from how we feel about who's doing what.

There's a good chance that our beliefs and expectations are beneath our emotional reactions. If a wife becomes angry because her husband isn't helping enough, she probably expects him to be more supportive of her. If a husband is asked to do something he believes is inappropriate for him, he might become angry or resentful because he thinks such tasks violate his manhood. In other words, one source of housework arguments relates to how partners think and feel about their chores and workload. If we can manage such negative emotions, we might find that work overload isn't intruding quite as much into how we think and feel about our partner.

First and foremost, be aware that the lifestyle of a parent is complicated, and it can affect your perspective. If you're feeling stressed out, it's probably because of all the roles you're trying to fill, and not necessarily because of something your spouse has done or not done. Taking your frustrations out on your spouse will only lead to arguments that have little to do with why you're stressed. Instead, partners need to discuss their issues and try to be supportive of each other. Emotional support helps to relieve stress and makes it easier to handle overwhelming circumstances. That's especially true for women, for whom emotional support is an important way to cope with problems. So pay attention to your partner's stress levels, and be prepared to intercede when help is needed.

For some marriages, having husbands take on more responsibilities is certainly important. However, trying to force them to change just their behavior may not be the most effective approach. There's likely to be a good deal of arguing and hard feelings from both sides as wives constantly have to remind their husbands of what they have to do. Besides, if he hasn't helped out regularly in the past, he's developed that as a habit, and habits can be hard to break. It might be easier for him to change behaviors and feelings by focusing on the beliefs that make him feel and act that way.

One such belief for men relates to their self-definition. Believing that a chore defines who we are is not rational. We all have things we have to do that we don't like or feel are beneath our dignity. But they have to get done, and we don't use them to define our self-image unless they are the only things we do. Nevertheless, some men see it that way. By being sensitive to role issues, a wife can avoid misinterpreting her husband's lack of help as laziness or insensitivity to her needs. In other words, she can avoid a reason for being angry and instead focus on chore-sharing solutions that work for both of them.

Some men also believe they have a choice as to how much housework they take on, and when they do help, it's a favor for their wives. With such thoughts, men give themselves permission to do less if they want to. These husbands need to realize that they really don't have a choice and getting married didn't mean they hired a domestic. Additionally, they should consider that roles are not as clearly delineated today as in the past, and housework can no longer be classified as a woman's domain. Besides, many women hold jobs today. They have had to redefine themselves and take on what has traditionally been a man's role, so men should expect to do the same regarding their domestic responsibilities.

Men should also keep in mind that when they don't pitch in, they really haven't taken the easy way out. Many wives gauge how they feel about their relationship by the support they receive from their husbands. When overloaded, they may feel abused and taken for granted, and interpret a lack of help as indicative of how their husbands feel about them. They're likely to resent such treatment, and that will come across in how they act toward their husbands. In other words, a husband who feels happy because he avoided chores probably won't feel happy for very long. Instead, he's much better off in the long run to simply ask his wife what he can do to help. She will appreciate the offer on a lot of different levels.

Staying on the same point, some wives believe their husband's lack of assistance indicates they don't love them. If he doesn't help out around the house enough, it may not reflect how he feels about his wife. Instead, she should try to take a broader perspective and consider the other ways he shows that he is caring and supportive, and use those as a way of judging her marriage. If she still feels unloved and unsupported, then her marriage might have problems that go beyond housework.

It's also important for wives to recognize that their husbands are expected to take on more chores, some of which challenge his masculinity, and at the same time they often have to live with less intimacy and attention. It's the loss of the latter that can make added chores and self-image issues especially difficult to handle. However, they may have an easier time reconciling themselves to these demands if they can choose the childcare or household chores to be done. That would allow them to select those that are more in line with how they see their roles. [13]

For husbands, it's important to keep in mind that their wives are often overburdened, and they won't have the time or energy to devote to their relationship as they did before children. The solution for both is to adjust their expectations and find some middle ground. Marriage is a partnership, and true partners acknowledge and try to satisfy the needs and interests of each other. Husbands must acknowledge that their wives need help, some empathy, and few added demands; and wives must accept that their husband might behave better if they receive some positive attention. In other words, some emotion work can help both handle this life stage better.

If both partners are agreeable to making an imbalanced workload more equitable, try to come up with a plan as to what is expected from each of you. Things go a lot smoother when couples are able to coordinate their activities, and each partner has a clear understanding of their roles and duties. When responsibilities are not clearly designated, the ambiguity that results can lead to misunderstandings and that can lead to conflicts. Note that tasks should not be randomly assigned, but rather based on competency. If some tasks are outside a partner's expertise, they may not be performed to the other partner's liking. That can lead to criticisms, and criticisms can be demotivating—not to mention aggravating.

As a simple exercise, list all the chores that have to be done and specify which ones each of you will be responsible for. It's a good idea to start by assigning chores based on preference. The remaining chores can then be assigned according to what seems appropriate and balanced. Importantly, both partners must commit to the agreed upon solution, and both should feel that they have been treated fairly. If not, you will eventually discard the arrangement and be back to where you started.

If a husband takes on added chores, he's not helping if they're not done to his wife's standards. When they're not done the way his wife wants, she will feel forced to do the work herself, and that defeats the purpose. If this is a problem for you, discuss the ways to do tasks properly so that they won't be done incorrectly and then become a source of contention. A successful conversation on this topic requires that wives instruct their husbands with patience, and that husbands listen and learn.

If you're overloaded and feeling stressed out, you might be able to help yourself by changing how you think about your various roles. We are talking about compartmentalizing and prioritizing. Those who successfully manage multiple roles learn to turn off thoughts about one when they're in the other. When you leave work, switch to thoughts about home and family, and vice versa. Learning to think compartmentally can help you focus better on what you have directly in front of you. It won't reduce your workload, but you will feel as though you're managing it better, and that can keep your stress levels more in check.

Before making the decision to have children, both partners must be personally committed to the idea, and their relationship should be on solid enough ground to handle how their lives will change. There will be a lot of pressure, and sometimes under pressure we can behave badly, and we may forget we're not the only two people living in the house. Marital disputes are a child's worst nightmare. If you and your spouse are having problems, and that could include how to raise children, work them out in private. Also, keep your roles as parent and spouse separate. Try not to let the issues you have with one contaminate how you feel about the other.

Your social circle can make a difference in how well you adjust to having children. Remember, we judge our competency and the quality of our relationship by making comparisons to the people around us. If most of our friends are childless or there is one partner at home full-time, we might compare ourselves to couples who have less stressful lifestyles. Such comparisons can make us think we're not capable of handling our own more complicated lives. We're not suggesting that such friendships should be abandoned, but you might find it helpful to spend time with people who share your lifestyle, or at the very least, use these couples as your standard. When you compare yourself to them, your expectations will be more in line with your actual situation, and you'll feel more normal when things are out of control. Furthermore, same-lifestyle couples can empathize and support each other when faced with problems, and you can learn from each other's experiences.

Some working mothers of young children might feel guilty because they hold full-time jobs. They might think they're not dedicating enough time to their child's welfare and development. However, as it turns out, kids with working moms turn out fine. There's no significant decrease in the amount or quality of time these mothers spend with their children as compared to non-working mothers. Preschool children spend a good deal of time on their own playing with toys or with siblings and friends, and not as much as we would believe interacting with their mothers. Of course, these mothers have to be concerned with the quality of care their children are receiving, but if they've selected a care provider carefully, they shouldn't feel badly that they're not with their children full time.

If you and your partner disagree on how to raise a child, it's important to confront this issue and find a solution as soon as possible. This can be an emotionally charged issue that can easily get out of hand, so it's best to follow some rules. First, as with all disputes, make sure this is done without the kids present. Second, wait until you and your partner are in a good place emotionally. Third, be prepared to negotiate and compromise so that you both get something that you want, and what you decide is in the best interests of the child. Whatever you decide, make sure you're consistent, so that your child is not confused as to what is expected of them.

Finally, we should mention that men establish their housework patterns early on in their marriages and hold onto these patterns when they get older. Whatever amount they do at the beginning of a marriage will stay about the same when they get to retirement. Consequently, women may want to try to train their prospective husbands from the start of the relationship, preferably before getting married. If he can't be trained, you will at least have an idea of what's in store for you. From there you can either adjust your expectations or negotiate for something you want in exchange for your extra labor. [14]

Steven and Joanne were living the good life. They had an expensive house in a prestigious Long Island neighborhood, a country club membership, expensive cars, and the like. Steve had a high-paying job in the financial industry and could afford their extravagant lifestyle. However, financial hard times came along, and they suffered along with everyone else. They had trouble making mortgage and car lease payments, but rather than downsize, they tried to hold onto the lifestyle they had gotten used to.

Soon after their financial difficulties began, Steven and Joanne ran into problems in their marriage. They found they were fighting about things they once could work out calmly together. Their arguments could be on almost any issue, although they never argued about money. When asked how they planned to handle their financial situation, they had no plans to change their lifestyle even though they knew they could no longer afford it. Their status in the community was extremely important, and they were embarrassed to think how it would look to their friends and neighbors if they had to now live like "normal people." Furthermore, Steven said that if they changed their lifestyle, he would feel like a failure, and he couldn't live with that.

However, while they both claimed to accept their situation, the financial hole they were digging had put them both under a lot of stress, and it was harming their marriage. That stress came out in a variety of negative emotions, much of which they targeted toward each other. As their biggest issue, they were privately blaming each other for their problems. Joanne was disappointed because she thought Steven was no longer capable of supporting them; Steven was angry because Joanne was not sympathetic to his problems and seemed to have lost respect for him. As a result of the frustration and hostility they both felt, they found themselves drifting apart.

Another aspect of managing a home that can have a profound effect on marriage is money. We all know that money plays a vital role in the quality of living. Those who have it are happier, have better health, and greater longevity. They're less likely to be victims of violent crime, or to have children who drop out of school or become pregnant as teenagers.

For many, it is a source of status and a way of defining themselves. In relationships, money can be used to show affection and support, and provide a reason to become or stay married. When couples feel good about their finances, they feel good about themselves and their marriage. While it does not guarantee happiness, not having money, or more precisely enough money, can strain a relationship to its breaking point.

When we talk about financial problems, we mean a prolonged money shortfall and heavy debt. The problem with debt is that it lingers. We often face stressful events that are difficult and can cause emotional turmoil, but they're usually short-lived. When the cause of our turmoil passes, the relationship often returns to normal. Debt, however, is usually not a short-term situation. It can drag on for years. We constantly feel the pressure to make payments, so that means we're likely to experience prolonged emotional stress, and stress leads to conflict. Debt that hangs around for a long time can wear down even the most resilient couples.

Some debt is avoidable. Buying a house, for example, is an ideal many couples strive for, and most of us feel it's worth the expense. It can also cement a relationship because it's a demonstration of partnership and commitment. Nevertheless, such a purchase can create economic pressure. We may find we have to increase our work hours, eliminate other things we'd like to buy, or cut down on doing things we enjoy doing, such as going to dinner or a movie. This is especially an issue for newly married couples, who, as just starting out, are likely to have the highest debt levels and very little discretionary money for play time.

It's avoidable debt that can be particularly damaging to a marriage. We are referring to buying something such as a house that's beyond our means or spending money in a one-sided manner (a husband buys a boat even though his wife hates boating). For the former, couples may have cutbacks that are too extreme; for the latter, one partner may resent having to give up something that's needed to pay a debt for something from which they receive no benefits. In fact, that kind of debt can tell a lot about their marriage. When one partner puts a couple into debt to meet his or her needs only, there's some question as to that person's commitment to their partner. Couples who end up divorced because of financial issues tend to spend more on items for themselves rather than for both partners.[15]

Regardless of how debt occurs, it can be detrimental to a marriage when it's extreme. Arguments are hard to avoid, and are often directly about money, such as how much is earned and how it's spent. These will often include accusations, such as the husband doesn't earn enough or the wife spends too much, or vice versa. Partners are likely to blame each other for their situation and scrutinize each other's purchases. They're also likely to feel less committed to their relationship. Again, if we think about marriage in terms of social exchanges, when there's not enough money in the household, we can feel that the costs of staying together outweigh the benefits.

The constant emotional strain can also bring to the forefront other problems in the marriage and lead to arguments that aren't directly related to money. Financial problems can affect how we think, act, and feel about our partner in general, causing hostility and marital dissatisfaction. Stressful events affect our moods and make us more sensitive, and, as a result, we don't think clearly and tend to focus on the things we don't like about our relationship. We might take out our frustrations on our partner or other family members. If our spouse says or does something we don't like, in non-stressful times we might let it pass, but under high-stress conditions we may not be able to.

Economic problems affect husbands and wives in different ways. Because a man sees his role as the breadwinner, he may think of himself as a failure when he cannot provide adequately for his family. How he feels about himself can then produce a range of other emotions, such as hostility and irritability, withdrawal, and depression, and these can affect how he treats his family. For women, prolonged financial distress tends to affect how they view their marriage overall. This may in part be due to the fact she's already overloaded with home-based responsibilities and adding money problems puts her closer to a breaking point. We would also guess that many women expect to be financially supported by their husbands because they also regard them as the breadwinners. When that doesn't happen, one of the primary benefits they're supposed to get out marriage is not delivered. From the emotional experiences faced by both husbands and wives, it's not uncommon for them to gradually lose touch with each other. [16]

For some couples, their financial burdens are extreme and no one's fault. Devastating illnesses, a bad job market, and the like can destroy families, and there's not much we can recommend that would solve such problems. However, for those whose financial difficulties are less extreme or are self-induced, it is possible to reduce some of the harm they can do to their marriage.

The ability to cope with such pressures depends on how couples approach them. For one, supportiveness can help limit the psychological impact and make it easier to focus on finding solutions. Secondly, it's extremely important that you don't blame each other, even if one partner is at fault. Accept the problem as one you both own, in the manner of a true partnership. Holding onto resentments and anger about your financial state of affairs is absolutely counterproductive. As we discussed, negativity blocks our ability to think clearly, and that makes it hard to work on problems. It can only harm your relationship and still the debt remains.

Supportive behavior and joint ownership of the problem is the first step, but obviously not the final one. There is the practical side of money management. We still have to come up with effective solutions. Working together to bring your spending more in line is essential, because it is hard to fight off the psychological demons that come along with prolonged and extreme debt. As we're not finance experts, there's not much practical advice we can give in this area. Nevertheless, there are many excellent books available that describe ways to budget money and solve debt problems. Additionally, we recommend that you speak to a financial consultant or an accountant who is more equipped to come up with approaches that can work for you.

If you are thinking of spending money you don't have for something you really don't need, we suggest you think again. Be realistic about what you can afford. The unnecessary debt you take on might not only prevent you from buying things you actually need, the resulting stress will take its toll on you and your relationship. Besides, the things we buy don't often make us as happy as we expect them to. After the initial excitement wears off, the pain of the debt will be worse than the long-term enjoyment of whatever you spent your money on. Nevertheless, if you still decide to take on needless debt, make sure it's for something both of you will benefit from. While our partner might initially agree to let us spend on something they don't want, the debt they have to keep servicing will soon make them forget they ever thought this was a good idea.

11

POWER AND CONTROL

Power and control can be an issue in all kinds of relationships. There are some in which the two parties consider themselves to be equals and treat each other as such. In many, however, one person might have the upper hand. The one who is higher in the pecking order very often has the ability to influence and manipulate the other person. When we dominate a relationship, decisions usually go in our favor and we often dictate what to do or talk about. Our emotional state can even influence the emotional state of the other person.

Establishing a hierarchy of power sometimes occurs because of the dynamics of the relationship and the type of people involved. Sometimes it's through force of personality and sometimes because of assets. One person either has certain personal characteristics that make them more forceful or more subservient, or one brings something to the relationship that the other person needs. While at times they may find their authority challenged, there is still a tendency for the dominating person to control the other.

Bill and Mary couldn't agree on anything. Regardless of what they were talking about, they would eventually end up in an argument. In fact, no issue was too small. They gave an example of how the previous week they had gone to the movies. Afterward, Bill gave his impression of the film, and Mary came back with almost the opposite opinion. They got into a fight about it and stayed angry at each other for the rest of the evening. That pattern had become pretty typical for them.

*Their problems began after Mary went back to work. She did so be-
cause they needed the extra money, but also to return to her career. While
Bill appreciated the extra money, he blamed her job as the reason for
their current problems. Before she was working, Bill said that their relationship was great and they had no trouble getting along. After she
started working, however, Mary changed. Bill said Mary seemed to disagree with him about everything, questioned every decision he made, and
no longer respected him. He said that the situation with Mary had become intolerable.*

*Mary agreed that she now acts differently with Bill, and she also
agreed that her job had something to do with it. But unlike Bill, she saw
the change in herself positively. Before she went back to work, she felt
subservient to Bill, and had become so dependent on him that she was
afraid to voice any disapproval. Mary hated how she felt about herself
and was thankful her job had given her more confidence and independence. She said that she still respects Bill, but she also feels she has a
right to her opinions and an equal say in their decisions.*

*Their problems actually stemmed from Bill's belief that men should be
dominant in a marriage, and this perspective formed the basis of his
expectations as to how a wife was supposed to behave. He was comfortable as long as he could control Mary but found it threatening when
Mary expected to be treated as his equal. He regarded her submissiveness as appropriate and any expression of independence or disagreement
with his decisions or opinions as disrespect. So any time Mary did not
agree with his point of view, they had a reason to argue. On Mary's part,
she went out of her way to disagree with any of his opinions because that
was a way to demonstrate her independence and equality. Bill had no
choice but to come to terms with that because Mary had no plans to
return to second-class status.*

Power struggles can be an issue in marriage. Some partners might
share power equally, and in others one partner accepts a more subservient
role and allows the other to be in control. However, for some couples, the
struggle for control is not settled because one partner refuses to submit
and be dominated by the other. The battle is ongoing, and the relationship
is often contentious, with continuous disagreements and skirmishes as
each partner struggles to gain either the upper hand or equality. Power
issues in marriage can be subtle; sometimes partners aren't even aware

that the real battle is for dominance or independence, not about the specific issue they're arguing about at the time.

Historically, power was not an issue. Men usually wore the pants, or at least that's how it appeared and what men believed. Their opinions on most things relating to the home and family were very often decisive. In many marriages, women didn't have much final say regarding most matters, including how the children were raised. Both men and women outwardly seemed to accept this arrangement, although we find it hard to believe that many women actually liked the idea.

Men's power derived from their social status and money. Couples accepted the idea that men were dominant and women submissive, but more importantly, men were usually the sole income earners. Money can be a source of power because it reflects the resources that partners bring to the marriage. Remember the notion of social exchanges, in which couples look for balance between what they're giving and receiving. When one partner brings more resources, they have more influence and are able to control the lives of the people around them. With few opportunities available, women had no choice but to submit to their husbands. As one positive, marriages were easier because couples had fewer reasons to argue because they both—or more accurately, women—knew their place.

The world is much different now. The women's movement has been whittling away at old gender definitions and has moved the issue of equality to the forefront. That in part has been achieved by the entry of women into the workforce. In the previous chapter we talked about how jobs taken by wives have affected the amount of housework expected of each partner. Taking on careers and earning money has also changed how women view themselves. They have a source of self-esteem and recognition, and that has helped them feel more independent and self-reliant. Such ego-gratifying benefits have also changed their priorities. A woman's sense of self-worth and well-being used to be driven by the quality of their home life, but it's now driven more by their jobs. While most women still define themselves as family members first and career persons second, they are starting to think more like men, especially if they have high-paying or prestigious positions.

Jobs have also provided women with options. Men primarily look at their jobs as a means of supporting their families and feeling productive. Married women can hold jobs for a couple of reasons. Some do so for the same reasons as men. Some, however, work as a hedge against divorce. If they feel vulnerable or are in an unhappy marriage, a job protects them from being abandoned without a means of support. Women are actually more likely to get a job, work longer hours, and invest more of themselves into their careers when they think the future of their marriage is in doubt.[1]

From this perspective, it can be argued that jobs have affected the stability of marriage. Working women don't have to stay in an unsatisfying marriage, and they no longer have to get married to be supported. Because they have some independence, they may not feel it's as important to work as hard on their marital problems. Furthermore, when both work outside the home, there is less time devoted to the marriage, particularly if they have demanding jobs. There are also more opportunities to meet people with whom love relationships can develop, so the potential for marriage-ending affairs is doubled when both work. Finally, because both husbands and wives won't suffer financial hardships to the same extent as when only one partner is working, divorce can be more of a consideration.

That said, it does not appear that divorce rates have increased because women hold jobs. When divorce occurs, it's primarily because the marriage is unhappy and not because the wife is working. The real change for working women seems to be on when to marry. They're more willing to delay marriage, particularly if they hold high-paying jobs. This is not to say that women are less interested in getting married, but they may put a little more effort into finding the right person and the right time, and not just jump at the first opportunity because they feel they need to. Still, however, the options to get out of an unsatisfying marriage are there, and husbands are aware of that.

In fact, it seems more the case that a working wife can be a benefit to the quality of the relationship. By contributing to the household income, she might be regarded by her husband as a more valued partner and more important to the success of their marriage. She's also likely to be a source of pride to her spouse and more worthy of his respect. Furthermore, because both partners face the same issues and problems related to working, there can be a greater sensitivity, flexibility, and responsiveness to each other's needs. All of this can make for closer emotional connections between them.[2]

However, whether or not her job is good or bad for a marriage can depend on why she's working. Wives who work because they want to are generally happy with their situation. But wives who feel forced to get a job, usually because of a financial need, are more likely to feel disappointed with her marital situation, especially if she's already overloaded with home responsibilities. She may come to see her husband as an inefficient provider. Such thoughts and feelings will affect how she treats her husband, and, in the spirit of reciprocity, that can lead him to be unhappy with her. He might also regard her attitude about working as a sign that she's unwilling to contribute to the household, and that becomes a reason to resent her. Such hostile feelings on both sides can put a strain on the relationship.

It can also depend on what a husband thinks about having a working wife. Some husbands may feel threatened by their increased prestige, especially if their wives earn more than they do. This is especially the case if a husband believes he's supposed to be the primary breadwinner for the family. He may see himself as a poor provider if she fills that role better than he does. Men are much more comfortable if they feel they can surpass their wives and much less so if it's the other way around. In fact, it's argued that the ultimate test of some marriages is when the wife earns more than her husband.

Some husbands might feel neglected because their wives can't provide the time and attention they want for themselves and the family. It's not that she's making more money or that he resents her success necessarily, but rather that he believes she is not fulfilling her role as a wife and homemaker. That can also mean there's pressure on him to take on more household chores. Picking up a greater portion of home responsibilities can interfere with their own personal and career goals, not to mention their self-image. Men with working wives actually seem to get less satisfaction out of their careers than men whose wives aren't working. They're sometimes required to put in fewer hours on their jobs, and that may limit their own career opportunities. Such a situation means partners can have conflicting goals and expectations, and that can put them at odds with each other.

Wives are not oblivious to the fact that their jobs can pose a risk to their marriage, especially if they're more successful than their husbands. Some will do things that are meant to reduce this risk. They may change jobs if their current one is too demanding or may limit their success by turning down promotions or reducing their time commitment. But even if they do nothing to limit their work aspirations, many wives will still worry as to whether their success is acceptable to their husbands. They watch their husbands' reactions and will do things to maintain their sense of masculinity, such as making them feel appreciated and emotionally supported.[3]

The point we're making is that women in the workforce, along with social movements for equality, have made gender relations more complicated. From the perspective of women as individuals, their improved status is what it should have always been. From the perspective of marriage, however, these changes have upset the power structure. They are in direct opposition to the traditional male-dominant and female-submissive roles, and so there's no longer a clearly defined power hierarchy. In some marriages, husbands are struggling to stay in control and hold onto what they see as their entitlement, while wives are struggling for the equality they think they deserve.

With equality, there are more opportunities for conflicts. Because both partners believe they should have a say in all decisions, couples are forced to do more negotiating and compromising, and that increases the chances for fighting. Furthermore, as each partner works hard to safeguard their equality, any social exchange imbalances become more of a point of contention. A wife who thinks she's working harder than she should around the house and a husband who thinks his wife doesn't respect him are more likely to confront their partner about these issues. This doesn't necessarily mean couples are less happy today, but anything that increases the chances of conflict puts their marriage at risk.[4]

Since the prestige of being male is not what it used to be and many wives have their own income, two ways to wield power have been eliminated for men. Nevertheless, money can still be used by partners to manipulate and control each other, and that's in how it's handled. We talked about money in the previous chapter as a problem when there's not enough of it. However, money can be a point of contention regardless of the family's financial status, such as when partners don't feel they have equal access to it. Money is such an important factor relating to marital health that when couples argue about it, the battles are more intense than when they argue about other topics, such as children. That's because money is not just about dollars: very often it's really about power and influence, and when we can't get to it, it's almost as bad as when we don't have enough.

There are two aspects of handling money. One is how it's stored. Couples can pool their money in a shared account or, if they both have incomes, they can keep their own money in separate accounts. If it's pooled, there's a second issue of who's managing it. They can manage it equally and have equal access to it, or it can be managed by either the husband or the wife. In some marriages, one partner will hand over all their money but keep some aside for their personal spending. In others, all the money is handed over to one partner, and the other partner is given an allowance to cover their personal or household expenses.

How money is stored and managed suggests different degrees of power by one partner over the other. Because both men and women understand that, they have different preferences on how it's handled. Pooled money very often implies that both partners are more invested in their relationship and committed to each other. However, it doesn't necessarily mean that one partner doesn't control the other. That can happen only when both have equal access to their pooled money. If one partner is the manager and doles out money to the other as they see fit, that is clearly an imbalance of control. Keep in mind that the one who manages the money very often has more say in how it's spent, more input in financial decision making, and feels a greater sense of independence.

There's a difference as to whether husbands or wives control the money. That's because money can have very different meanings to men and women. It's these differences that are often the cause of conflict in a marriage. For example, while couples may think they're arguing about the way money is spent, it's likely that the real problem is what money means to each partner. A wife might buy an expensive pair of shoes as a way of expressing her independence, while a husband might become angry because such spending suggests he's lost some control.

When women manage the money, they treat it like a responsibility, similar to other household chores. For men, money translates into status. They're prone to have their identities and sense of self-worth defined by their income and earning power. That's one reason why it can be an issue when their wives earn more than they do. They can think they are less appreciated by their wives, and that can leave them feeling embarrassed and jealous. These feelings can come out in a lot of different situations, so it's not always apparent that a couple's problem really revolves around the amount made by each partner.

Men also tend to believe they own the money earned by the couple. That may be a reason why they can see money as a source of power, and it may also be why they believe they are more entitled to spend it than do their wives. Many wives seem to agree with that, because they can often feel inhibited about spending, sometimes thinking they're not entitled to it. Ownership and power is also why many men may prefer to merge money into a single pool. When it's pooled together, he can be the sole manager, and that means he has more control in deciding how it's spent. Wives, on the other hand, like to have at least some money kept separately. In that way she can take some of her husband's control away from him.

We should point out that having one partner who controls all the money is not a problem in all marriages. Some couples are perfectly comfortable having a single partner take on that responsibility. In fact, money won't even become a point of contention for couples unless one partner believes the allocation of money between them is unfair. If a husband distributes the money, but doesn't make his wife feel like she's getting less than he gives to himself or less than she has a right to, she's typically fine with that. However, if he tends to indulge himself and at the same time keeps his wife on a tight budget, she will not be happy with that situation. Under these conditions, the arguments that can occur between partners are likely to be intense, because again they're not actually arguing about money but about being controlled and manipulated.[5]

Charlie and Cathy were school teachers who were married for many years. Throughout their marriage, Cathy was pretty much in control of most of the activities in their lives and made most of the decisions for them. She took her role as dominant partner seriously and would often worry about making the right decisions, but still she believed that it was important for her to take control of their lives.

Charlie was a music teacher and a laid-back kind of guy who spent a good deal of his free time playing his trumpet. He sometimes resented Cathy's dominance, but liked the idea that he didn't have to deal with all the things Cathy took on. In his mind, Charlie got to be free of the responsibility of dealing with the burdens of life. Plus, having Cathy in control meant he could blame her when things didn't go well.

Their life took a turn when Charlie's father suffered a heart attack. Because the father's illness left him unable to work, the family asked

Charlie to take over the business. Charlie agreed and found himself in charge of a very large staff of people. He got a significant increase in the amount of money he made. Charlie began to like being in charge, and his sense of self-control and self-confidence were greatly enhanced.

With this change in his lifestyle, Charlie began to complain openly about Cathy's control over his life. Cathy was confused by the changes in Charlie. She continually hounded him to find out what was going on. When they came into therapy, Cathy said she believed that Charlie had major psychological problems and was in need of medication, but as there was no evidence of psychopathology in Charlie, there was no need for a psychiatric consultation. It was clear that Charlie no longer needed Cathy to run his life, and he openly objected to her continued attempts to do so. In one session Charlie said that he was angry because during an argument, Cathy threw a Xanax tablet down his throat.

The problem was the balance of power had shifted dramatically. Charlie refused to remain submissive because he felt belittled by Cathy's dominance. Cathy didn't want to surrender control, in part because she felt threatened by Charlie's independence, but also because she wanted to play a dominant role in their relationship. Because they were unable to face the real issue, they argued about a series of things with no resolution. They left therapy, tried other therapists with no success, and eventually got divorced.

Controlling the household assets is not the only way partners can dominate a relationship. As we mentioned, it can come about through the strength of one partner's personality or the willing submissiveness of the other. However they get there, when relationships are unequal and unfair, it's usually the husband who has the upper hand. Certainly there are some marriages in which the wife dominates her husband, but that's not very typical. Most women give more than they receive in their marriage, and that's a pretty good indication that husbands often have more power.

Consistent with the traditions of their gender, men really like the idea of being the boss, and even if they really aren't the boss, they tend to believe they are. Most women, on the other hand, are not as concerned about being dominant as they are about being treated as subservient. It's not that wives reject power and wouldn't like to be in control. In fact, they don't mind over-benefiting at all, even if what they receive puts their marriage out of balance. The more they receive, the happier they are and the better they actually feel about many other seemingly unrelated aspects of their marriage, such as sexual satisfaction.

As we've mentioned throughout, equality and fairness are important components to a healthy marriage. When neither partner believes they are dominated, both reap a lot of benefits. Couples have stronger emotional bonds and feel like true companions, often because there's mutual respect. As a result, partners are nicer to each other, have more productive ways of communicating, and are more open and supportive of each other. Partners are also more prone to feel like they own their problems jointly, and that makes it easier for them to find solutions that have both of their needs in mind.

A relationship that's one-sided is not satisfying. When we believe we are dominated by our partner, we're likely to have our self-confidence gradually erode, and that can fuel a host of other problems. We may believe we have no control over our marriage, and sometimes over our own lives, and that can lead to overdependency and feelings of helplessness. We're also likely to lose interest in our relationship because our own needs are secondary to our partner's. That means they're usually unmet, but we might feel powerless to improve the situation. Furthermore, as no one likes thinking they are being treated like a second-class citizen, very often we'll feel angry and resentful toward our partner. While we might suppress these emotions because we're afraid of our partner's reaction, we're not likely to feel intimate or emotionally connected.

Even the dominant partner is not really happy in a dominant-submissive relationship. As we've mentioned throughout, interactions between partners are reciprocal. So if one partner is unhappy because they feel manipulated, the other will be made to feel just as unhappy. Furthermore, domination often leads to discomfort. Most people who have more power than they should usually have a hunch they're taking advantage. They might get there out of a sense of righteousness, but more likely they'll get it by seeing how their partner behaves toward them. When we dominate our partner, our partner can be resentful, or worse, will shut down. They might be unwilling to voice opinions or present new ideas, and we don't get to know their true thoughts and feelings. In other words, interactions with a partner in such a relationship can be uninteresting, even frustrating, because we don't get much feedback from them. Unfortunately, a dominating partner may not realize that what they lose in the quality of their relationship is not made up for by the benefits of being the boss.[6]

Nevertheless, there are some marriages that work even though they're out of balance. Some spouses seem to be perfectly happy having a partner who occupies the dominant role. In the case of traditional marriages, for example, both husbands and wives are comfortable with the idea that the husband is dominant. These couples share the old-style perspective of male and female roles. They have a set of expectations about how each partner should behave, and they find their respective roles to be natural and even preferred. While they might admit to themselves that their relationship is unfair, they're not likely to voice that opinion, and seem willing to live with things as they are because that's the way of the world. However, we should point out that these relationships are acceptable only if the husband is dominant. Neither partner likes the arrangement when the wife is dominant, possibly because this represents too extreme a departure from traditional male and female roles.

However, the reality is couples who hold onto traditional gender roles are not as satisfied with their marriages as those who have a more contemporary view. Modern-thinking couples are sometimes referred to as androgynous, because the two partners share a number of personal traits. Both husbands and wives possess some degree of what might be considered masculine traits, such as means-ends problem solving, and feminine traits, such as emotional expressiveness. Androgynous couples do better because they can identify with each other. As we mentioned in a previous chapter, when two people have similar ways of thinking, they have an easier time communicating because they understand each other. In contrast, those who are more traditional might have difficulty at times seeing their partner's side of issues. When conflicts arise, they are not as well equipped to handle them because they see the world primarily from the perspective of their different gender roles.

A modern view of male and female roles is particularly important when wives work full time. Husbands who regard their wives as their equals tend to be more nurturing and supportive, and more likely to pitch in around the house, and that helps their wives deal with their workload pressures. The income their wives bring home, even if it's more than their own, is also seen as less of a threat to their manhood than it is a way of improving their quality of life. These couples actually tend to encourage each other in their careers and support them in their goals. They're also better at developing strategies to deal with the pressures of their demanding lifestyles without getting on each other's nerves. That's because there's a lot more flexibility in their thinking. Without being bogged down in old gender definitions, they can work through compromises without worrying whether their decisions detract from their self-images.

Modern-thinking couples also have their difficulties, but their problems tend to be different than those faced by traditional-thinking couples. Women who expect equality and reject traditional gender roles won't sacrifice their personal happiness to save their marriage out of respect for the institution. They are particularly vigilant of their relationship and will watch carefully how much their husbands contribute to home maintenance, how involved they are with their children, how committed they are to their marriage, and so on. When things are unfair and out of balance, wives will react strongly. Not only will inequities cause a lot of disagreements, they can have the unintended consequence of causing their husbands to pull back emotionally. This reaction can make the wife even more angry and resentful and less happy in her marriage.[7]

While the edge goes to modern thinkers, both traditional and modern couples can still be happy. What's most important is that their perspectives are in harmony, that is, modern thinkers are married to modern thinkers and traditional thinkers to traditional thinkers. It's not hard to imagine that much bigger problems can arise when couples are mixed, especially if the husband is extremely traditional and the wife is not. Consider, for example, how such a couple would deal with housework. A traditional-thinking husband would feel it is woman's work, while his egalitarian-thinking wife would demand that he do his share. In these marriages, partners have a very hard time understanding each other, and there are a lot of opportunities for conflicts. Very often their conflicts can't be resolved because the two partners believe very different things. Ultimately, all the turbulence can lead them to prefer to spend less time together and can weaken their commitment to the relationship.[8]

As we said, a relationship can also be imbalanced because of a partner's personality traits and emotional issues, and these relationships can be abusive. Individuals who strive to control their partners tend to rely on negative communication styles to achieve their goal, and these can be hard to tolerate. When dealing with issues with their partners, would-be dominators tend to be condescending, take on superior airs, and are often self-absorbed. When they interact with others, they will often use verbally abusive language and other aggressive tactics to get others to submit to them. They're not only interested in making their partners behave a certain way but also want to control what they think, believe, and feel.

With such a partner, one can often feel beaten into submission. Here's an example of how a dominating partner might respond to an unwillingness to follow their demands: "How can you not accept what I'm saying? What's wrong with you?" The first statement implies that our own opinions are wrong or don't matter. The second statement is where the abuse can come in because it suggests we lack the intelligence to grasp the issue. We can try to stand up for our rights, but very often we will give in to avoid aggravation and further humiliation. While the dominant partner might see this as a victory, it's really not. The losing partner is likely to hold onto negative thoughts and feelings about their relationship. They may also resort to a few defensive techniques to try to improve their position and achieve some balance, such as passive-aggressiveness or emotional withdrawal. Regardless of whether they respond with revenge or submission, it's not good for the relationship.

There are some marriages in which one partner comes to dominate the other without wanting to. In these cases, it's the submissive partner who causes the imbalance. They might put themselves in a subservient position because they're overly dependent on their partner. They may lack confidence in themselves or are insecure about their relationship, so they behave subserviently because they're afraid their partner will leave them. These couples probably won't have many arguments about who's in charge, but the relationship is not likely to be enjoyable to either partner. Overdependency can be stifling to the partner in the dominant role, and that may cause them to fluctuate between feelings of resentment and guilt for having been put in that position. Unhappiness for the submissive partner may initially stem more from their feelings of insecurity about the relationship rather than their lack of power, but may ultimately stem from feeling that their needs are not being satisfied.

The most difficult situation is one in which the struggle for control is never fully resolved. One partner might continually try to force the other to think and act in a certain way, while the other either tries to avoid being dominated or tries to exert their own dominance. These relationships are often characterized by a lot of arguing and hostility. Almost any issue can lead to a confrontation because partners are always battling for position, and their arguments can be especially intense when they're trying to make decisions. Even in periods of calm, their negative emotions can lie just below the surface because both partners are continually on their guard. Because their arguments are really about power and control, they can have a very hard time resolving conflicts. [9]

As with other problems, dealing with power issues in a marriage is not easy. Part of the problem has to do with changing some behaviors and attitudes. However, as the bigger issue, couples might not even be aware that a power problem exists. Partners who are having trouble getting along might believe they're just not suited for each other when in reality they're actually caught up in a power struggle. As an example of what we mean, couples who fight about money might think they're arguing about how it's spent, but in fact they're fighting about the right of each partner to spend it. In other words, they think they're arguing about one thing when they're really arguing about something else.

Furthermore, while we might be aware that our relationship is uneven and unfair, we still have to be willing to do something about it. That can be a difficult proposition for the one who holds the power. Dominating partners like being in control, but they can also feel entitled to their position. They might believe that the success of their relationship depends on their ability to make all the decisions for the couple. They might also feel they have a right to treat their partner as they see fit and believe it's perfectly acceptable to contribute less to managing the home. They may feel they deserve to be emotionally supported, or that their partner should be affectionate and attentive to them regardless of how they're treated in return.

Nevertheless, if we can acknowledge the problem exists and we want to fix it, the first step will be to adjust our thinking. Husbands who believe in traditional male roles have to accept the fact that the old ways of defining men and women may be obsolete. Others might have to come to the realization that people cannot really be controlled unless they want to be. We might believe we can control our partners and manage their lives for them, and we're doing it because that's what is best for them. However, the person who is being controlled is not likely to see it that way. The one being controlled will find their relationship aggravating and their feelings toward their partner less than loving. Forcing someone to behave or think in a particular way is actually a very good way to alienate a partner. Besides, the odds are good we will be continually disappointed because people fight against being manipulated, and they might do that by purposely not doing what we would like them to do.

This is not to say that we can't influence our partner. Influence means that we present information that can help our partner understand an issue more fully, and as a result they can come to a better course of action. Because they're better informed, they're more prone to make decisions that can satisfy their own needs. In contrast, control means that we make the decision about what is to be done and our partner does what we tell them to do. The reality is we can help our partners develop and change only if they feel they're in charge of making the change. If they feel we're directing the change, they're more likely to feel manipulated.

Even if we could control our partner, it's really not in our personal interests to do so. When we try to control another person, we're deciding we know the best way for that person to live. However, a way of thinking or acting that's best for us might not be best for another person. Secondly, while we may believe we have our partner's best interests at heart, that's not always the case. Very often we're working from our own agenda, and we want our partner to live and act in a certain way because it fills our own needs, not theirs. Finally, if we try to get someone to act a certain way, we become responsible for what happens to them and how they feel as a result. Taking on the responsibility for outcomes suffered by our partner is one we should be happy to avoid, because when things don't go according to our plan, we get and deserve all the blame.

Taking the idea of control in a slightly different direction, we should mention that it's also not possible to make a spouse stay in a marriage if he or she doesn't want to. Some of us might think we can force an unhappy partner to stay, or we can accomplish the same by being submissive and bending to all of their demands. Even if they give in initially, it's not likely to be for the long term, and the relationship can never be satisfying to either party.

When you allow yourself to be dominated by another person, you set yourself up for a number of emotional problems. You will lose respect for yourself, your confidence will suffer, and you surrender control of your life and your relationship. Furthermore, your partner is not likely to respect you, and when you're not respected, you leave yourself open to being exploited.

If that is the state of your relationship, you really have no choice but to accept the fact that you cannot control how your partner feels about you and what he or she will do. However, as difficult as it might seem at the time, if they don't want to stay and your relationship ends, you will survive. In fact, you give yourself an opportunity to prosper, because you can look for a relationship that might be more fulfilling. After all, when your partner no longer wants to be with you, satisfying your needs is the last thing they have in mind.

For many of the same reasons, it's wise to avoid becoming overly dependent on your partner. Dependency is a difficult balancing act. At moderate levels, it can be a demonstration of commitment, respect, and emotional connectedness. However, when taken to an extreme, it can be suffocating to your spouse and you can be regarded as needy, and that's never a good thing. One way to protect yourself from overdependency is to pursue interests that are yours alone and that add personal value to your life. Another is by maintaining close relationships with your own friends.

Sometimes we can become overdependent because we believe we're supposed to be very closely tied to our spouse, but we can overdo it. Try to keep in mind that it's not possible for any one person to satisfy all of your needs. Expecting that from a spouse puts a lot of pressure on them, and you're likely to be disappointed because they won't always be able to deliver. If you're on the other side of this issue—that is, you have a partner who is overly dependent on you—you might want to help that person become more independent. Encouraging them to adopt personal interests or socialize with their own friends is helpful. However, you may also want to focus your attention on making them feel more secure and loved because that might be the reason why they've become overdependent.[10]

If you're in a continuous power struggle and don't like it, you can try to discuss the issue with your partner. However, be aware that such conversations are likely to be confrontational, since a domineering person likes the position they hold and will often resort to hostile tactics to stay right where they are. Be patient, stay calm, and stick to your guns. Clearly express the point that you expect to be treated as an equal and your partner cannot always have their way or tell you what to do. It might also be worthwhile to point out how being treated as an inferior makes you feel more resentful than loving, and that means you're less interested in doing things that make them happy.

Beyond discussing the issue, do not allow yourself to be forced into doing something you don't want to do. When a situation arises, calmly explain that you will do this instead of that, and don't allow your partner to draw you into an argument about it. To learn how to be effective in this regard, you might want to consider assertiveness training. There are a number of excellent books available for developing this skill. If you find these approaches don't work for you, you may need help from a marriage professional. They might be in a better position to determine the changes one or both of you have to make to achieve a more equitable relationship. Regardless of how you decide to approach this problem, it's important for your personal well-being and the goodness of your marriage that you do something. Keep in mind that while submitting to your partner's demands will certainly be less stressful in the short term, in the long term you'll be much happier if you can find ways to make your relationship more balanced and fair.

If you occupy a submissive role in your marriage and you're comfortable with that, well, frankly we're not. A willingness to be submissive can signal other problems, such as a lack of confidence and self-esteem, attachment anxiety, or a fear of abandonment. Additionally, these emotional issues tend to occur when we're younger. As we get older, we may not feel quite as vulnerable, but by then we've already established a pattern of being dominated by our partner that may be harder to change. If you feel your emotional state or personal traits are at the core of your submissiveness, these are the issues you will need to deal with first and foremost, and you will be much happier for the effort.

If you're fortunate enough to read this before you marry, use the opportunity to take a very close look at yourself and your partner. You might want to compare your opinions and beliefs with those of your prospective partner on men's and women's roles. Try to determine whether they lean toward submissiveness, equality, or dominance, and compare that with what is comfortable for you as their partner. While you might be able to tolerate inconsistencies in your views before marriage while you're still under the spell of romantic love, you will have a much harder time accepting these differences as you settle into a long-term relationship.

12

THE ROOTS OF MARITAL CONFLICTS

From all that we've talked about in previous chapters, three fundamental points should be apparent. First, men and women are very different, and these differences are apparent in their approach to marriage. What the two genders find important, how they react to various situations, and what they want and expect from their relationship suggest they come from two distinct worlds. Viewed objectively, it's a miracle they can live together at all, let alone find happiness in that arrangement.

However, it's possible that their differences allow them to work well as a partnership. Because they bring unique gender-driven sets of behaviors, emotions, beliefs, and thought patterns to each situation, men and women are complementary to each other. One partner may be particularly well equipped to handle some issues, while the other may be better in other situations. While they may have trouble understanding each other at times, their distinct styles give them pretty broad coverage of life's varied challenges when considered as a team.

As a second point, there are unlimited ways men and women can run into problems in a relationship. Their innate differences might be a cause, but it's just as likely that any two people would have as much trouble getting along. Choose any one friend or family member of either gender and imagine what it would be like to live with that person for thirty or forty years. From that perspective, it's understandable that many couples are struggling. Yet, as we pointed out from the beginning, marriage is probably the best coupled arrangement one can hope for.

Nevertheless, that doesn't deny the fact that marriage can be difficult. There are small problems, large problems, and small ones that will turn into large ones if not handled effectively. Many can be resolved if we expend some effort and focus on the right things. Yet, that's the rub. Determining what to focus on isn't easy because there's no single answer that applies to all couples, and not all problems are what they appear to be.

While we'd like to believe some factors are more critical than others to a marriage's success, that doesn't seem to be the case. Researchers have tried to rank them, but the results aren't consistent. Some argue that intimacy, sexual and emotional, are the essential ingredients. Others point to what we described as the cornerstones, including commitment, trust, support, and fidelity. Then there's the ability to communicate effectively, manage expectations, and maintain a positive bias toward our partners. There are the more practical aspects such as financial stability and help-ing around the house. We also have to consider fairness, kindness, and other forms of positive interaction as essential, and let's not forget shared interests and time spent together.

They're all important, but one isn't necessarily more than another. It depends on the couple and their values and beliefs. One couple may have sexual problems, and they regard sex as most important for a good mar-riage. Another may feel equality is the greatest concern, while money ranks highest for others. Then there's the fact that problems are usually interrelated, so that one problem is linked to or the cause of another problem. A couple may have sexual issues because a wife feels she isn't respected, which inhibits her sexual desire. Additionally, an apparently simple problem can actually be the result of much larger issues. Take, for example, the case of a husband who doesn't take out the trash when asked. Such a problem should be easy to solve. Just take out the trash, and the problem is gone.

However, it's just not that simple. Emotions are at the heart of virtual-ly all marital problems, even those that appear to have no emotional underpinnings. But it's not just emotions, its intense emotions. In the above example, there are probably emotional reasons why he doesn't take out the trash. Maybe he thinks his wife treats him like a child or she's too controlling, and not taking out the trash is his passive-aggressive way of getting revenge. While he might eventually get around to it, his anger and resentment are still present and will likely emerge in other interactions with his wife. Acknowledging the role of emotions is an important first step to improving many relationships. From there, we can see that solving any problem requires that we deal with the emotions that are behind the problem.

So how do we fix our emotional issues? It would seem that all we have to do is control or change them. The husband should just take out the trash and stop feeling angry or resentful about it, and the wife should stop getting angry that he doesn't do it immediately. However, that's not likely to work, because the emotions we experience might have something else beneath them. Consequently, trying to change them directly might still not get at the heart of the issue. Besides, keeping our emotions in check all the time is extremely difficult.

To fully grasp what we're getting at, we need to discuss what actually happens when we experience emotions. An emotion is not simply a reaction to something our partner has said or done. Instead, the specific emotion we experience may be affected by the ideas that we hold in our heads. In other words, our emotions, and the thoughts and behaviors that spring from these emotions, are the product of what we believe. The idea that our belief systems are the triggers of our emotions is the fundamental principle behind Rational Emotive Behavior Therapy (REBT), developed by the renowned psychologist Albert Ellis.[1]

An example of trying to lose weight may help to illustrate the point. Suppose while growing up we learned to associate food with family closeness, or certain foods such as candy were used as rewards for good deeds. We've developed a belief about food that goes beyond its life-sustaining purpose. If we don't try to change our beliefs about food, we cannot change the emotions these beliefs produce, we will eventually return to the same pattern of eating. That's why diets that focus just on the behavior, such as reducing calories or avoiding certain foods, are not effective for many people over time.

Beliefs are also what lie beneath the wants, needs, and expectations of each partner. Beliefs are what we hold to be true about what marriage should be like and how our partner should think and act. They're also the things we expect and deserve from our relationship. We want our partner to be more interested in sex, we expect them to help around the house, or we need them to embrace all of our friends and family members. These are the things we believe a partner is supposed to do in marriage.

When our wants, needs, or expectations are satisfied, we feel good about our relationship because we think our partner loves us and wants to make us happy. However, when they're not met, they become a source of contention. Unmet needs, wants, and expectations are really what make us unhappy in our marriage. It truly doesn't matter who takes out the trash. However, it does matter what it says about how our partner feels about us when they don't. Additionally, because we're not dealing with the real reason why we're upset, problems will linger. We might stay angry even after our partner has taken out the trash because we had to ask them repeatedly to do it. We might interpret that as our partner doesn't pay attention or care about what we want.

An essential point about beliefs is that some are perfectly acceptable, but some are not. Acceptable beliefs are rational, and when they're beneath our needs, wants, and expectations, we have a right to have them fulfilled. We have a right to be supported by our partner or treated with affection and respect. However, the ones that work against our relationship are irrational. It is irrational to believe our partner should love us and treat us with consideration no matter what we do or how we treat them. Some people actually believe that; they call it unconditional love.

As the major difference, needs, wants and expectations based on rational beliefs can be satisfied, but they can't be if they're based on irrational beliefs. Because irrational beliefs cannot be satisfied, they can cause a lot of negative emotions, such as anger or frustration. That's because we keep waiting to get what we want or expect and it doesn't happen. These negative emotions also linger and can infect other aspects of a relationship. Because we had to repeatedly ask our partner to take out the trash, we're too annoyed to be nice to them.

If our beliefs are behind our emotions, then one way to resolve some marital problems is to figure out which beliefs are irrational and eliminate them. Although it takes practice, it's not that difficult to accomplish. Many people in therapy have been taught how to do it and have found the technique to be quite helpful. Throughout the remainder of this chapter we'll go through the details of this process. But before we do, it's worthwhile to get into a very brief discussion of how our thoughts and emotions are related to each other and how they're affected by our beliefs.

THOUGHT PROCESSES

Cognition, or thinking, includes memory, problem solving, and creativity. Thoughts are experienced as internal speech, that is, they're the things we say to ourselves in our heads. They're also the primary drivers of human behavior. Before we do something, a thought pops up in our minds to perform that action. Thoughts often occur as a response to something in our environment. We see or hear something, and that causes us to think about it. Thinking about situations and events as they occur is the means by which we attempt to understand and interpret what we're seeing or hearing. It is our ability to think that also allows us to solve problems and make decisions. Our personal experiences are stored in our memory, and we use these experiences to guide our decisions.

Thoughts can be conscious and unconscious. Conscious thoughts are essentially those that we are aware of; they are the ones that we say to ourselves. Conscious thinking is rational—that is, it follows the rules of logic and can be analyzed and understood. We use conscious-rational thinking to solve problems, plan for the future, and deal with our day-to-day needs and challenges. The unconscious contains information about which we have no awareness. A lot of what we've learned and experienced over the years (thoughts, memories, and beliefs) is stored in our unconscious, even though we might not be aware that such has happened.

EMOTIONS

A good way to think about emotions is that they're changes in normal functioning, typically as a reaction to events that are occurring in our environment or in our own heads. Emotions are highly subjective and are linked to our thought processes. Emotions and thoughts actually work together and feed on each other. A positive or negative emotion will trigger thoughts that are consistent with that emotion. For example, if your partner has made you angry (a negative emotion), you might think about all the other times they've made you angry in the past (negative thoughts). Conversely, if you have a negative thought about someone, you will also experience a corresponding negative emotion about that person.

The way thoughts and emotions play off each other explains why we can experience a chain reaction of negativity. A negative thought produces a negative emotion, which then produces another negative thought, followed by another negative emotion, and so on. Such thinking patterns cause us to become angry and ruminate about an event, repeating it over and over again in our minds, and as a result getting angrier and angrier. Consequently, we might hold onto negative emotions for quite a while, sometimes causing us to feel badly for days.

Dr. Ellis distinguished two types of emotions, which we refer to as adaptive and non-adaptive. Adaptive emotions enrich our lives by highlighting and magnifying our experiences, and include feelings such as joy, sadness, and happiness. Adaptive emotions lead us to focus on the events that caused the emotion. When we feel sad because a loved one dies, we think about that person in terms of our past experiences or how much we enjoyed being with them. When our partner does something nice, we're happy, and we think about doing something nice for them in return.

Non-adaptive emotions, on the other hand, interfere with our ability to deal with situations, and include depression, anger, anxiety, and jealousy. These emotions freeze us into inactivity, causing us to dwell on how we're feeling rather than work on the issues that have produced these feelings. If we're angry at our partner because of something they've said or done, we tend to focus on how badly they treat us rather than on what they can do to treat us better. Because non-adaptive emotions make us focus inward and away from the world, they can often lead us to feel isolated and helpless.

Not all negative emotions are non-adaptive. It would be nonsensical to say that we can never be annoyed or disappointed. If our partner does something that is obviously hostile or hurtful, there might be something wrong with us if we didn't get annoyed. The key difference between adaptive and non-adaptive emotions is how we function when we're experiencing them. If we're annoyed at our partner and that emotion makes us think of a way to deal with the problem, it's adaptive. However, if we're angry and we focus only on how we're feeling, or we ruminate on other bad things our partner does and never think of ways to fix the problem, then it's non-adaptive. Non-adaptive emotions are also more intense, and that's makes them particularly problematic. Remember what we talked about in a previous chapter: intense negative emotions can narrow our perceptions and cloud our judgment. Consequently, they prevent us from thinking accurately about our problem.

BELIEFS

Beliefs are the principles that we accept as truths about how the world and other people operate. Our beliefs are the driving force behind how we think, feel, and behave. If I believe that *I am ugly*, this says something about how I will think and act in my relationships with others. Beliefs are also an essential part of how we deal with other people. If we know our friends hold conservative beliefs on politics, we have a pretty good idea how they would react to a new social policy.

Because beliefs reveal so much about us and affect how we think, act, and feel, they play a critical role in our personal relationships. In marriage, our beliefs serve as the rules we follow for interacting with our partner and serve as the basis for our expectations. They make their presence felt in virtually all aspects of our relationship, from the most intimate forms of expression down to the most mundane household chores. Some of these are particularly well ingrained, while others we might hold onto a little more loosely. But they're always present, and they influence how we feel, think, and behave toward our partner.

As we mentioned, Ellis postulated two kinds of beliefs—rational and irrational. A belief is rational if it satisfies the following conditions: (1) it conforms to the rules of logic, (2) it is consistent with our general experiences, and (3) it is consistent with our personal goals. Irrational beliefs are those that violate any one of these rules—that is, they do not conform to the rules of logic, are not consistent with our general experience, or are not consistent with our goals.

If we believe that we and our partners make mistakes, we hold a rational belief. It is rational because it is logical, given what we know about human behavior. It is consistent with our experiences both with others and with what we have personally experienced, because we know that people make mistakes. It is also consistent with our goals. If we are open to the possibility that mistakes happen, we're better prepared to deal with them when they do. On the other hand, if we believe that our partner should never make mistakes, we hold an irrational belief. It is irrational because it is illogical if one understands human nature. It is inconsistent with our experiences because we all make mistakes and have seen others do the same. It also interferes with our goals because it prevents us from planning for mistakes and leads us to become upset when they happen.

Everyone holds both rational and irrational beliefs. It is normal and a part of human nature to think irrationally from time to time. In fact, we can hold both irrational and rational beliefs about the same issue, even if the two contradict each other. Here's an example of how that can happen. If you ask people if they expect that every person would like them, they would probably say no, pointing out that no one can be liked by everyone. Now, imagine there's a party with a hundred guests, and all of the guests decide to give their evaluation of that person. The first ninety-nine heap large doses of praise and adulation but the last one rejects that person. How do you imagine that person would react to this last guest? He or she would probably spend time wondering why that hundredth person did not have the same positive reaction that the others did. He or she might conclude that there must be something wrong with this person for not feeling the same way as the others. So, even though we hold the rational belief that no one can be loved by everyone, we can also be surprised, or disappointed, or upset when we find that someone doesn't like us. We can hold the irrational belief that everyone must approve and admire us even as we also hold the rational belief that such is not possible.

There will be times when irrationality and the unconscious, with its illogical and unpredictable nature, will dominate our thoughts and actions, while rationality will dominate at other times. When we become aware of our irrational thoughts, we can often see them for what they are. Unfortunately, that doesn't mean that we can immediately switch our thinking from irrational to rational. Many of us have experienced times when we might feel or think something that we know is irrational, but we claim that we just can't help it. We might excuse it by saying that's just who we are and what we believe. In other words, we can see that the thought or feeling is irrational but have trouble changing our beliefs.

A primary feature of irrational beliefs is absoluteness. Irrational beliefs often contain the words *should* and *must* and imply a demand about the world and the people in it. Absolutes are irrational because they violate the three rules we discussed above. People are fallible and have limited abilities, and thus they cannot perform exactly the same way all the time. They're inconsistent with our experiences because we understand the world has some randomness to it. They work against our self-interests because we might ruminate over our disappointment and anger when things don't go as we expect.

That's not to say that absolutes have no value at all. They're useful as standards of behavior. For example, we may aspire never to lie. However, to expect or demand that we or other people must never lie is irrational. Our point here is that we don't need to set low standards for behavior, but it's wise to set these standards realistically so that we we'll be less upset when the things don't go as we want them to. It's also wise to accept the possibility that we and others will sometimes fall short of our standards, as we will fall short of theirs.

THE RELATIONSHIP BETWEEN BELIEFS AND EMOTIONS

We tend to think that our emotions are singularly and directly linked to a situation or event, meaning that how we feel is exclusively and directly a result of what we're seeing or hearing. However, we don't believe this reflects what really happens when we have an emotional reaction. Ellis argued that our belief systems come in between what we see or hear, and how we then react emotionally. It's our interpretation of an event that causes us to react in a certain way, and our interpretation is affected by our beliefs.

Here's an example that may explain how beliefs determine emotions. Suppose a professor gives three students a grade of B for a course. Upon receiving the grade, the first student becomes elated, the second student becomes depressed and agitated, and the third student is indifferent. If getting a grade of B was exclusively and directly the cause of the emotions, the three students should have similar reactions. Since they react differently, something else must be going on.

If the three different emotional reactions were caused by three different beliefs, the situation becomes understandable. The student who was elated may have not expected to get a B, and was thrilled to get a grade that was better than he expected. The student who became depressed and agitated probably expected a grade of A and possibly believed anything less was unacceptable. The student who was indifferent probably saw grades as unimportant to his or her life and therefore did not care what grade was received.

It's not the event of getting a B grade that led to the emotions and behaviors each student experienced. Instead, it was a result of what each believed that grade meant. So, while emotions can appear to be a reaction to something, the beliefs we hold in our heads actually provide the reason we feel as we do. This is the central idea proposed by Dr. Ellis: it's not the events of the world that cause our emotions but rather the significance we attach to those events.

Adaptive emotions, those which lead us to focus on the events that cause them, typically have rational beliefs behind them. Here's an example of a wife who's annoyed at her husband and has a rational belief behind her feelings. She says to her friend, "I don't like it when my husband comes home late without calling. I think that he is not being considerate of me, and I'd better talk to him about it and ask that he change his behavior." The rational belief expressed here is that people will sometimes not consider others when it would be better for their relationship if they did. There is no insistence that her husband *must* change his behavior. There is only the expression of the desire that it would be better for their relationship if he did. The emotion is adaptive because she is thinking about ways to fix this problem.

Non-adaptive emotions, on the other hand, are caused by irrational beliefs. In the above example, we referred to annoyance. Anger, as we mentioned earlier, is much more intense and will have irrational beliefs as its main underpinning. It will often lead to repeated negative thoughts that will dominate one's thinking and feelings. For example, another wife might say to her friend, "My husband is an inconsiderate thoughtless person who never thinks of anyone else but himself. I can't tell you how many times he's done things like this to me since we've been married. I'm really getting sick of it, and he must do something about it right away."

There are a few irrational beliefs working in this example. For one, the wife describes her husband in absolute terms (he never thinks of anyone else) and demands that he behave differently (he must change). When we think of our partners in terms of absolutes, we make demands that they behave just as we want them to. Unfortunately, most people, including our partners, are usually reluctant to bend to the will of others, especially those who demand that they do so. Even if they appear to be cooperative, they're likely to harbor resentments and have other negative thoughts about us because we forced them to do something they didn't want to.

The wife's anger might also lead her to ruminate over the situation, reviewing in her mind the occasions in the past when her husband had been inconsiderate, and these thoughts further feed her anger. She starts a chain of negative thoughts and negative emotions that can gradually get her to a boiling point. By the time her husband arrives home, she's ready to attack. She might get herself so worked up that her emotions and reaction are out of proportion to the wrongdoing. Her husband can then be expected to respond with his own anger and hostility, and that can cause the problem to turn into a major and prolonged argument.

Arguments that stem from irrational beliefs rarely find their way to solutions. As in the above example, partners will generally resort to an attack-counterattack approach, which often causes an argument to escalate. It's not unusual for couples to develop a habit of relying on ineffective communication styles when dealing with conflicts. Each partner comes to expect that arguments will include accusations and other forms of negativity, and they are predisposed before the argument starts to respond in that same manner.

When we understand how thoughts and emotions spring from beliefs, it's clear that some of the problems couples face in their marriage, especially those that keep coming up over and over again, can result from irrational beliefs held by one or both partners. As we said, needs, wants, and expectations that are supported by irrational beliefs usually stay unsatisfied, and because they're unsatisfied, we stay unhappy. While we'll never get rid of all of our irrational beliefs, we can at least identify the ones that are particularly detrimental to our relationship. We can then fight against their damaging effects by replacing them with more rational beliefs.

IDENTIFYING IRRATIONAL BELIEFS

In order to uncover our beliefs, we have to work backward. We first have to examine the emotions that emerge from a situation before we can identify their underlying beliefs. Once we're aware of how we feel, we can then figure out why we feel that way. We can use the emotions we're feeling as an indicator as to what types of thoughts are occupying our minds. As we mentioned previously, one way to determine a belief's rationality is by asking three questions.

(1) *Is the belief logical?* A belief is not logical if it cannot be supported by evidence or falls outside what is accepted as the bounds of human experience. For example, any belief that contains *should* or *must* cannot be logical because these concepts are absolutes and do not describe human behavior.

(2) *Is the belief consistent with my experiences?* There are likely to be many past occasions where our partner has not behaved the way we may have wanted them to. So expecting them to do so clearly does not fit with our experiences. We may want them to behave in a certain way, but we have to be prepared for the possibility that they won't.

(3) *Does holding this belief help me obtain my goals?* Assuming that our goal is to have a good relationship, an emotion that prevents us from solving a problem works against our personal interests.

We have to be careful as we go through this process, because it's not always easy to tell whether a belief is rational or irrational. We might think we feel a particular way because of a rational belief, but an irrational belief can actually be what's causing our thoughts and emotions. Suppose we're angry because our partner did something we didn't like. We might feel our anger is justified because what they did was hurtful or inconsiderate. But what's actually underlying our reaction is that our partner's actions make us feel insecure about our relationship. We want them to act in a certain way so that we can feel more secure. These are irrational beliefs because we can't force other people to act in a particular way, and our fears of rejection may be of our own creation.

We are not saying that we can't have preferences as to how we would like our partner to behave. Nor are we saying we can't be annoyed or that we shouldn't confront our partner when we're annoyed. We're saying that *demanding* or *expecting* them to be a certain way can get us into trouble. When we prefer something, we are prepared for the possibility that we might not get it and can make appropriate plans for choosing alternatives. When we demand something, we are not prepared for not getting what we want, and this lack of preparedness can only lead to non-adaptive emotions.

Even if we can identify our irrational beliefs and we agree that they should be discarded, sometimes it's hard to put that into practice. The problem is, while we may agree in principle, we may also believe that a particular belief is irrational for other people, but not be for ourselves or for this situation. That's because we all have reasons why we think and act the way we do, and we think our reasons are rational. And even if we acknowledge that some of the things we believe are not rational, we might still hold onto them, using the excuse that we can't help it but that's just how we feel or what we believe. That, of course, doesn't make such a belief rational, but it does give us an excuse to hold onto it. We can find it hard to surrender the reasons for the way we think and act, even if they get in our way.

Here's an example of how difficult it can be to surrender an irrational belief because we don't see it as irrational. A close friend suffered an injury that required a good deal of therapy afterward. Her family was extremely protective, and while she was in rehabilitation, they claimed that the therapists were working her too hard, and that was causing a lot of pain. The therapists didn't understand that she wasn't like other people. In truth, they weren't working her too hard, and she was capable of handling all that was asked. When asked if, in general, rehabilitation required hard work and could sometimes be painful, the family completely agreed. However, they claimed to know what this person was capable of and that she shouldn't be in pain. The treatment she was receiving may be right for others but not for their family member. Their reason was that she was different from other patients, which, of course, she wasn't.

MINIMIZING IRRATIONAL BELIEFS

Self-reflection and self-monitoring are the key tools for changing irrational beliefs. Only through exploring our own thoughts and asking ourselves questions can we gain the insight we need to identify and change irrational beliefs. Self-reflection means listening to the voice inside of our heads and analyzing the content. As we said, we experience thinking as an internal monologue, and it's important to listen, not only for the words, but also to the tone and intensity of our conversation with ourselves.

Self-reflecting also means reviewing previous events in your mind, things that have happened to you and situations you found yourself in. Think about the problems you've faced with your partner and how you reacted to those situations. Think about the emotions you experienced and try to uncover what thoughts and beliefs triggered those feelings. As you try to understand the source of your feelings, try to determine whether any irrational beliefs and non-adaptive emotions dominated your thoughts.

Sometimes we might think the thoughts we have are beyond our control. People often say something to the effect of "I can't help what I think. It's just how my mind works." Such rationales deny responsibility for our own thoughts. We also deny ourselves the right to choose to think differently if we want to. The fact that we can exert control over our personal thoughts, behaviors, and emotions is an extremely important rational belief. Just as we cannot control the thoughts, feelings, and actions of other people, with few exceptions we can decide how we think, feel, or behave. We can't just pay lip service to this fact; we must *truly believe* that we have freedom to choose what we believe, how we feel, and how we act. If we don't accept this fact, then we must also admit that we can't change our irrational beliefs. Then we must also admit that we have no choice but to continue to live with their accompanying emotions and the problems they can lead to.

Once irrational beliefs are identified, they need to be disputed and countered. By that we mean you must acknowledge that the belief is irrational, and then you must find a more rational belief to replace it. Point out to yourself how this belief is illogical and destructive. For example, suppose you're angry with your partner for being late. Rather than being absorbed by your anger, ask yourself why you're angry. Is it because they're always late? If you know that to be the case, then you should admit to yourself that it's irrational to expect them not to be.

Keep in mind that irrational beliefs are well ingrained and have a tenacious quality, so you need to be forceful with yourself. If it's done correctly, you will find that you're more capable of accepting situations as they really are even when they're not to your liking. You will also have room to plan alternatives and make provisions to deal with these situations in more constructive ways. In the above example, you can be prepared for when your partner is supposed to arrive, but you can also be mentally prepared that it will be later than that. If you're prepared for the latter, you won't be quite as angry.

Once we're able to recognize an irrational thought, we can take the next step to replace it. Here's how we might counter an irrational belief. Each of us probably had the experience at one time or another of feeling our partner doesn't understand us, and we ask ourselves that exact question. The reality is our partner completely understands what we are saying, but they just refuse to agree with it. Our irrational belief is that only through agreeing with our opinion is our partner understanding us.

Rather than asking, "Why doesn't my spouse understand me?" the following is a more rational counter: "Not everyone can understand everything I or anybody says. Maybe my partner understands me, but they don't agree with me. Maybe I am being unreasonable to expect her to agree with me on this issue."

Here's another irrational belief: "Why doesn't my partner do things my way (or the right way)?" The replacing rational belief might be, "People do whatever they want to do. I can't control others. It would be easier for me if my spouse did what I wanted. But they don't have to, and I would be better off not demanding or expecting that they do."

There are lots of possible irrational beliefs, probably as many as there are people. Nevertheless, we have provided a few examples of the more common irrational beliefs and their rational counter beliefs. We have also offered suggestions for follow-up conversations you can have with yourself to move difficult situations in a positive direction. You can use this list in table 12.1 as a starting point for your own list of irrational beliefs that might be operating in your marriage, and then come up with their rational substitutes.

Once you're able to replace an irrational belief with a more rational one, you will find that your emotional reaction will be different. You won't be as angry, upset, or frustrated, and you won't be emotionally

Table 12.1. Examples of Irrational Beliefs and Countering Rational Beliefs

Irrational Belief	Countering Rational Belief
I hate when things go wrong/not my way.	I may not like what's happening, but not everything will go as I would like. The world is an unpredictable place that I can't control. I would prefer if things went smoothly, but I can handle it when they don't.
My partner must stop putting unreasonable demands on me.	My partner is sometimes self-centered and makes demands to meet his own needs, but not all the time. If a demand is unreasonable, we can discuss that, or I can propose something I want in return for giving in to his demands.
My partner always yells and argues with me about everything.	He is entitled to his opinions, just as I am, but we don't argue about everything. It would be a good idea to talk about our communication styles so our discussions are easier.
My partner never helps me, and that really makes me angry.	He does some nice things for me, but I would like him to help me more around the house. It's better if I focus my attention on finding things that he can do to help me.

agitated for days. Instead, you're likely to feel better about yourself and less disenchanted with your spouse. You'll also find that, because you're not as emotionally rattled, you'll have an easier time communicating with your partner about your issues. So when you find that you're experiencing non-adaptive emotions over something your partner has said or done, challenge yourself. Think about why you feel the way you do, what's really at the heart of why you're so upset. Then look to make adjustments to the beliefs that are beneath your reaction.

It's important to keep in mind that to become truly proficient at identifying irrational beliefs, it takes careful personal examination and a lot of practice. In fact, it will probably be necessary to have the same talk with yourself over and over again for each belief you're trying to change. Don't put yourself down if that's your experience. Be honest and forceful with yourself, and at the same time, be patient. The old behaviors or emotions can return because the beliefs you're trying to change are well ingrained, and it will take time to get rid of them.

So far we've been discussing your irrational beliefs and what you can do to change them. There's also the other side. What can you do when your partner holds irrational beliefs? It can be the case that your wants, needs, or expectations are completely reasonable. However, if your partner, even after repeated requests, is either unwilling or unable to be or do what you reasonably want, need, or expect, then you have to consider your options.

For one, you might still have to conclude that your underlying beliefs are irrational. Even if most people would consider them to be reasonable, the fact that they won't be fulfilled by your partner suggests they may not be rational, because they don't fit within the bounds of your relationship. At that point, you can try to change your beliefs—that is, you can acknowledge that you will not get what you believe you're entitled to, and you have to adjust your expectations. Alternatively, if what you want or need is too important to give up, you can try talking to your partner about your needs. If you're still unable to come to a satisfactory solution, then you have to decide whether having a particular need unfulfilled is something you can live with or whether you must leave the relationship.

As we said, sometimes a want, need or expectation can masquerade as rational but it really isn't. To reiterate, a clue to rationality is your emotional reaction. Suppose you think your spouse isn't affectionate enough. You certainly have a right to expect affection, so your need appears rational. However, if your emotional reaction is intense or you ruminate over the issue, there may be an underlying irrational belief. You might believe your partner should always be affectionate with you regardless of what is happening in their life, and when he or she is not, that means your partner doesn't love you. The irrational belief is that your partner should always be affectionate. No one feels affectionate all of the time, so it's irrational to think your partner should. Sometimes we might link a lack of affection with feelings of being rejected, and we might link rejection with an irrational belief that we can't survive without our partner. That's irrational also, because everyone physically and psychologically survives the loss of a loved one, despite how difficult it might be when it first happens.

Such a situation is certainly unfortunate, but still there's not much that can be done about it. However, while we can't change other people, we can change how we react to them. Once we replace the irrational thought, such as not being able to survive without someone, with a more rational one, such as, there will be pain but it will go away, we can then think more clearly about our futures. By paying careful attention to your emotional reaction, you will at least have an idea as to whether the underlying belief is rational or irrational. From there you have a better chance of making the correct decision about how best to proceed.

As a final comment, there is no such thing as a cure-all. This approach might not work on every problem in your marriage. Some problems may require that you take a different direction or seek professional assistance, or you may have trouble gaining the cooperation of your partner in dealing with their irrational beliefs. Nevertheless, it can be helpful for many problems, and its applicability is wide-ranging. As its greatest benefit, it can reduce the intensity of emotional reactions, so arguments are less likely to escalate or get blown out of proportion, and it will be easier to work your way toward solutions because you won't feel so hostile.

This is a critical point, because many marital problems result from how strongly we react to some wrongdoing. When we're emotionally overcharged, we create an environment of reciprocity, ineffective communication, and residual negative feelings. So it's really a matter of how well we handle the things we don't like in our marriage that determines whether or not it will be successful.

13

SOME FINAL THOUGHTS

Throughout the previous chapters, we've focused on the major issues that can affect marriages. We have also tried to lay out specific ways of handling many of the problems that might arise. Even though we've covered quite a few topics, we're sure we missed more than a few. There are so many specific issues that can crop up in intimate relationships, and each relationship has its own unique set of issues, that it's impossible to deal with them all in a single volume. Nevertheless, in this chapter we looked at marriage from a broader perspective. There are general ways of thinking that can enhance our relationship and others that prevent us from living as well as we can. What follows are some of the guiding principles that are behind all successful relationships. Some of these we touched upon in previous chapters, but they are worth repeating, if only as a reminder of their importance.

MARRIAGE IS A SOCIAL CONTRACT

In every relationship, including marriage, we have a social contract. By that we mean we have a set of rules, expectations, and boundaries that define that relationship. The standards of our contracts can vary, depending upon the type of relationship. The contract we have with a spouse would be very different from one with a friend, and that contract would be different from one with a casual acquaintance. The contractual aspects of our relationships have implications for how we interact and communicate with others.

Social contracts specify our rights and responsibilities. For example, when interviewing for a job, we ask about the responsibilities, that is, the tasks we're expected to perform, and about our rights, that is, the benefits and compensation. We then make an informed judgment as to whether we want to make the commitment to that job. If we made the correct assessment of our rights and responsibilities, we'll like it, but if we've made the wrong assessment, we'll soon be back in the job market.

While romantic ideals make it hard to think about intimate relationships in contractual terms, the same rules apply. If we keep in mind that many problems in marriage spring from unmet needs, taking a contractual approach means we know exactly what we want and expect from our relationship, and we're aware of what we will be expected to give in return. You may find, for example, that you are being asked to agree to do things that you really don't want to do. Or you might discover that you have some needs that your partner may not be aware of, and others that they're not capable of satisfying. Of course, it's best to get all this squared away before you marry, but if not, late is better than never.

Assessing the rights and responsibilities of a contract requires that we know our personal agendas. We all have an agenda, that is, a set of wants and needs, and there are certain things we don't want or need from a relationship. Understanding our agenda and using that as a framework for evaluating a relationship simply means we're operating with our own best interests in mind. Unless we're fully in touch with our own needs and desires, we cannot work at having them fulfilled. In other words, we can't have a beneficial relationship if we don't know the exact terms of the contract that we are agreeing to.

Discovering our full agenda may not be as easy as it might seem, because we may not be conscious of all the things we really want or need. For example, most of us want the love and approval of others, but this may not be something we'd put on our list. Some might escape our consciousness because they're threatening. We may not want to recognize certain goals and desires because we believe we don't have a right to ask for or want them. This can stem from a lack of self-confidence or a belief that they're beyond what we're realistically entitled to. There may be others we're conscious of, but we tone down their importance for fear they may lead to rejection or ridicule. You may be highly ambitious but will downplay that because you believe it makes you appear conceited or opportunistic.

Just as we have unconscious aspects of our personal agenda, we can have unconscious aspects of our marriage contract. These unconscious aspects often involve negative behavior patterns, which are motivated by inappropriate negative emotions. Rather than risk harming the relationship, we prefer to keep them out of our conscious thoughts. Or they may be things we'd rather not admit to ourselves because of what they say about who we are. However, because they're associated with negative behaviors and emotions, they're often at the center of problems. Here's an example of what we mean. Let's say we look down on our partner because they're too dependent on us. However, we may be a cause of their overdependency because we strive to dominate and control them. Every time they try to act or think independently, we lash out at them, so they learn to be dependent. We would have to admit that we have a need to be in control, possibly because we're afraid they will leave us unless we force them to stay.

Getting a full understanding of our own agenda requires self-reflection. Spend time thinking about what you really want from your relationship, remembering to be completely honest with yourself. Along with spelling out your agenda, you can use self-reflection to discover the less obvious contract terms that might be destructive. You can then try to replace these with more positive thoughts and behaviors that are healthier for your relationship. Following up from the above example, we would put aside our insecurities that lead us to control our partner and allow them to think and act independently.

To have a contract that's complete and truly meaningful, we also need to understand what's expected of us—that is, we need to know our partner's agenda. Discuss with your partner what they want and expect to get out of the relationship. That's a conversation that won't be completed all at once. It might take some time for both of you to bring out all the elements of your agendas. Yet this will be time well spent, since armed with such knowledge, you and your partner will have a better chance of meeting each other's needs.

Knowing each other's full agenda also lets both partners know what their relationship may not provide. It's an extremely rare marriage that can satisfy all the needs of both partners. As we've mentioned, sometimes we may not want to do some of the things that our partners expect of us, or our needs may run counter to those of our partner's. For example, one partner might like to spend a lot of time with friends while another prefers to stay at home. While it may be unpleasant, still both of you are better off knowing what needs might not be met, so you can adjust your expectations or decide the relationship cannot work for you.

NEGOTIATING SOLUTIONS

Negotiating may also seem odd when talking about an intimate relationship, but it actually fits quite well. In fact, couples in happy marriages do a lot of negotiating with each other. A husband might trade off sex for housework, or both partners might agree to take turns doing what the other wants. It can be an effective way to resolve conflicts because both partners can have their needs addressed.

To be clear, negotiation is not compromise. In a negotiation, each person gets something in exchange for giving something their partner wants. In compromise, neither partner actually gets what they want. They often settle on some middle ground between two ends of an issue, with the result that neither is satisfied with the solution. With negotiated solutions, both partners have their needs met, and they have an opportunity to feel like they're contributing to the relationship.

Effective negotiation requires that both partners know their agenda. You have to know what you're negotiating for and not be sidetracked by incidental issues. Effective negotiation also requires that we make every effort to state our issue in a clear and precise way. If it's about something that we'd like our partner to change, it's best to frame problems in terms of what our partner does (behavior) and not who they are (personality). For example, you can negotiate about how money is spent, but you cannot negotiate about your partner being careless about money any more than you can negotiate their height or age. Besides, stating a problem in terms of personality can be taken as an attack on our partner's character, and that can lead them to retaliate by taking shots at our character.

When presenting a problem, limit the conversation to the issue at hand. Couples will sometimes use one conflict as an opportunity to express their frustration and dissatisfaction with their relationship in general. It is as if all the issues that are unpleasant and/or unresolved are carried around in a big bag. When a problem comes up, the entire contents of the bag are dumped onto the floor and/or on each other. For instance, suppose a couple has two dinner invitations for a Saturday night. In trying to decide which one to accept, the discussion becomes heated and one person says to the other, "You always insist on having things your way. You're stubborn, just like your mother."

There is no appropriate response to this accusation. If you're stubborn, not much can be done at that moment to fix that. Later on you could work on being more open to alternative ways of thinking. Also, whether or not you learned this behavior from your mother is irrelevant, and that kind of comment only fuels anger. Importantly, the discussion has moved off target, and it's not possible to negotiate because you're no longer talking about the original issue.

Negotiations are most effective when they have a quid pro quo component. If you have something you want from your partner, there's a good chance your partner also wants something from you. It's easier to come to a solution if you come up with a few things you'd like to receive and a few things you're willing to give in return. Here it's a good idea to offer options because that allows your partner to pick ones that are most acceptable. Keep in mind that the overriding principle in a negotiated solution is that you obtain something that meets your needs, and at the same time you give something that meets the needs of your partner.

As an important part of a negotiation, both partners must feel the solution is fair and was arrived at together, with full consideration of each other's thoughts, beliefs, emotions, and values. Each partner has to believe the decision was not forced upon them. Intimidating a partner into agreement or giving in without being truly comfortable will not solve the problem. Furthermore, a truly negotiated solution will make an issue go away. Sometimes you might think you have reached a negotiated solution, only to find that the same issue surfaces later on. Typically that means one or the other partner has not found the final decision to be completely acceptable. When you and your partner are satisfied with the outcome, you can avoid facing the same problems over and over.

LEARN TO FORGIVE

It's understandable to be insulted, hurt, or angry when our partner has treated us badly. However, as difficult as it might be at times, the path to our personal well-being and the health of our relationship includes learning how to forgive. When we don't forgive, we hold a grudge. When we hold a grudge, we leave ourselves open to ruminating about the event. We rehash the episode in our minds, and as we do so, we hold onto all the negative emotions.

Ruminating stems from irrational beliefs. It is not a logical or rational process because past injustices cannot be changed, nor can we alleviate the unpleasantness surrounding them. Furthermore, as we've mentioned in an earlier chapter, ruminating fuels itself because negative thoughts and emotions start a chain reaction of negativity. These negative emotions then guide how we treat our partner, and sometimes others as well. Yet, we haven't solved anything; the hurt remains because what's done often can't be repealed. The best we can do with past mistakes, our own and our partner's, is to learn from them and try to avoid making the same ones again.

Because ruminating causes us to hold onto a negative event, it fuels grudges. Holding a grudge is a waste of effort and actually runs counter to our own self-interests. We sacrifice control over our lives because we allow ourselves to be ruled by negative emotions. We also set ourselves up to exacerbate the problem by taking revenge, which is always a bad idea. It has been suggested that taking revenge is like drinking a cup of poison and expecting the other person to die.

Forgiving can be a lot easier if we keep in mind that everybody makes mistakes. When we stay angry with our partner because of mistakes, we find it hard to accept their apologies. We may also find it difficult to maintain positive feelings about them, and that will interfere with our ability to enjoy our relationships. On the other hand, when we truly accept the idea that mistakes will happen, we have a much easier time letting go of the negative emotions. We also give our brains the chance to work on fixing the problem because it's not cluttered with negativity. Of course, if we're continually disappointed because of what we perceive as the things our partner does wrong, we might have to admit that our expectations are too high.

Fight the temptation to dwell on the negatives, and leave past events in the past. Try to appeal to your rational side, and don't let irrational beliefs or non-adaptive emotions get in your way. The most important thing to remember about forgiving is that it is something you do for yourself, not just for your partner. You may have been justified in your anger, but how do you justify feeling bad twice? That's what happens when you decide not to forgive—you feel bad because of what had happened and you feel bad still when you hold onto the anger. We all feel better when we don't have negative thoughts clouding up our brains.

UNDERSTANDING THE PROCESS OF CHANGE

When people try to change, they usually keep track of their progress by monitoring the behavior or emotion they want to change. For instance, people who want to overcome depression will note how often they feel depressed and whether or not it's happening less frequently. If their depressive episodes decline, they judge themselves as having made progress. However, if their depression returns, they will think they've relapsed. Their conclusion is that they have made no progress at all, or worse, that they've failed.

This is an example of all or none, or dichotomous thinking. It's a very unrealistic view of how change actually takes place, and can work against achieving our goal of improvement. We might think that we've failed, and that may lead us to give up trying. We can also come away with a sense of powerlessness, thinking things cannot be changed or that we don't have what it takes to make changes, and so we are destined to live with our problems forever.

It's much more realistic to think about improvement in your relationship as an up-and-down process. Real progress is not a steady upward change; it's more accurately described as a sawtooth curve—that is, some movement upward, then downward, then upward, and so forth. There will always be some sliding back, which is then followed by improvement. We might even find that as we try to change something, the behavior we're trying to change actually gets a little worse in the first stages. That is because we can be resistant to change. When we accept the reality as to how change progresses, we take some of the pressure off of ourselves when we're not as far along as we want to be, and we're less likely to give up trying.

As an additional point, if there are a lot of things you want to change, don't try to do it all at once. In fact, you're better off trying to work on one issue at a time. Your first goal is to prioritize what you'd like to work on. Find the one issue that you feel would have the most impact on your life, or the one that may be easiest to fix, and focus your attention on that. Note that of these two options, we recommend first going with the easier-to-fix problem. This can build your confidence, and you're then likely to feel you have a better chance for success with the next problem you take on.

DON'T BELIEVE IN MAGIC

When you realize that change can be slow, you surrender your belief in magic. Magic is best described as action without work. We watch a magician place a blanket over a person, he or she then says a few words, and that person disappears. The magician has not expended any effort that we can detect to make the person disappear—it just happened. To expect that change will be instantaneous or easy is tantamount to believing in magic.

This may sound silly, but sometimes we can't help think, or at least hope, that magic is real. As proof, go to the self-help section in any book store. Check out the books on losing weight, quitting smoking, having a better sex life, and the like. You will notice that the titles suggest changing these patterns is easy. You might come across a title such as *Eat All You Want to Eat and Still Lose All the Weight You Want to Lose*. Books like these become best sellers because things would be much easier if their claims were real.

Unfortunately, changing habits takes planning, thinking, a lot of effort, and most importantly, perseverance. Habits have staying power, and they have that because they have actually provided benefits over the years. If you need to lose weight, you probably love food or profit emotionally from eating; if you smoke, you probably do it because it feels good. To combat their persistence, we need to come up with a plan and stick with it through all of the ups and downs. Even though we may acknowledge that change won't happen overnight, we may still be unrealistic as to how long it can actually take. So we have to keep reminding ourselves to be patient, that change comes slowly, and don't expect magic.

LEARNING TO COPE

That brings us to learning how to cope with failure. When things are not moving according to our plan, we can approach our lack of success from two different angles. We can adopt an active strategy, that is, we stick with our plan and give it more time, or try alternative approaches and not become discouraged. In active coping, we do something to deal with the event and/or its circumstances. By confronting the situation head on, we have an opportunity to come up with a solution.

The alternative is to take a passive approach. When we don't get the success we're hoping for, we can withdraw or let our emotions lead us to inaction. We might believe we're either incapable of fixing the problem or that too much effort is required. Or we can react with anger, frustration, and impatience. If we're trying to change something in our relationship, very often we'll direct our negative emotions to our partner, because we might see them as the reason for failure. Passive coping is rarely of any value. In fact, it can make us feel worse. We might conclude our marriage is doomed to stay as it is because we can't figure out how to fix it.

Even if we choose an active coping strategy, we have to make sure we focus on the right things. We can take an emotion-focused approach, where we try to control our anger and the frustration that block us from making progress. However, the problem with an emotion-focused strategy is that we don't get at the heart of what's causing the emotions. Unless we deal with the underlying causes, we will continue to experience these negative emotions.

Alternatively, we can use the more effective situation-focused approach, in which we attack our irrational beliefs. As we have mentioned, in order to change something about our marriage, we must focus on the thought patterns and beliefs that are at the root of what we want to change. Situation-focused coping helps us identify the irrational beliefs and destructive behaviors that cause the non-adaptive negative emotions. We can then work on replacing these with rational beliefs so that we reduce our non-adaptive negative emotions.

If you are experiencing negative emotions, such as anger or frustration, because you are not further along in reaching your goal, focus on your beliefs and not on your emotions. You might, for example, find out that you expected improvement to come more quickly or easily. If that is your irrational belief, you can adjust your thinking about how fast or easy changes can be achieved. The right coping skills can help you set up more realistic expectations about your goals and make it easier for you to persevere in the face of less than expected success.

THE TYRANNY OF *SHOULDS* AND *MUSTS*

The essence of irrationality is to think of our relationships in terms of absolute conditions and demands. That's precisely what we do when we use the words *should* or *must* in the context of how our partners are to think and act. People can be oppositional, prefer to think and choose on their own, and can never be absolutely controlled. In other words, most people don't think they *should* or *must* do anything.

When we use *must or should* regarding our own or our partner's actions, the demands they imply set expectations, and we might set standards that are unrealistic. When these expectations aren't met, we can experience frustration, anger, and disappointment, and these get in the way of solving problems. Instead, it is much more helpful to think in terms of the possibility that our partners will do what they choose to do, regardless of our suggestions. When we make provisions for the possibility of outcomes other than what we desire, we manage our expectations so that they're more in line with reality. In that way we're not disappointed, nor are we quite as upset when our partner won't do what we want them to.

The renowned psychologist Albert Ellis coined a few words so that his patients would remember the important concepts they represented. These words helped to get a patient's attention and emphasized the irrational thinking they imply. He referred to our tendency to repeatedly insist on things being what we want them to be instead of what they are as *musterbating* and *shoulding*. When patients would repeatedly insist that something *must* or *should* happen in a certain way, Dr. Ellis would tell them that they were *musterbating* or *shoulding* on themselves. These particular plays on words are not only easy to remember, they also help to emphasize the negative and self-destructive aspects of irrational thinking.

Dr. Ellis also coined the term *awfulizing* to refer to a person's tendency to think of every negative event as the worst thing that ever happened to them or anyone else. Again, his purpose was to help the patient recognize her or his own irrational thinking and become aware of the negative impact it has on her or him. When we use words like *musterbate* and *awfulize,* or we *should on ourselves,* we spend all of our time focusing on the negative events, and we do not spend time to figure out what we can or cannot do about these negative events.

Many of us waste valuable time, effort, and resources trying to control the uncontrollable. Or we allow ourselves to become impatient and frustrated because things that are beyond our control are not cooperating with our desires. People who rant and rave while sitting in traffic only manage to ruin their mood and raise their blood pressure, not to mention the stress level of those riding along with them. In certain situations, some may let their frustration build up until they find themselves falling into depression, ill-health, or a chronic bad mood.

When it comes to partners, you must accept the reality that what you see is what you get. If they have traits that you don't like, you can either accept them with their faults and keep them in your life, or move out. They can change their thinking patterns and behaviors if they want to, but you can't turn them into something different unless they want to do it themselves. Acknowledging this fact may lead you away from trying to change them, and that can help you avoid disappointments and frustrations. Besides, you can then spend time and effort trying to change things that can be changed, and that means you might discover more ways to improve your relationship and your own life.

ACCEPTANCE IS FUNDAMENTAL TO IMPROVEMENT

When we say acceptance we mean the recognition of reality. If we have problems in our marriage, we can't do much about them until we accept the fact that they exist. Acceptance does not mean that we approve, desire, or have any positive feeling toward what we are accepting. It's simply an acknowledgment that something exists. Lack of acceptance, on the other hand, is very often the denial of reality. As its most damaging feature, it leaves people unprepared to deal with problems, and unattended problems usually don't get better by themselves; they usually get much worse.

It is important to point out that acceptance is an *active* process, not a passive one. Sometimes we might not acknowledge that a problem exists because we're just not aware of it. We might notice that periodically there is tension or uneasiness in our relationship, but we think that it just happens and it's nothing to worry about. Well, sometimes that's true, but sometimes it's not. Again, this points to the need for constant monitoring and the value of self-reflection so that we stay in touch with the state of our union.

True acceptance also tends to come in stages, and it can require a good deal of effort. Often the things we need to accept are offensive and unpleasant to us, or we think they're beyond our control, and this makes their acceptance difficult. While there will certainly be some things we may never completely accept, we can become better at it by dealing with the irrational beliefs that cause us to deny what we need to accept.

On the other hand, when we refuse to accept situations that are difficult or can't be controlled, such as rejection by someone we love, we will find that not only have we wasted our time, we're no closer to a solution and as a result no happier. The more we accept the things we cannot change, the better are the chances that we can cope with those situations.

IT TAKES TWO TO ARGUE

Acceptance also includes taking responsibility for our emotions and behaviors. Responsibility is the recognition of the connection between what we do and what happens as a result of what we do. There is nothing inherently good or bad about responsibility. We can have good or bad outcomes from our choices, but responsibility in and of itself is simply a rational thinking process in which we admit to ourselves that what we say and do produces outcomes.

A key point regarding responsibility is acknowledging that both partners have a role in how their relationship functions at any given point in time. As we've mentioned throughout, many problems in relationships result from reciprocity. We do or say something to our partner, or vice versa, and there is a response in kind. When we run into a conflict or a conflict escalates, it often results from how partners react to each other rather than the issue that started the conflict. Once we acknowledge reciprocity, we can realize that we own problems together with our partner.

When partners recognize ownership is shared, they're more likely to work as a team to solve them, so they're likely to have an easier time coming to solutions. Partners are also less likely to blame each other for problems. After all, it's hard to blame someone else if you realize you're just as much at fault. We should point out that, while responsibility is a positive thing, blame is not. When we blame ourselves or our partner, we imply the need for punishment and retribution. In that way blame produces negative emotions, and these interfere with rational thinking and make it hard to fix a problem.

Blame also produces guilt in most people. Guilt, like physical pain, can have a positive function. It warns us that there is something that needs our attention. If we've said or done something that's wrong, guilt makes us think twice about doing the same thing again. It's also a sign of a well-developed conscience. However, at its extreme, guilt can be debilitating. When we feel guilty, we focus all of our attention on ourselves, but not in a good way. The emphasis is on how terrible we feel and how awful we are, and on how we should be punished and treated with disdain. Such thoughts not only lead to a good deal of needless suffering, they're also counterproductive. Just as with blame, guilt inhibits rational thinking and makes it more difficult to focus on making changes that would eliminate the source of our guilt. When we stop blaming, we stop the guilt, and we and our partner have an easier time focusing on the problem at hand rather than how we feel about it.

STAY VIGILANT

So, once you've put in place the corrective measures we've been talking about, your marriage will be perfect the rest of the way, right? Well, not really. There's no such thing as perfect when it comes to people or relationships. The road to a rewarding marriage, like psychological well-being, has no final destination. It's a journey without end, and while we are living and breathing, there will always be room for improvement.

A key point here is that the world is constantly fluctuating and evolving. Our partners can change, we can change, and we can be faced with new situations and challenges. Many of the needs, interests, personal tastes, and values we had as young adults are different than those we had as children, and they're likely to be different again when we get older. When we acknowledge that things constantly change, we open ourselves to the possibility of adjusting our thinking to fit situations as they stand in the present rather than rely on solutions that applied to the past. However, that also means we have to stay vigilant. We have to keep monitoring our relationship to make sure we are working on problems as they arise and are still manageable.

Don't be disillusioned by the fact that the struggle is never likely to end. Instead, be proud of yourself for deciding to get on the road. Take comfort in the fact that you are trying to make your relationship better, and you are learning to dodge the various pitfalls and problems that come along. With practice, you will become more effective and efficient at resolving issues, and from there you will come to feel more in control of your relationship, and you will derive more satisfaction from the day-to-day living with your partner.

NOTES

1. INTRODUCTION

1. Teachman, Tedrow, and Crowder, 2000; Cherlin, 2004; Glenn, Uecker, and Love, 2010; Copen, Daniels, Vespa, and Mosher, 2012.

2. Rogers and Amato, 1997; Teachman, Tedrow, and Crowder, 2000; Goldstein and Kenny, 2001; Wilcox, 2009.

3. Rogers and Amato, 1997; Teachman, Tedrow, and Crowder, 2000; Ventura, 2009.

4. Glenn, 1998; Wilcox and Dew, 2010.

5. Glenn, 1998; Twenge, 2006; Twenge and Campbell, 2003; Horton, Bleau, and Drwecki, 2006; Amato, Booth, Johnson, and Rogers, 2007; Twenge and Campbell, 2008; Twenge, Konrath, Foster, Campbell, and Bushman, 2008; Twenge and Campbell, 2009.

6. Coontz, 2005.

7. Gottman, Coan, Carrere, and Swanson, 1998.

8. Stack and Eshleman, 1998; Brown, 2000; Carrére, Buehlman, Gottman, Coan, and Ruckstuhl, 2000; Waite and Gallagher, 2000; Amato and Previti, 2003; Pinquart, 2003; Hawkins and Booth, 2005; Burstein, 2007; Diefenbach and Opp, 2007; Vernon, 2010.

9. Amato and Previti, 2003.

10. Brody, Neubaum, and Forehand, 1988.

2. MARRIED, LIVING TOGETHER, AND LIVING ALONE

1. Brown and Booth, 1996; Horwitz, White, and Howell-White, 1996; Marks and Lambert, 1998; Prigerson, Maciejewski, and Rosenheck, 1999; Spitze and Ward, 2000; Coyne, Rohrbaugh, Shoham, Sonnega, Nicklas, and Cranford, 2001; Kiecolt-Glaser and Newton, 2001; Simon, 2002; Robels and Kiecolt-Glaser, 2003; Frech and Williams, 2007.

2. Kiecolt-Glaser, Glaser, Cacioppo, MacCallum, Snydersmith, Kim, and Malarkey, 1997; Xinhua, 1997; Kiecolt-Glaser and Newton, 2001; Simon, 2002; Holt-Lunstad, Birmingham, and Jones, 2008.

3. Brown and Booth, 1996; Horwitz and White, 1998; Brines and Joyner, 1999; Bumpass and Lu, 2000; Christopher and Sprecher, 2000; Skinner, Bahr, Crane, and Call, 2002; Stanley, Whitton, and Markman, 2004; Rhoades, Stanley, and Markman, 2006; Huang, Smock, Manning, and Bergstrom-Lynch, 2011; Kulik and Havusha-Morgenstern, 2011.

4. Smock, 2000; Smock and Manning, 2004; Manning and Smock, 2005; Rhoades, Stanley, and Markman, 2009; Yabiku and Gager, 2009.

5. Nock, 1995; Brown and Booth, 1996; Brines and Joyner, 1999; Smock, 2000; Skinner, Bahr, Crane, and Call, 2002; Brown, 2004; Rhoades, Stanley, and Markman, 2009; Brown and Kawamura, 2010.

6. Kiecolt-Glaser, Glaser, Cacioppo, MacCallum, Snydersmith, Kim, and Malarkey, 1997; Wickrama, Lorenz, Conger, and Elder 1997; Cohen, Frank, Doyle, Skoner, Rabin, and Gwaltney, 1998; Baker, Helmers, O'Kelly, Sakinofsky, Abelsohn, and Tobe, 1999; Kiecolt-Glaser and Newton, 2001; Holt-Lunstad, Birmingham, and Jones, 2008.

7. Margolin, Christensen, and John, 1996; Dhabhar and McEwen, 1997; Carels, Sherwood, and Blumenthal, 1998; Gottman and Notarius, 2000; Kiecolt-Glaser, Bane, Glaser, and Malarkey, 2003; Whitson and El-Sheikh, 2003.

8. Johnson and Booth, 1998; Hawkins and Booth, 2005.

9. McCarthy and Ginsberg, 2007.

10. Coleman, Ganong, and Fine, 2000; Skinner, Bahr, Crane, and Call, 2002; Sweeney, 2002b; McCarthy and Ginsberg, 2007; Poortman and Lyngstad, 2007; Ragsdale, Brandau-Brown, and Bello, 2010.

11. Buunk and Mutsaers, 1999; Knox and Zusman, 2001; Schmiege, Richards, and Zvonkovic, 2001; Ono, 2006.

12. Falke and Larson, 2007; Ambert, 1986; Skinner, Bahr, Crane, and Call, 2002.

13. Brown and Booth, 1996; Skinner, Bahr, Crane, and Call, 2002; Xu, Hudspeth, and Bartkowski, 2006; Stanley, Rhoades, Amato, Markman, and Johnson, 2010.

3. TRANSITIONING FROM LOVERS
TO PARTNERS

1. Ellis and Harper, 1961; Riggio and Weiser, 2008.

2. Cobb, Larson, and Watson, 2003; Spivey, 2010.

3. Cobb, Larson, and Watson, 2003.

4. Porges, 1998; Bartels and Zeki, 2004; Aron, Fisher, Mashek, Strong, Li, and Brown, 2005; Zeki, 2007; Schneiderman, Zilberstein-Kra, Leckman, and Feldman, 2011.

5. Grote and Frieze, 1998; Sprecher, 1999; Huston, Caughlin, Houts, Smith, and George, 2001; Wilcox and Dew, 2010.

6. Nock, 1995; Botwin, Buss, and Shackelford, 1997; Amato, 2009; Wilcox and Dew, 2010.

7. Helms, Proulx, Klute, McHale, and Crouter, 2006; Wilcox and Nock, 2006.

8. Lehrer, 2008; Glenn, Uecker, and Love, 2010.

9. Larson and Holman, 1994.

10. Brines and Joyner, 1999; Wilcox and Nock, 2006; Riggio and Weiser, 2008.

11. Fletcher, Simpson, Thomas, and Giles, 1999; Murray, Holmes, and Griffin, 1996; Fletcher, Simpson, and Thomas, 2000.

12. Fletcher, Simpson, and Thomas, 2000; McNulty and Karney, 2002; McNulty and Karney, 2004; Pascale, Primavera, and Roach, 2112; Huston, Caughlin, Houts, Smith, and George, 2001; Amato and Previti, 2003.

13. Glenn, 1998; Gottman and Levenson, 2000; Gottman and Notarius, 2000; Van Laningham, Johnson, and Amato, 2001; Umberson, Williams, Powers, Chen, and Campbell, 2005.

4. THE FOUR CORNERSTONES

1. Van Lange, Rusbult, Drigotas, Arriaga, Witcher, and Cox, 1997; Agnew, Van Lange, Rusbult, and Langston, 1998; Johnson, Caughlin, and Huston, 1999; Amato and of DeBoer, 2001; Arriaga and Agnew, 2001; Le and Agnew, 2003; Burgoyne, Reibstein, Edmunds, and Routh, 2010.

2. Van Lange, Rusbult, Drigotas, Arriaga, Witcher, and Cox, 1997; Agnew, Van Lange, Rusbult, and Langston, 1998; Arriaga and Agnew, 2001; Le and Agnew, 2003; Etcheverry and Le, 2005; Schoebi, Karney, and Bradbury, 2011.

3. Huston, 2000; Stanley, Markman, and Whitton, 2002; Previti and Amato, 2003; Frye, McNulty, and Karney, 2008.

4. Amato and Rogers, 1999; Stanley, Markman, and Whitton, 2002; Le and Agnew, 2003.

5. Nock, 1995; Van Lange, Rusbult, Drigotas, Arriaga, Witcher, and Cox, 1997.

6. Wieselquist, Rusbult, Foster, and Agnew, 1999.

7. Rempel, Ross, and Holmes, 2001; Campbell, Simpson, Boldry, and Rubin, 2010.

8. Rempel, Ross, and Holmes, 2001; Knobloch, 2008; Campbell, Simpson, Boldry, and Rubin, 2010; Theiss, 2011.

9. Rempel, Ross, and Holmes, 2001; Simpson, 2007; Campbell, Simpson, Boldry, and Rubin, 2010.

10. Rempel, Ross, and Holmes, 2001; Simpson, 2007; Knobloch, 2008; Campbell, Simpson, Boldry, and Rubin, 2010.

11. Wiederman, 1997; Widmer, Treas, and Newcomb, 1998; Christopher and Sprecher, 2000; Amato and Previti, 2003; Previti and Amato, 2004; Blow and Hartnett, 2005.

12. Atwood and Seifer, 1997; Wiederman, 1997; Atkins, Baucom, and Jacobson, 2001; Blow and Hartnett, 2005.

13. Atwood and Seifer, 1997; Liu, 2000; Atkins, Baucom, and Jacobson, 2001; Allen, Atkins, Baucom, Snyder, Gordon, and Glass, 2005; Atkins, Yi, Baucom, and Christensen, 2005; Blow and Hartnett, 2005; Allen, Rhoades, Stanley, Markman, Williams, Melton, and Clements, 2008.

14. Fraley and Shaver, 2000; Rusbult and Van Lange, 2003; Allen and Baucom, 2004; Previti and Amato, 2004; Atkins, Yi, Baucom, and Christensen, 2005; Allen and Rhoades, 2008; Allen, Rhoades, Stanley, Markman, Williams, Melton, and Clements, 2008; DeWall, Lambert, Slotter, Pond, Deckman, Finkel, Luchies, and Fincham, 2011.

15. Olson, Russell, Higgins-Kessler, and Miller, 2002; Allen and Rhoades, 2008.

16. Edwards, Nazroo, and Brown, 1998; Conger, Rueter, and Elder, 1999; Dehle, Larsen, and Landers, 2001; Dehle and Landers, 2005; Verhofstadt, Buysse, and Ickes, 2007.

17. Rampage, 1994; Pasch, Bradbury, and Davila, 1997; Edwards, Nazroo, and Brown, 1998; Neff and Karney, 2005; Verhofstadt, Buysse, and Ickes, 2007.

18. Amato and Rogers, 1997; Pasch and Bradbury, 1998; Gottman and Levenson, 2000; Amato and Previti, 2003; Amato, 2010.

5. SEX AND INTIMACY

1. Risch, Riley, and Lawler, 2003; Little, McNulty, and Russell, 2010.

2. Call, Sprecher, and Schwartz, 1995; Yeh, Lorenz, Wickrama, Conger, and Elder, 2006.

3. Trudel, 2002; Zimmerman, Holm, Daniels, and Haddock, 2002; Sinikka and Umberson, 2008.

4. Rampage, 1994; Christopher and Sprecher, 2000; Greeff and Malherbe, 2001; McCarthy, Ginsberg, and Fucito, 2006; McNulty and Fisher, 2008; Sinikka and Umberson, 2008; Theiss, 2011.

5. Rampage, 1994.

6. Call, Sprecher, and Schwartz, 1995; MacNeil and Byers, 2005; Sinikka and Umberson, 2008.

7. Laumann, Paik, and Rosen, 1999; Zimmerman, Holm, Daniels, and Haddock, 2002; Trudel, 2002; Bancroft, Loftus, and Long, 2003; McCarthy, Ginsberg, and Fucito, 2006; Sinikka and Umberson, 2008.

8. Garcia and Khersonsky, 1996; Garcia and Khersonsky, 1997; Wiederman and Hurst, 1997; Langlois, Kalakanis, Rubenstein, Larson, Hallam, and Smoot, 2000; Sangrador and Yela, 2000; Smolak, 2003; Zeki, 2007; McNulty, Neff, and Karney, 2008; Meltzer and McNulty, 2010.

9. Call, Sprecher, and Schwartz, 1995; Kernoff-Mansfield, Koch, and Voda, 1998; Christopher and Sprecher, 2000; Liu, 2000; Liu, 2003; Bancroft, Loftus, and Long, 2003; Potter, 2007; Sinikka and Umberson, 2008.

10. Purnine and Carey, 1997; Gossmann, Julien, Mathieu, and Chartrand, 2003; McNulty and Fisher, 2008; Simms and Byers, 2009.

11. Yeh, Lorenz, Wickrama, Conger, and Elder, 2006; Yabiku and Gager, 2009.

12. Rampage, 1994; Friedman, Dixon, Brownell, Whisman, and Wilfley, 1999; Bancroft, Loftus, and Long, 2003; Weller and Dziegielewski, 2004; MacNeil and Byers, 2005; Markey and Markey, 2006; Knobloch, 2008; Sinikka and Umberson, 2008; Theiss, 2011.

13. Nicholas, 2004; Rathus, Nevid, Fichner-Rathus, Herold, and McKenzie, 2005.

6. PARTNERS, FAMILIES, AND FRIENDS

1. Berkman, 1995; Ross, 1995; Pinquart, 2003.

2. Kalmijn, 2003; Kearns and Leonard, 2004; Kalmijn and Vermunt, 2007.

3. Wills, 1981; Kalmijn 2003; Cunningham and Thornton, 2006.

4. Kearns and Leonard, 2004.

5. Driscoll, Davis, and Lipetz, 1972.

6. Lepore, 1992.

7. Umberson, Chen, House, Hopkins, and Slaten, 1996; Kawachi and Berkman, 2001; Marks, Huston, Johnson, and Macdermid, 2001; Pinquart, 2003.

8. Kalmijn, 2003; Kearns and Leonard, 2004; Cornwell, 2011.

9. Sullivan, 1996; Rogers and Amato, 1997; Kalmijn and Bernasco, 2001; Voorpostel, van der Lippe, and Gershuny, 2009, 2010.

10. Kalmijn and Bernasco, 2001; Crawford, Houts, Huston, and George, 2002.

11. Bittman and Wajcman, 2000; Kalmijn and Bernasco, 2001; Gager and Sanchez, 2003; Mattingly and Bianchi, 2003; Amato, 2004; Nomaguchi, Milkie, and Bianchi, 2005; Voorpostel, van der Lippe, and Gershuny, 2010.

7. OUR PERSONAL BAGGAGE

1. Jockin, McGue, and Lykken, 1996; Bouchard and Loehlin, 2001; Robins, Caspi, and Moffitt, 2002; Spotts, Lichtenstein, Pedersen, Neiderhiser, Hansson, Cederblad, and Reiss, 2005.

2. Houts, Robins, and Huston, 1996; Blum and Mehrabian, 1999; Murray, Holmes, Bellavia, Griffin, and Dolderman, 2002; Watson, Klohnen, Casillas, Nus Simms, Haig, and Berry, 2004; Spotts, Lichtenstein, Pedersen, Neiderhiser, Hansson, Cederblad, and Reiss, 2005.

3. Murray, Holmes, Bellavia, Griffin, and Dolderman, 2002; Anderson, Keltner, and John, 2003; Gonzaga, Campos, and Bradbury, 2007.

4. Gonzaga, Campos, and Bradbury, 2007.

5. Botwin, Buss, and Shackelford, 1997; Nemechek and Olson, 1999; Gattis, Berns, Simpson, and Christensen, 2004.

6. Geist and Gilbert, 1996; Botwin, Buss, and Shackelford, 1997; Karney and Bradbury, 1997; Bouchard, Lussier, Sabourin, 1999; Nemechek and Olson, 1999; Caughlin, Huston, and Houts, 2000; Robins, Caspi, and Moffitt, 2000; Dehle and Weiss, 2002; Donnellan, Conger, and Bryant, 2004; Fisher and McNulty, 2008.

7. Botwin, Buss, and Shackleford, 1997; Robins, Caspi, and Moffitt, 2002; Twenge and Campbell, 2003; Donnellan, Conger, and Bryant, 2004; Horton, Bleau, and Drwecki, 2006; Twenge, Konrath, Foster, Campbell, and Bushman, 2008.

8. Klohnen and Bera, 1998; Davila, Karney, and Bradbury, 1999; Campbell, Simpson, Boldry, and Kashy, 2005; Hollist and Miller, 2005.

9. Bandura, 1977; Tasker and Richards, 1994; Amato, 1996; Feng, Giarrusso, Bengtson, and Frye, 1999; Sanders, Halford, and Behrens, 1999; Conger, Cui, Bryant, and Elder, 2000; Stith, Rosen, Middleton, Busch, Lundeberg, and Carlton, 2000; Wolfinger, 2000; Perren, Von Wyl, Bergin, Simoni, and Von

Klitzing, 2005; Topham, Larson, and Holman, 2005; Riggio and Fite, 2006; Riggio and Weiser, 2008.

8. COMMUNICATION AND CONFLICT

1. Kluwer, Heesink, and Van De Vliert, 1997; Graber, Laurenceau, Miga, Chango, and Coan, 2011.
2. Arriaga and Rusbult, 1998; Laurenceau, Barrett, and Rovine, 2005.
3. Gottman, 1993; Huston, Caughlin, Houts, Smith, and George, 2001; Amato and Previti, 2003; Overall, Fletcher, Simpson, and Sibley, 2009.
4. Markman, Rhoades, Stanley, Ragan, and Whitton, 2010.
5. Simmons, Gordon, and Chambless, 2005; Markman, Rhoades, Stanley, Ragan, and Whitton, 2010.
6. Arriaga and Rusbult, 1998; Weger, 2005.
7. Amato and Rogers, 1997; Gottman and Notarius, 2000; Kiecolt-Glaser and Newton, 2001; Menchaca and Dehle, 2005; Lawrence, Pederson, Bunde, Barry, Brock, Fazio, Mulryan, Hunt, Madsen, and Dzankovic, 2008; Thompson, 2008.
8. Noller and Feeney, 1994.
9. Knobloch, 2008; Riggio and Weiser, 2008; Overall, Fletcher, Simpson, and Sibley, 2009.

9. PERCEPTIONS AND ATTRIBUTIONS

1. Harvey and Weary, 1984.
2. Baucom and Epstein, 1990.
3. Fowers, Lyons, and Montel, 1996; Murray, Holmes, and Griffin, 1996; Murray and Holmes, 1997; Jacobson, Christensen, Prince, Cordova, and Eldridge, 2000; Karney and Bradbury, 2000; Shapiro, Gottman, and Carrere, 2000; Strom, 2003; Neff and Karney, 2005b.
4. Gottman, 1993.
5. Fowers, Lyons, and Montel, 1996; Karney and Bradbury, 2000; Fincham, Paleari, and Regalia, 2002.
6. Murray and Holmes, 1997; McNulty, O'Mara, and Karney, 2008.
7. Murray, Holmes, and Griffin, 1996; Neff and Karney, 2005b.
8. Murray, Holmes, and Griffin, 1996; Carrére, Buehlman, Gottman, Coan, and Ruckstuhl, 2000; McNulty and Karney, 2001; Miller, Niehuis, and Huston, 2006; Frye and Karney, 2002.

9. Wills, 1981; Frye and Karney, 2002.

10. Murray, Holmes, and Griffin, 1996; McNulty and Karney, 2001; McNulty and Karney, 2002; Neff and Karney, 2002, 2005b, 2009; Murray, Bellavia, Rose, and Griffin, 2003.

10. MANAGING THE HOME AND FAMILY

1. Coltrane, 2000.

2. Shelton and John, 1996; Risman and Johnson-Sumerford, 1998; Coltrane, 2000; Bianchi, Milkie, Sayer, and Robinson, 2001; Frisco and Williams, 2003.

3. Bianchi, Milkie, Sayer, and Robinson, 2001; Baxter, Haynes, and Hewitt, 2010.

4. Thibaut and Kelley, 1959; Greenstein, 1996; Shelton and John, 1996; Gager, 1998; Milkie and Peltola, 1999; Coltrane, 2000; Lavee and Katz, 2002; Frisco and Williams, 2003.

5. Shelton and John, 1996; Kroska, 1997.

6. Frisco and Williams, 2003.

7. Sanchez and Thomson, 1997; Coltrane, 2000.

8. Shapiro, Gottman, and Carrere, 2000; Guttman and Lazar, 2004; Perren, Von Wyl, Burgin, Simoni, and Von Klitzing, 2005.

9. Guttmann and Lazar, 2004; Perren, Von Wyl, Burgin, Simoni, and Von Klitzing, 2005; Gager and Yabiku, 2010; Umberson, Pudrovska, and Reczek, 2010.

10. Hyde, Essex, Clark, and Klein, 2001; Klein, Izquierdo, and Bradbury, 2007; Milkie, Kendig, Nomaguchi, and Denny, 2010.

11. Hyde, DeLamater, and Hewitt, 1998; Bianchi, 2000; Shapiro, Gottman, and Carrere, 2000; Nomaguchi, Milkie, and Bianchi, 2005; Milkie, Raley, and Bianchi, 2009; Higgins, Duxbury, and Lyons, 2010.

12. Gottman and Notarius, 2000; Kaczynski, Lindahl, Malik, and Laurenceau, 2006.

13. Doherty, Kouneski, and Erickson, 1998; Guttmann and Lazar, 2004.

14. Bianchi, 2000; Erdwins, Buffardi, Casper, and O'Brien, 2001; Klein, Izquierdo, and Bradbury, 2007.

15. Schaninger and Buss, 1986; Prelec and Loewenstein, 1998; Conger, Rueter, and Elder, 1999; Dew 2007, 2008.

16. Tesser and Beach, 1998; Conger, Rueter, and Elder, 1999; Moen and Yu, 2000; Neff and Karney, 2004, 2009; Dew, 2007; Dakin and Wampler, 2008; Atwood, 2012; Dew, Britt, and Huston, 2012.

11. POWER AND CONTROL

1. Vogler, 2005; Atwood, 2012.

2. Hiedemann, Suhomlinova, and O'Rand, 1998; Sayer and Bianchi, 2000; South, 2001; Schoen, Astone, Rothert, Standish, and Kim, 2002; Sweeney, 2002a.

3. Oppenheimer, 1997; Hyde, Essex, Clark, and Klein, 2001; Bremmer and Kesselring, 2004.

4. Rogers and Amato, 2000.

5. Call, Sprecher, and Schwartz, 1995; Pahl, 1995; Amato and Rogers, 1997; Heimdal and Houseknecht, 2003; Vogler, 2005; Burgoyne, Reibstein, Edmunds, and Routh, 2010; Atwood, 2012; Dew, Britt, and Huston, 2012.

6. Longmore and DeMaris, 1997; Halloran, 1998; Gottman and Notarius, 2000; Kulik, 2002; DeMaris, 2007, 2010.

7. Sprecher and Felmlee, 1997; Rogers and Amato, 2000; Nock, 2001; Kulik, 2004; Wilcox and Nock, 2006; DeMaris, Mahoney, and Pargament, 2010; Hankins and Hoekstra, 2010.

8. Helms, Proulx, Klute, McHale, and Crouter, 2006.

9. Halloran, 1998.

10. Felmlee, 1994; Sprecher and Felmlee, 1997.

12. THE ROOTS OF MARITAL CONFLICTS

1. Ellis and Harper, 1961; Ellis, 1994, 1999.

REFERENCES

Agnew, C. R., Van Lange, P. A. M., Rusbult, C. E., and Langston, C. A. Cognitive interdependence: Commitment and the mental representation of close relationships. *Journal of Personality and Social Psychology*, 74, 4 (1998), 939–954.

Allen, E. S., Atkins, D., Baucom, D. H., Snyder, D., Gordon, K. C., and Glass, S. P. Intrapersonal, interpersonal, and contextual factors in engaging in and responding to extramarital involvement. *Clinical Psychology: Science and Practice*, 12 (2005), 101–130.

Allen, E. S., and Baucom, D. H. Adult attachment and patterns of extradyadic involvement. *Family Process*, 43 (2004), 467–488.

Allen, E. S., and Rhoades, G. K. Not all affairs are created equal: Emotional involvement with an extradyadic partner. *Journal of Sex and Marital Therapy*, 43 (2008), 307–317.

Allen, E. S., Rhoades, G. K., Stanley, S. M., Markman, H. J., Williams, T., Melton, J., and Clements, M. L. Premarital precursors of marital infidelity. *Family Processes*, 47 (2008), 243–259.

Amato, P. R. Explaining the intergenerational transmission of divorce. *Journal of Marriage and the Family*, 58 (1996), 628–640.

Amato, P. R. Tension between institutional and individual views of marriage. *Journal of Marriage and Family*, 66 (2004), 959–965.

Amato, P. R. Institutional, companionate, and individualistic marriage: A social psychological perspective on marital change. In Peters, H. E., Kamp Dush, C. M. (Eds.), *Marriage and family: Complexities and perspectives*. New York: Columbia University Press (2009), 75–90.

Amato, P. R. Research on divorce: Continuing trends and new developments. *Journal of Marriage and Family*, 72, 3 (June 2010), 650–666.

Amato, P. R., and DeBoer, D. D. The transmissions of marital instability across generations: Relationship skills or commitment to marriage? *Journal of Marriage and the Family*, 63 (2001), 1038–1051.

Amato, P. R., and Previti, D. People's reasons for divorcing: Gender, social class, the life course, and adjustment. *Journal of Family Issues*, 24 (2003), 602–626.

Amato, P. R., and Rogers, S. J. A longitudinal study of marital problems and subsequent divorce. *Journal of Marriage and the Family*, 59, 3 (August 1997), 612–624.

Amato, P. R., and Rogers, S. J. Do attitudes toward divorce affect marital quality? *Journal of Family Issues*, 20 (1999), 69–86.

Ambert, A. M. Being a stepparent: Live-in and visiting stepchildren. *Journal of Marriage and the Family*, 48 (1986), 795–804.

Anderson, C., Keltner, D., and John, O. P. Emotional convergence between people over time. *Journal of Personality and Social Psychology*, 84 (2003), 1054–1068.

Aron, A., Fisher, H., Mashek, D. J., Strong, G., Li, H., and Brown, L. L. Reward, motivation, and emotion systems associated with early stage intense romantic love: An fMRI study. *Journal of Neurophysiology*, 94 (2005), 327–337.

Arriaga, X. B., and Agnew, C. R. Being committed: Affective, cognitive, and conative components of relationship commitment. *Personality and Social Psychology Bulletin*, 27 (2001), 1190–1203.

Arriaga, X. B., and Rusbult, C. E. Standing in my partner's shoes: Partner perspective-taking and reactions to accommodative dilemmas. *Personality and Social Psychology Bulletin*, 9 (1998), 927–948.

Atkins, D. C., Baucom, D. H., and Jacobson, N. S. Understanding infidelity: Correlates in a national random sample. *Journal of Family Psychology*, 15 (2001), 735–749.

Atkins, D. C., Yi, J., Baucom, D. H., and Christensen, A. Infidelity in couples seeking marital therapy. *Journal of Family Psychology*, 19, 3 (2005), 470–473.

Atwood, J. D. Couples and money: The last taboo. *The American Journal of Family Therapy*, 40 (2012), 1–19.

Atwood, J. D., and Seifer, M. Extramarital affairs and constructed meanings: A social constructionist therapeutic approach. *American Journal of Family Therapy*, 25 (1997), 55–74.

Baker, B., Helmers, K., O'Kelly, B., Sakinofsky, I., Abelsohn, A., and Tobe, S. Marital cohesion and ambulatory blood pressure in early hypertension. *American Journal of Hypertension* 12 (February 1999), 227–230.

Bancroft, J., Loftus, J., and Long, J. S. Distress about sex: A national survey of women in heterosexual relationships. *Archives of Sexual Behavior* 32, 1 (2003), 193–209.

Bandura, A. *Social learning theory*. Englewood Cliffs, NJ: Prentice Hall (1977).

Bartels, A., and Zeki, S. The neural correlates of maternal and romantic love. *Neuroimage*, 21 (2004), 1155–1166.

Baucom, D. H., and Epstein, N. *Cognitive-behavioral marital therapy*. Philadelphia: Brunner/Mazel (1990).

Baxter, J., Haynes, M., and Hewitt, B. Pathways into marriage: Cohabitation and the domestic division of labor. *Journal of Family Issues*, 31, 11 (2010), 1507–1529.

Berkman, L. F. The role of social relations in health promotion. *Psychosomatic Medicine*, 57 (1995), 245–254.

Bianchi, S. M. Maternal employment and time with children: Dramatic change or surprising continuity? *Demography*, 37 (2000), 139–154.

Bianchi, S. M., Milkie, M. A., Sayer, L. C., and Robinson, J. P. Is anyone doing the housework? Trends in the gender division of household labor. *Social Forces*, 79 (2001), 191–228.

Bittman, M., and Wajcman, J. The rush hour: The character of leisure time and gender equity. *Social Forces*, 79, 1 (2000), 165–189.

Blow, A. J., and Hartnett, K. Infidelity in committed relationships II: A substantive review. *Journal of Marital and Family Therapy*, 31 (2005), 217–233.

Blum, J. S., and Mehrabian, A. Personality and temperament correlates of marital satisfaction. *Journal of Personality*, 67 (1999), 93–125.

Botwin, M. D., Buss, D. M., and Shackelford, T. K. Personality and mate preferences: Five factors in mate selection and marital satisfaction. *Journal of Personality*, 65 (1997), 107–136.

Bouchard, G., Lussier, Y., and Sabourin, S. Personality and marital adjustment: Utility of the five-factor model of personality. *Journal of Marriage and the Family*, 61 (1999), 651–660.

Bouchard, T. J., and Loehlin, J. C. Genes, evolution and personality. *Behavior Genetics*, 31, 3 (2001), 243–273.

Bremmer, D., and Kesselring, R. Divorce and female labor force participation: Evidence from time-series data and cointegration. *Atlantic Economic Journal*, 32, 3 (2004), 175–190.

Brines, J., and Joyner, K. The ties that bind: Principles of cohesion in cohabitation and marriage. *American Sociological Review*, 64, 3 (June 1999), 333–355.

Brody, G. H., Neubaum, E., and Forehand, R. Serial marriage: A heuristic analysis of an emerging family form. *Psychological Bulletin*, 103 (1988), 211–222.

Brown, S. L. The effect of union type on psychological well-being: Depression among cohabitors versus marrieds. *Journal of Health and Social Behavior*, 41, 3 (2000), 241–255.

Brown, S. L. Moving from cohabitation to marriage: Effects on relationship quality. *Social Science Research*, 33 (2004), 1–19.

Brown, S. L., and Booth, A. Cohabitation versus marriage: A comparison of relationship quality. *Journal of Marriage and the Family*, 58, 3 (August 1996), 668–678.

Brown, S. L., and Kawamura, S. Relationship quality among cohabitors and marrieds in older adulthood. *Social Science Research*, 39, 5 (2010), 777–786.

Bumpass, L., and Lu, H. Trends in cohabitation and implications for children's family contexts. *Population Studies*, 54 (2000), 29–41.

Burgoyne, C. B., Reibstein, J., Edmunds, A. M., and Routh, D. A. Marital commitment, money and marriage preparation: What changes after the wedding? *Journal of Community and Applied Social Psychology*, 20 (2010), 390–403.

Burstein, N. R. Economic influences on marriage and divorce. *Journal of Policy Analysis and Management* 26, 2 (2007), 387–429.

Buunk, B. P., and Mutsaers, W. The nature of the relationship between remarried individuals and former spouses and its impact on marital satisfaction. *Journal of Family Psychology*, 13 (1999), 165–174.

Call, V., Sprecher, S., and Schwartz, P. The incidence and frequency of marital sex in a national sample. *Journal of Marriage and Family*, 57, 3 (1995), 639 –653.

Campbell, L., Simpson, J. A., Boldry, J., and Kashy, D. A. Perceptions of conflict and support in romantic relationships: The role of attachment anxiety. *Journal of Personality and Social Psychology*, 88 (2005), 510–531.

Campbell, L., Simpson, J. A., Boldry, J. G., and Rubin, H. Trust, variability in relationship evaluations, and relationship processes. *Journal of Personality and Social Psychology*, 99, 1 (2010), 14–31.

Carels, R. A., Sherwood, A., and Blumenthal, J. A. Psychosocial influences on blood pressure during daily life. *International Journal of Psychophysiology*, 28 (1998), 117–129.

Carrére, S., Buehlman, K. T., Gottman, J. M., Coan, J. A., and Ruckstuhl, L. Predicting marital stability and divorce in newlywed couples. *Journal of Family Psychology*, 14, 1 (March 2000), 42–58.

Caughlin, J. P., Huston, T. L., and Houts, R. M. How does personality matter in marriage? An examination of trait anxiety, interpersonal negativity, and marital satisfaction. *Journal of Personality and Social Psychology*, 78 (2000), 326–336.

Cherlin, A. J. The deinstitutionalization of American marriage. *Journal of Marriage and Family*, 66, 4 (2004), 848–861.

Christopher, S., and Sprecher, S. Sexuality in marriage, dating and other relationships: A decade review. *Journal of Marriage and the Family*, 62 (2000), 999–1017.

Cobb, N. P., Larson, J. H., and Watson, W. L. Development of the attitudes about romance and mate selection scale. *Family Relations*, 52, 3 (July 2003), 222–231.

Cohen, S., Frank, E., Doyle, W. J., Skoner, D. P., Rabin, B. S., and Gwaltney, J. M. Jr. Types of stressors that increase susceptibility to the common cold in healthy adults. *Health Psychology*, 17, 3 (May 1998), 214–223.

Coleman, M., Ganong, L., and Fine, M. Reinvestigating remarriage: Another decade of progress. *Journal of Marriage and Family*, 62, 4 (November 2000), 1288–1307.

Coltrane, S. Research on household labor: Modeling and measuring the social imbeddedness of routine family work. *Journal of Marriage and Family*, 62 (2000), 1208–1233.

Conger, R. D., Cui, M., Bryant, C. M., and Elder, G. Competence in early adult romantic relationships: A developmental perspective on family influences. *Journal of Personality and Social Psychology*, 79 (2000), 224–237.

Conger, R. D., Rueter, M. A., and Elder, G. H., Jr. Couple resilience to economic pressure. *Journal of Personality and Social Psychology*, 76 (1999), 54–71.

Coontz, S. *Marriage, a history: From obedience to intimacy, or how love conquered marriage.* New York: Viking Press (2005).

Copen C. E., Daniels, K., Vespa, J., Mosher, W. D. First Marriages in the United States: Data from the 2006–2010 National Survey of Family Growth. *National Health Statistics Reports*, 49 (March 2012), 1–21.

Cornwell, B. Independence through social networks: Bridging potential among older women and men. *The Journals of Gerontology, Series B: Psychological Sciences and Social Sciences*, 66, 6 (2011), 782–794.

Coyne, J. C., Rohrbaugh, M. J., Shoham V., Sonnega, J. S., Nicklas, J. M., and Cranford, J. A. Prognostic importance of marital quality for survival of congestive heart failure. *The American Journal of Cardiology*, 88, 5 (September 2001), 526–529.

Crawford, D. W., Houts, R. M., Huston, T. L., and George, L. J. Compatibility, leisure, and satisfaction in marital relationships. *Journal of Marriage and Family*, 64 (2002), 433–449.

Cunningham, M., and Thornton, A. The influence of parents' marital quality on adult children's attitudes toward marriage and its main and moderating effects. *Demography*, 43, 4 (November 2006), 659–672.

Dakin, J., and Wampler, R. Money doesn't buy happiness, but it helps: Marital satisfaction, psychological distress, and demographic differences between low- and middle-income clinic couples. *The American Journal of Family Therapy*, 36 (2008), 300–311.

Davila, J., Karney, B. R., and Bradbury, T. N. Attachment change processes in the early years of marriage. *Journal of Personality and Social Psychology*, 76, 5 (1999), 783–802.

Dehle, C., and Landers, J. E. You can't always get what you want, but can you get what you need? Personality traits and social support in marriage. *Journal of Social and Clinical Psychology*, 24, 7 (2005), 1051–1076.

Dehle, C., Larsen, D., and Landers, J. E. Social support in marriage. *American Journal of Family Therapy*, 29 (2001), 307–324.

Dehle, C., and Weiss, R. L. Associations between anxiety and marital adjustment. *The Journal of Psychology*, 136, 3 (2002), 328–338.

DeMaris, A. The role of relationship inequity in marital disruption. *Journal of Social and Personal Relationships*, 24 (2007), 177–195.

DeMaris, A. The 20-year trajectory of marital quality in enduring marriages: Does equity matter? *Journal of Social and Personal Relationships*, 27 (2010), 449–471.

DeMaris, A., Mahoney, A., and Pargament, K. I. Sanctification of marriage and general religiousness as buffers of the effects of marital inequity. *Journal of Family Issues*, 31 (2010), 1255–1278.

Dew, J. P. Two sides of the same coin? The differing roles of assets and consumer debt in marriage. *Journal of Family and Economic Issues*, 28 (2007), 89–104.

Dew, J. P. Debt change and marital satisfaction change in recently married couples. *Family Relations*, 57, 1 (January 2008), 60–71.

Dew, J. P., Britt, S., and Huston, S. Examining the relationship between financial issues and divorce. *Family Relations*, 61 (October 2012), 615–628.

DeWall, C. N., Lambert, N. M., Slotter, E. B., Pond, R. S., Jr., Deckman, T., Finkel, E. J., Luchies, L. B., and Fincham, F. D. So far away from one's partner, yet so close to romantic alternatives: Avoidant attachment, interest in alternatives, and infidelity. *Journal of Personality and Social Psychology*, 101, 6 (2011), 1302–1316.

Dhabhar, F. S., and McEwen, B. S. Acute stress enhances while chronic stress suppresses cell-mediated immunity in vivo: A potential role for leukocyte trafficking. *Brain, Behavior and Immunity*, 11 (1997), 286–306.

Diefenbach, H., and Opp, K. D. When and why do people think there should be a divorce?: An application of the factorial survey. *Rationality and Society*, 19 (2007), 485–517.

Doherty, W. J., Kouneski, E. F., and Erickson, M. E. Responsible fathering: An overview and conceptual framework. *Journal of Marriage and Family*, 60, 2 (May 1998), 277–292.

Donnellan, M. B., Conger, R. D., and Bryant, C. M. The Big Five and enduring marriages. *Journal of Research in Personality*, 38 (2004), 481–504.

Driscoll, R., Davis, K. E., and Lipetz, M. E. Parental interference and romantic love: The Romeo and Juliet Effect. *Journal of Personality and Social Psychology*, 24 (1972), 1–10.

Edwards, A. C., Nazroo, J. Y., and Brown, G. W. Gender differences in marital support following a shared life event. *Social Science and Medicine*, 46, 8 (April 1998), 1077–1085.

Ellis, A. *Reason and emotion in psychotherapy*, revised and updated. Secaucus, NJ: Carol Publishing Group (1994).

Ellis, A. *How to make yourself happy and remarkably less disturbable.* Atascadero, CA: Impact Publishers (1999).

Ellis, A., and Harper, R. *A guide to rational living.* Englewood Cliffs, NJ: Prentice-Hall (1961).

Erdwins, C. J., Buffardi, L. C., Casper, W. J., and O'Brien, A. S. The relationship of women's role strain to social support, role satisfaction, and self-efficacy. *Family Relations*, 50 (2001), 230–238.

Etcheverry, P. E., and Le, B. Thinking about commitment: Accessibility of commitment and prediction of relationship persistence, accommodation, and willingness to sacrifice. *Personal Relationships*, 12 (2005), 103–123.

Falke, S. I., and Larson, J. H. Premarital predictors of remarital quality: Implications for clinicians. *Contemporary Family Therapy*, 29 (2007), 9–23.

Felmlee, D. H. Who's on top? Power in romantic relationships. *Sex Roles*, 31 (1994), 275–295.

Feng, D., Giarrusso, R., Bengtson, V. L., and Frye, N. Intergenerational transmission of marital quality and marital stability. *Journal of Marriage and the Family*, 61 (1999), 451–464.

Fincham, F. D., Paleari, F. G., and Regalia, C. Forgiveness in marriage: The role of relationship quality, attributions, and empathy. *Personal Relationships*, 9 (2002), 27–37.

Fisher, T. D., and McNulty, J. K. Neuroticism and marital satisfaction: The mediating role played by the sexual relationship. *Journal of Family Psychology*, 22 (2008), 112–122.

Fletcher, G. J. O., Simpson, J. A., and Thomas, G. Ideals, perceptions, and evaluations in early relationship development. *Journal of Personality and Social Psychology*, 79 (2000a), 933–940.

Fletcher, G. J. O., Simpson, J. A., and Thomas, G. The measurement of perceived relationship quality components: A confirmatory factor analytic approach. *Personality and Social Psychology Bulletin*, 26 (2000b), 340–354.

Fletcher, G. J. O., Simpson, J. A., Thomas, G., and Giles, L. Ideals in intimate relationships. *Journal of Personality and Social Psychology*, 76, 1 (1999), 72–89.

Fowers, B. J., Lyons, E. M., and Montel, K. H. Positive marital illusions: Self-enhancement or relationship enhancement? *Journal of Family Psychology*, 10, 2 (1996), 192–208.

Fraley, R. C., and Shaver, P. R. Adult romantic attachment: Theoretical developments, emerging controversies, and unanswered questions. *Review of General Psychology*, 4 (2000), 132–154.

Frech, A., and Williams, K. Depression and the psychological benefits of entering marriage. *Journal of Health and Social Behavior*, 48, 2 (June 2007), 149–163.

Friedman, M. A., Dixon, A. E., Brownell, K. D., Whisman, M. A., and Wilfley, D. E. Marital status, marital satisfaction, and body image dissatisfaction. *International Journal of Eating Disorders*, 26 (1999), 81–85.

Frisco, M. L., and Williams, K. Perceived housework equity, marital happiness and divorce in dual-earner households. *Journal of Family Issues*, 24, 1 (January 2003), 51–73.

Frye, N. E., and Karney, B. R. Being better or getting better? Social and temporal comparisons as coping mechanisms in close relationships. *Personality and Social Psychology Bulletin*, 28 (2002), 1287–1299.

Frye, N. E., McNulty, J. K., and Karney, B. R. When are constraints on leaving a marriage related to negative behavior within the marriage? *Journal of Family Psychology*, 22, 1 (2008), 153–161.

Gager, C. T. The role of valued outcomes, justifications, and comparison referents in perceptions of fairness among dual-earner couples. *Journal of Family Issues*, 19 (1998), 622–649.

Gager, C. T., and Sanchez, L. Two as one?: Couples' perceptions of time spent together, marital quality, and the risk of divorce. *Journal of Family Issues*, 24 (2003), 21–50.

Gager, C. T., and Yabiku, S. T. Who has the time? The relationship between household labor time and sexual frequency. *Journal of Family Issues*, 31, 2 (2010), 135–163.

Garcia, S. D., and Khersonsky, D. "They are a lovely couple": Perceptions of couple attractiveness. *Journal of Social Behavior and Personality*, 11 (1996), 667–682.

Garcia, S. D., and Khersonsky, D. "They are a lovely couple": Further examination of perceptions of couple attractiveness. *Journal of Social Behavior and Personality*, 12, 2 (1997), 367–380.

Gattis, K. S., Berns, S., Simpson, L. E., and Christensen, A. Birds of a feather or strange birds? Ties among personality dimensions, similarity, and marital quality. *Journal of Family Psychology*, 18 (2004), 564–574.

Geist, R. L., and Gilbert, D. G. Correlates of expressed and felt emotion during marital conflict: Satisfaction, personality, process, and outcome. *Personality and Individual Differences*, 21 (1996), 49–60.

Glass, S. P., and Wright, T. L. Sex differences in type of extramarital involvement and marital dissatisfaction. *Sex Roles*, 12 (1985), 1101–1120.

Glenn, N. D. The well-being of persons remarried after divorce. *Journal of Family Issues*, 2 (1981), 61–75.

Glenn, N. D. The course of marital success and failure in five American 10-year marriage cohorts. *Journal of Marriage and Family*, 60, 3 (August 1998), 569–576.

Glenn, N. D., Uecker, J. E., and Love, R. W. B., Jr. Later first marriage and marital success. *Social Science Research*, 39, 5 (September 2010), 787–800.

Goldstein, J. R., and Kenney, C. T. Marriage delayed or marriage forgone? New cohort forecasts of first marriage for U.S. women. *American Sociological Review*, 66 (2001), 506–519.

Gonzaga, G. C., Campos, B., and Bradbury, T. Similarity, convergence, and relationship satisfaction in dating and married couples. *Journal of Personality and Social Psychology*, 93 (2007), 34–48.

Gossmann, I., Julien, D., Mathieu, M., and Chartrand, E. Determinants of sex initiation frequencies and sexual satisfaction in long term couples' relationships. *The Canadian Journal of Human Sexuality*, 12, 3–4 (2003), 169–181.

Gottman, J. M. The roles of conflict engagement, escalation, and avoidance in marital interaction: A longitudinal view of five types of couples. *Journal of Consulting and Clinical Psychology*, 61, 1 (February 1993), 6–15.

Gottman, J. M., Coan, J., Carrere, S., and Swanson, C. Predicting marital happiness and stability from newlywed interactions. *Journal of Marriage and the Family*, 60 (1998), 5–22.

Gottman, J. M., and Levenson, R. W. The timing of divorce: Predicting when a couple will divorce over a 14-year period. *Journal of Marriage and the Family*, 62 (2000), 737–745.

Gottman, J. M., and Notarius, C. Decade review: Observing marital interaction. *Journal of Marriage and the Family*, 62 (2000), 927–947.

Graber, E. C., Laurenceau, J. P., Miga, E., Chango, J., and Coan, J. Conflict and love: Predicting newlywed marital outcomes from two interaction contexts. *Journal of Family Psychology*, 25, 4 (2011), 541–550.

Greeff, A. P., and Malherbe, H. L. Intimacy and marital satisfaction in spouses. *Journal of Sex and Marital Therapy*, 27 (2001), 247–257.

Greenstein, T. N. Gender ideology and perceptions of the fairness of the division of household labor: Effects on marital quality. *Social Forces*, 74, 3 (March 1996), 1029–1042.

Grote, N. K., and Frieze, I. H. Remembrance of things past: Perceptions of marital love from its beginnings to the present. *Journal of Social and Personal Relationships*, 15 (1998), 91–109.

Guttmann, J., and Lazar, A. Criteria for marital satisfaction: Does having a child make a difference? *Journal of Reproductive and Infant Psychology*, 22, 3 (August 2004), 147–155.

Halloran, E. C. The role of marital power in depression and marital stress. *The American Journal of Family Therapy*, 26 (1998), 3–14.

Hankins, S., and Hoekstra, M. Lucky in life, unlucky in love? The effect of random income shocks on marriage and divorce. *The Journal of Human Resources*, 46, 2 (2010), 403–426.

Harvey, J. H., and Weary, G. Current issues in attribution theory and research. *Annual Review of Psychology*, 35 (1984), 427–459.

Hawkins, D. N., and Booth, A. Unhappily ever after: Effects of long-term, low-quality marriages on well-being. *Social Forces*, 84, 1 (September 2005), 445–465.

Heimdal, K. R., and Houseknecht, S. K. Cohabiting and married couples' income organization: Approaches in Sweden and the United States. *Journal of Marriage and Family*, 65, 3 (August 2003), 525–538.

Helms, H. M., Proulx, C. M., Klute, M. M., McHale, S. M., and Crouter, A. C. Spouses' gender-typed attributes and their links with marital quality: A pattern analytic approach. *Journal of Social and Personal Relationships*, 23 (2006), 843–863.

Hiedemann, B., Suhomlinova, O., and O'Rand, A. Economic independence, economic status, and empty nest in midlife marital disruption. *Journal of Marriage and the Family*, 60, 1 (1998), 219–231.

Higgins, C. A., Duxbury, L. E., and Lyons, S. T. Coping with overload and stress: Men and women in dual-earner families. *Journal of Marriage and Family*, 72, 4 (August 2010), 847–859.

Hollist, C. S., and Miller, R. B. Perceptions of attachment style and marital quality in midlife marriage. *Family Relations*, 54, 1 (January 2005), 46–57.

Holt-Lunstad, J., Birmingham, W., and Jones, B. Q. Is there something unique about marriage? The relative impact of marital status, relationship quality, and network social support on ambulatory blood pressure and mental health. *Annals of Behavioral Medicine*, 35 (2008), 239–244.

Horton, R. S., Bleau, G., and Drwecki, B. Parenting narcissus: Does parenting contribute to the development of narcissism? *Journal of Personality*, 74 (2006), 345–376.

Horwitz, A. V., and White, H. R. The relationship of cohabitation and mental health: A study of a young adult cohort. *Journal of Marriage and Family*, 60, 2 (May 1998), 505–514.

Horwitz, A. V., White, H. R., and Howell-White, S. Becoming married and mental health: A longitudinal study of a cohort of young adults. *Journal of Marriage and Family*, 58, 4 (November 1996), 895–907.

Houts, R. M., Robins, E., and Huston, T. L. Compatibility and the development of premarital relationships. *Journal of Marriage and the Family*, 58 (1996), 7–20.

Huang, P. M., Smock, P. J., Manning, W. D., and Bergstrom-Lynch, C. A. He says, she says: Gender and cohabitation. *Journal of Family Issues*, 32, 7 (July 2011), 876–905.

Huston, T. L. The social ecology of marriage and other intimate unions. *Journal of Marriage and the Family*, 62 (2000), 298–316.

Huston, T. L., Caughlin, J. P., Houts, R. M., Smith, S. E., and George, L. J. The connubial crucible: Newlywed years as predictors of marital delight, distress, and divorce. *Journal of Personality and Social Psychology*, 80 (2001), 237–252.

Hyde, J. S., DeLamater, J. D., and Hewitt, E. C. Sexuality and the dual-earner couple: Multiple roles and sexual functioning. *Journal of Family Psychology*, 12 (1998), 354–368.

Hyde, J. S., Essex, M. J., Clark, R., and Klein, M. H. Maternity leave, women's employment, and marital incompatibility. *Journal of Family Psychology*, 15, 3 (2001), 476–491.

Jockin, V., McGue, M., and Lykken, D. T. Personality and divorce: A genetic analysis. *Journal of Personality and Social Psychology*, 71 (1996), 288–299.

Jacobson, N. S., Christensen, A., Prince, S. E., Cordova, J., and Eldridge, K. Integrative behavioral couple therapy: An acceptance-based, promising new treatment for couple discord. *Journal of Consulting and Clinical Psychology*, 68 (2000), 351–355.

Johnson, D. R., and Booth, A. Marital quality: A product of the dyadic environment or individual factors? *Social Forces*, 76, 3 (March 1998), 883–904.

Johnson, M. P., Caughlin, J. P., and Huston, T. L. The tripartite nature of marital commitment: Personal, moral, and structural reasons to stay married. *Journal of Marriage and Family*, 61, 1 (February 1999), 160–177.

Kaczynski, K. J., Lindahl, K. M., Malik, N. M., and Laurenceau, J. P. Marital conflict, maternal and paternal parenting, and child adjustment: A test of mediation and moderation. *Journal of Family Psychology*, 20, 2 (2006), 199–208.

Kalmijn, M. Shared friendship networks and the life course: An analysis of survey data on married and cohabiting couples. *Social Networks*, 25 (2003), 231–249.

Kalmijn, M., and Bernasco, W. Joint and separated lifestyles in couple relationships. *Journal of Marriage and the Family*, 63 (2001), 639–654.

Kalmijn, M., and Vermunt, J. K. Homogeneity of social networks by age and marital status: A multilevel analysis of ego-centered networks. *Social Networks*, 29 (2007), 25–43.

Karney, B. R., and Bradbury, T. N. Neuroticism, marital interaction, and the trajectory of marital satisfaction. *Journal of Personality and Social Psychology*, 72 (1997), 1075–1092.

Karney, B. R., and Bradbury, T. N. Attributions in marriage: State or trait? A growth curve analysis. *Journal of Personality and Social Psychology*, 78 (2000), 295–309.

Kawachi, I., and Berkman, L. F. Social ties and mental health. *Journal of Urban Health*, 78, 3 (2001), 458–467.

Kearns, J. N., and Leonard, K. E. Social networks, structural interdependence, and marital quality over the transition to marriage: A prospective analysis. *Journal of Family Psychology*, 18, 2 (2004), 383–395.

Kernoff-Mansfield, P. K., Koch, P. B., and Voda, A. M. Qualities midlife women desire in their sexual relationships and their changing sexual response. *Psychology of Women Quarterly*, 22 (1998), 285–303.

Kiecolt-Glaser, J. K., Bane, C., Glaser, R., and Malarkey, W. B. Love, marriage, and divorce: Newlyweds' stress hormones foreshadow relationship changes. *Journal of Consulting and Clinical Psychology*, 71 (2003), 176–188.

Kiecolt-Glaser, J. K., Glaser, R., Cacioppo, J. T., MacCallum, R. C., Snydersmith, M., Kim, C., and Malarkey, W. B. Marital conflict in older adults: Endocrinological and immunological correlates. *Psychosomatic Medicine*, 59 (1997), 339–349.

Kiecolt-Glaser, J. K., and Newton, T. L. Marriage and health: His and hers. *Psychological Bulletin*, 127 (2001), 472–503.

Klein, W., Izquierdo, C., and Bradbury, T. N. Working relationships: Communicative patterns and strategies among couples in everyday life. *Qualitative Research in Psychology*, 4 (2007), 29–47.

Klohnen, E., and Bera, S. Behavioral and experiential patterns of avoidantly and securely attached women across adulthood: A 31-year longitudinal perspective. *Journal of Personality and Social Psychology*, 66 (1998), 502–512.

Kluwer, E. S., Heesink, J. A. M., and Van De Vliert, E. The marital dynamics of conflict over the division of labor. *Journal of Marriage and Family*, 59, 3 (August 1997), 635–653.

Knobloch, L. K. The content of relational uncertainty within marriage. *Journal of Social and Personal Relationships*, 25 (2008), 467–495.

Knox, D., and Zusman, M. E. Marrying a man with baggage: Implications for second wives. *Journal of Divorce and Remarriage*, 35 (2001), 67–79.

Koch, P. B., Kernoff-Mansfield, P., Thurau, D., and Carey, M. "Feeling frumpy": The relationships between body image and sexual response changes in midlife women. *The Journal of Sex Research*, 42, 3 (August 2005), 215–223.

Kroska, A. The division of labor in the home: A review and reconceptualization. *Social Psychology Quarterly*, 60, 4 (December 1997), 304–322.

Kulik, L. Marital equality and the quality of long-term marriage in later life. *Aging and Society*, 22 (July 2002), 459–481.

Kulik. L. Perceived equality in spousal relations, marital quality, and life satisfaction: A comparison of elderly wives and husbands. *Families in Society*, 85, 2 (April–June 2004), 243–250.

Kulik, L., and Havusha-Morgenstern, H. Does cohabitation matter? Differences in initial marital adjustment among women who cohabited and those who did not. *Families in Society*, 92, 1 (January–March 2011), 120–127.

Langlois, J. H., Kalakanis, L., Rubenstein, A. J., Larson, A., Hallam, M., and Smoot, M. Maxims or myths of beauty? A meta-analytic and theoretical review. *Psychological Bulletin*, 126 (2000), 390–423.

Larson, J. H., and Holman, T. B. Premarital predictors of marital quality and stability. *Family Relations*, 43, 2 (April 1994), 228–237.

Laumann, E. O., Paik, A., and Rosen, R. C. Sexual dysfunctions in the United States: Prevalence and predictors. *Journal of the American Medical Association*, 281 (1999), 537–544.

Laurenceau, J., Barrett, L., and Rovine, M. The interpersonal process model of intimacy in marriage: A daily-diary and multilevel modeling approach. *Journal of Family Psychology*, 19 (2005), 314–323.

Lavee, Y., and Katz, R. Division of labor, perceived fairness, and marital quality: The effect of gender ideology. *Journal of Marriage and Family*, 64, 1 (2002), 27–39.

Lawrence, E., Pederson, A., Bunde, M., Barry, R. A., Brock, R. L., Fazio, E., Mulryan, L., Hunt, S., Madsen, L., and Dzankovic, S. Objective ratings of relationship skills across multiple domains as predictors of marital satisfaction trajectories. *Journal of Social and Personal Relationships*, 25 (2008), 445–466.

Le, B., and Agnew, C. R. Commitment and its theorized determinants: A meta-analysis of the Investment Model. *Personal Relationships*, 10 (2003), 37–57.

Lehrer, E. L. Age at marriage and marital instability: Revisiting the Becker–Landes–Michael hypothesis. *Journal of Population Economics*, 31 (2008), 463–484.

Lepore, S. J. Social conflict, social support, and psychological distress: Evidence of cross-domain buffering effects. *Journal of Personality and Social Psychology*, 63 (1992), 857–867.

Little, K. C., McNulty, J. K., and Russell, V. M. Sex buffers intimates against the negative implications of attachment insecurity. *Personality and Social Psychology Bulletin*, 36, 4 (2010), 484–498.

Liu, C. A theory of marital sexual life. *Journal of Marriage and Family*, 62 (2000), 363–374.

Liu, C. Does the quality of marital sex decline with duration? *Archives of Sexual Behavior*, 32, 1 (2003), 55–60.

Longmore, M. A., and DeMaris, A. Perceived inequity and depression in intimate relationships: The moderating effect of self-esteem. *Social Psychology Quarterly*, 60 (1997), 172–184.

MacNeil, S., and Byers, E. S. Dyadic assessment of sexual self-disclosure and sexual satisfaction. *Journal of Social and Personal Relationships*, 22 (2005a), 193–205.

MacNeil, S., and Byers, E. S. Dyadic assessment of sexual self-disclosure and sexual satisfaction in heterosexual dating couples. *Journal of Social and Personal Relationships*, 22 (2005b), 169–181.

Manning, W. D., and Smock, P. J. Measuring and modeling cohabitation: New perspectives from qualitative data. *Journal of Marriage and Family*, 67 (2005), 989–1002.

Margolin, G., Christensen, A., and John, R. S. The continuance and spillover of everyday tensions in distressed and nondistressed families. *Journal of Family Psychology*, 10 (1996), 304–321.

Markey, C. N., and Markey, P. M. Romantic relationships and body satisfaction among young women. *Journal of Youth and Adolescence*, 35 (2006), 271–279.

Markman, H. J., Rhoades, G. K., Stanley, S. M., Ragan, E. P., and Whitton, S. W. The premarital communication roots of marital distress and divorce: The first five years of marriage. *Journal of Family Psychology*, 24, 3 (2010), 289–298.

Marks, N. F., and Lambert, J. D. Marital status continuity and change among young and midlife adults: Longitudinal effects on psychological well-being of adults. *Journal of Family Issues*, 19, 6 (November 1998), 652–686.

Marks, S. R., Huston, T. L., Johnson, E. M., and Macdermid, S. M. Role balance among white married couples. *Journal of Marriage and Family*, 63, 4 (November 2001), 1083–1098.

Mattingly, M. J., and Bianchi, S. M. Gender differences in the quantity and quality of free time: The U.S. experience. *Social Forces*, 81, 3 (March 2003), 999–1030.

McCarthy, B. W., and Ginsberg, R. L. Second marriages: Challenges and risks. *The Family Journal: Counseling and Therapy for Couples and Families*, 15, 2 (April 2007), 119–123.

McCarthy, B. W., Ginsberg, R. L., and Fucito, L. M. Resilient sexual desire in heterosexual couples. *The Family Journal: Counseling and Therapy for Couples and Families*, 14, 1 (January 2006), 59–64.

McCranie, E., and Kahan, J. Personality and multiple divorce: A prospective study. *Journal of Nervous and Mental Disease*, 17, 1 (1986), 161–164.

McNulty, J. K., and Fisher, T. D. Gender differences in response to sexual expectancies and changes in sexual frequency: A short-term longitudinal study of sexual satisfaction in newly married couples. *Archives of Sexual Behavior*, 37 (2008), 229–240.

McNulty, J. K., and Karney, B. R. Attributions in marriage: Integrating specific and global evaluations of a relationship. *Personality and Social Psychology Bulletin*, 27 (2001), 943–955.

McNulty, J. K., and Karney, B. R. Expectancy confirmation in appraisals of marital interactions. *Personality and Social Psychology Bulletin*, 28 (2002), 764–775.

McNulty, J. K., and Karney, B. R. Positive expectations in the early years of marriage: Should couples expect the best or brace for the worst? *Journal of Personality and Social Psychology*, 86 (2004), 729–743.

McNulty, J. K., Neff, L. A., and Karney, B. R. Beyond initial attraction: Physical attractiveness in newlywed marriage. *Journal of Family Psychology*, 22, 1 (2008), 135–143.

McNulty, J. K., O'Mara, E. M., and Karney, B. R. Benevolent cognitions as a strategy of relationship maintenance: "Don't sweat the small stuff" . . . . but it is not all small stuff. *Journal of Personality and Social Psychology*, 94 (2008), 631–646.

Meltzer, A. L., and McNulty, J. K. Body image and marital satisfaction: Evidence for the mediating role of sexual frequency and sexual satisfaction. *Journal of Family Psychology*, 24, 2 (2010), 156–164.

Meltzer, A. L., McNulty, J. K., Novak, S. A., Butler, E. A., and Karney, B. J. Marriages are more satisfying when wives are thinner than their husbands. *Social Psychological and Personality Science* 2, 4 (2011), 416–424.

Menchaca, D., and Dehle, C. Marital quality and physiological arousal: How do I love thee? Let my heartbeat count the ways. *The American Journal of Family Therapy*, 33 (2005), 117–130.

Milkie, M. A., Kendig, S. M., Nomaguchi, K. M., and Denny, K. D. Time with children, children's well-being, and work-family balance among employed parents. *Journal of Marriage and Family*, 72, 5 (October 2010), 1329–1343.

Milkie, M. A., and Peltola, P. Playing all the roles: Gender and the work family balancing act. *Journal of Marriage and the Family*, 61 (1999), 476–490.

Milkie, M. A., Raley, S. B., and Bianchi, S. M. Taking on the second shift: Time allocations and time pressures of U.S. parents with preschoolers. *Social Forces*, 88, 2 (December 2009), 487–518.

Miller, P. J. E., Niehuis, S., and Huston, T. L. Positive illusions in marital relationships: A 13-year longitudinal study. *Personality and Social Psychology Bulletin*, 32 (2006), 1579–1594.

Moen, P., and Yu, Y. Effective work/life strategies: Working couples, work conditions, gender, and life quality. *Social Problems*, 47 (2000), 291–326.

Murray, S. L., Bellavia, G. M., Rose, P., and Griffin, D. W. Once hurt, twice hurtful: How perceived regard regulates daily marital interactions. *Journal of Personality and Social Psychology*, 84 (2003), 126–147.

Murray, S. L., and Holmes, J. G. A leap of faith? Positive illusions in romantic relationships. *Personality and Social Psychology Bulletin*, 23 (1997), 586–604.

Murray, S. L., Holmes, J. G., Bellavia, G., Griffin, D. W., and Dolderman, D. Kindred spirits? The benefits of egocentrism in close relationships. *Journal of Personality and Social Psychology*, 82 (2002), 563–581.

Murray, S. L., Holmes, J. G., and Griffin, D. W. The self-fulfilling nature of positive illusions in romantic relationships: Love is not blind, but prescient. *Journal of Personality and Social Psychology*, 71 (1996), 1155–1180.

Neff, L. A., and Karney, B. R. Judgments of a relationship partner: Specific accuracy but global enhancement. *Journal of Personality*, 70 (2002), 1079–1112.

Neff, L. A., and Karney, B. R. How does context affect intimate relationships? Linking external stress and cognitive processes within marriage. *Personality and Social Psychology Bulletin*, 30 (2004), 134–148.

Neff, L. A., and Karney, B. R. Gender differences in social support: A question of skill or responsiveness? *Journal of Personality and Social Psychology*, 88 (2005a), 79–90.

Neff, L. A., and Karney, B. R. To know you is to love you: The implications of global adoration and specific accuracy for marital relationships. *Journal of Personality and Social Psychology*, 88 (2005b), 480–497.

Neff, L. A., and Karney, B. R. Stress and reactivity to daily relationship experiences: How stress hinders adaptive processes in marriage. *Journal of Personality and Social Psychology*, 97, 3 (2009), 435–450.

Nemechek, S., and Olson, K. R. Five-factor personality similarity and marital adjustment. *Social Behavior and Personality*, 27 (1999), 309–318.

Nicholas, L. J. The association between religiosity, sexual fantasy, participation in sexual acts, sexual enjoyment, exposure, and reaction to sexual materials among Black South Africans, *Journal of Sex and Marital Therapy*, 30, 1 (2004), 37–42.

Nock, S. The marriages of equally dependent spouses. *Journal of Family Issues*, 22, 6 (2001), 755–775.

Nock, S. L. Commitment and dependency in marriage. *Journal of Marriage and the Family*, 57 (1995), 503–514.

Noller, P., and Feeney, J. A. Relationship satisfaction, attachment, and nonverbal accuracy in early marriage. *Journal of Nonverbal Behavior*, 18, 3 (Fall 1994), 199–221.

Nomaguchi, K. M., Milkie, M. A., and Bianchi, S. M. Time strains and psychological well-being: Do dual-earner mothers and fathers differ? *Journal of Family Issues*, 26, 6 (2005), 756–792.

Olson, M. M., Russell, C. S., Higgins-Kessler, M., and Miller, R. B. Emotional processes following disclosure of an extramarital infidelity. *Journal of Marital and Family Therapy*, 28 (2002), 423–434.

Ono, H. Homogamy among the divorced and the never married on marital history in recent decades: Evidence from vital statistics data. *Social Science Research*, 35 (2006), 356–383.

Oppenheimer, V. K. Women's employment and the gain to marriage: The specialization and trading model. *Annual Review of Sociology*, 23 (1997), 431–453.

Overall, N. C., Fletcher, G. J. O., Simpson, J. A., and Sibley, C. G. Regulating partners in intimate relationships: The costs and benefits of different communication strategies. *Journal of Personality and Social Psychology*, 96 (2009), 620–639.

Pahl, J. His money, her money: Recent research on financial organization in marriage. *Journal of Economic Psychology*, 16 (1995), 361–376.

Pascale, R., Primavera, L. H., and Roach, R. *The retirement maze*. Lanham, MD: Rowman and Littlefield Publishers, Inc. (2012).

Pasch, L. A., and Bradbury, T. N. Social support, conflict, and the development of marital dysfunction. *Journal of Consulting and Clinical Psychology*, 66 (1998), 219–230.

Pasch, L. A., Bradbury, T. N., and Davila, J. Gender, negative affectivity, and observed social support behavior in marital interaction. *Personal Relationships*, 4 (1997), 361–378.

Perren, S., Von Wyl, A., Burgin, D., Simoni, H., and Von Klitzing, K. Intergenerational transmission of marital quality across the transition to parenthood. *Family Process*, 44, 4 (2005), 441–459.

Pinquart, M. Loneliness in married, widowed, divorced, and never-married older adults. *Journal of Social and Personal Relationships*, 20 (2003), 31–53.

Poortman, A. R., and Lyngstad, T. H. Dissolution risks in first and higher order marital and cohabiting unions. *Social Science Research*, 36 (2007), 1431–1446.

Porges, S. W. Love: An emergent property of the mammalian autonomic nervous system. *Psychoneuroendocrinology*, 23 (1998), 837–861.

Potter, J. E. A 60-year-old woman with sexual difficulties. *Journal of the American Medical Association*, 297, 6 (February 2007), 620–633.

Prelec, D., and Loewenstein, G. The red and the black: Mental accounting of savings and debts. *Marketing Science*, 17 (1998), 4–28.

Previti, D., and Amato, P. R. Why stay married? *Journal of Marriage and Family*, 65 (2003), 561–572.

Previti, D., and Amato, P. R. Is infidelity a cause or a consequence of poor marital quality? *Journal of Social and Personal Relationships*, 21 (2004), 217–230.

Prigerson, H. G., Maciejewski, P. K., and Rosenheck, R. A. The effects of marital dissolution and marital quality on health and health services use among women. *Medical Care*, 37 (1999), 858–873.

Purnine, D. M., and Carey, M. P. Interpersonal communication and sexual adjustment: The roles of understanding and agreement. *Journal of Consulting and Clinical Psychology*, 65 (1997), 1017–1025.

Ragsdale, J. D., Brandau-Brown, F., and Bello, R. Attachment style and gender as predictors of relational repair among the remarried: Rationale for the study. *Journal of Family Communication*, 10 (2010), 158–173.

Rampage, C. Power, gender, and marital intimacy. *Journal of Family Therapy*, 16 (1994), 125–137.

Rathus, S. A., Nevid, J. S. Fichner-Rathus, L., Herold, E. S., and McKenzie, S. W. *Human sexuality in a world of diversity* (2nd ed.). New Jersey: Pearson Education (2005).

Reczek, C., Liu, H., and Umberson, D. Just the two of us? How parents influence adult children's marital quality. *Journal of Marriage and Family*, 72, 5 (October 2010), 1205–1219.

Rempel, J. K., Ross, M., and Holmes, J. G. Trust and communicated attributions in close relationships. *Journal of Personality and Social Psychology*, 81, 1 (2001), 57–54.

Rhoades, G. K., Stanley, S. M., and Markman, H. J. Pre-engagement cohabitation and gender asymmetry in marital commitment. *Journal of Family Psychology*, 20 (2006), 553–560.

Rhoades, G. K., Stanley, S. M., and Markman, H. J. Couples' reasons for cohabitation: Associations with individual well-being and relationship quality. *Journal of Family Issues*, 30 (2009), 233–258.

Riggio, H. R., and Fite, J. E. Attitudes toward divorce: Embeddedness and outcomes in personal relationships. *Journal of Applied Social Psychology*, 36 (2006), 2935–2962.

Riggio, H. R., and Weiser, D. A. Attitudes toward marriage: Embeddedness and outcomes in personal relationships. *Personal Relationships*, 15 (2008), 123–140.

Risch, G. S., Riley, L. A., and Lawler, M. G. Problematic issues in the early years of marriage: Content for premarital education. *Journal of Psychology and Theology*, 31 (2003), 253–269.

Risman, B. J., and Johnson-Sumerford, D. Doing it fairly: A study of post gender marriages. *Journal of Marriage and Family*, 60, 1 (February 1998), 23–40.

Robels, T. F., and Kiecolt-Glaser J. K. The physiology of marriage: Pathways to health. *Physiology and Behavior*, 79 (2003), 409–416.

Robins, R. W., Caspi, A., and Moffitt, T. E. Two personalities, one relationship: Both partners' personality traits shape the quality of their relationship. *Journal of Personality and Social Psychology*, 79 (2000), 251–259.

Robins, R. W., Caspi, A., and Moffitt, T. E. It's not just who you're with, it's who you are: Personality and relationship experiences across multiple relationships. *Journal of Personality*, 70 (2002), 925–964.

Rogers, S. J., and Amato, P. R. Is marital quality declining? The evidence from two generations. *Social Forces*, 75, 3 (1997), 1089–1100.

Rogers, S. J., and Amato, P. R. Have changes in gender relations affected marital quality? *Social Forces*, 79, 2 (2000), 731–753.

Ross, C. E. Reconceptualizing marital status as a continuum of social attachment. *Journal of Marriage and Family*, 57, 1 (February 1995), 129–140.

Rusbult, C. E., and Van Lange, P. A. M. Interdependence, interaction, and relationships. *Annual Review of Psychology*, 54 (2003), 351–375.

Sanchez, L., and Thomson, E. Becoming mothers and fathers: Parenthood, gender, and the division of labor. *Gender and Society*, 11, 6 (December 1997), 747–772.

Sanders, M. R., Halford, W. K., and Behrens, B. C. Parental divorce and premarital couple communication. *Journal of Family Psychology*, 13 (1999), 60–74.

Sangrador, J. L., and Yela, C. What is beautiful is loved: Physical attractiveness in love relationships in a representative sample. *Social Behavior and Personality*, 28 (2000), 207–218.

Sayer, L. C., and Bianchi, S. M. Women's economic independence and the probability of divorce: A review and reexamination. *Journal of Family Issues*, 21 (2000), 906–943.

Schaninger, C. M., and Buss, W. C. A longitudinal comparison of consumption and finance handling among happily married and divorced couples. *Journal of Marriage and the Family*, 48 (1986), 129–136.

Schmiege, C. J., Richards, L. N., and Zvonkovic, A. M. Remarriage: For love or money? *Journal of Divorce and Remarriage*, 36 (2001), 123–140.

Schneiderman, I., Zilberstein-Kra, Y., Leckman, J. F., and Feldman, R. Love alters autonomic reactivity to emotions. *Emotion*, 11, 6 (2011), 1314–1321.

Schoebi, D., Karney, B. R., and Bradbury, T. N. Stability and change in the first 10 years of marriage: Does commitment confer benefits beyond the effects of satisfaction? *Journal of Personality and Social Psychology*, 21 (November 2011), 1–14.

Schoen, R., Astone, N. M., Rothert, K., Standish, N. J., and Kim, Y. J. Women's employment, marital happiness, and divorce. *Social Forces*, 81, 2 (2002), 643–662.

Shapiro, A. F., Gottman, J. M., and Carrere, S. The baby and the marriage: Identifying factors that buffer against decline in marital satisfaction after the first baby arrives. *Journal of Family Psychology*, 14, 1 (2000), 59–70.

Shelton, B. A., and John, D. The division of household labor. *Annual Review of Sociology*, 22 (1996), 299–322.

Simmons, R. A., Gordon, P. C., and Chambless, D. L. Pronouns in marital interaction: What do "You" and "I" say about marital health? *Psychological Science*, 16, 12 (2005), 932–936.

Simms, D. C., and Byers, E. S. Interpersonal perceptions of desired frequency of sexual behaviours. *The Canadian Journal of Human Sexuality*, 18 (2009), 1–12.

Simon, R. W. Revisiting the relationships among gender, marital status, and mental health. *American Journal of Sociology*, 107, 4 (January 2002), 1065–1096.

Simpson, J. A. Psychological foundations of trust. *Current Directions in Psychological Science*, 16 (2007), 264–268.

Sinikka, E., and Umberson, D. The performance of desire: Gender and sexual negotiation in long-term marriages. *Journal of Marriage and Family*, 70, 2 (2008), 391–406.

Skinner, K. B., Bahr, S. J., Crane, D. R., and Call, V. R. Cohabitation, marriage, and remarriage: A comparison of relationship quality over time. *Journal of Family Issues*, 23, 1 (January 2002), 74–90.

Smock, P. J. Cohabitation in the United States: An appraisal of research themes, findings, and implications. *Annual Review of Sociology*, 26 (2000), 1–20.

Smock, P. J., and Manning, W. D. Living together unmarried in the United States: Demographic perspectives and implications for family policy. *Law and Policy*, 26, 1 (January 2004), 87–117.

Smolak, L. Body image in children and adolescents: Where do we go from here? *Body Image*, 1 (2003), 15–28.

South, S. J. Time-dependent effects of wives' employment on marital dissolution. *American Sociological Review*, 66, 2 (2001), 226–245.

Spitze, G., and Ward, R. Gender, marriage, and expectations for personal care. Research on Aging, 22 (2000), 451–469.

Spivey, C. Desperation or Desire? The role of risk aversion in marriage. *Economic Inquiry*, 48, 2 (April 2010), 499–516.

Spotts, E. L., Lichtenstein, P., Pedersen, N., Neiderhiser, J. M., Hansson, K., Cederblad, M., and Reiss, D. Personality and marital satisfaction: A behavioural genetic analysis. *European Journal of Personality*, 19 (2005), 205–227.

Sprecher, S. "I love you more today than yesterday": Romantic partners' perceptions of changes in love and related affect over time. *Journal of Personality and Social Psychology*, 76 (1999), 46–53.

Sprecher, S., and Felmlee, D. The balance of power in romantic heterosexual couples over time from "his" and "her" perspectives. *Sex Roles*, 37 (1997), 361–379.

Stack, S., and Eshleman, J. R. Marital status and happiness: A 17-nation study. *Journal of Marriage and the Family*, 60 (1998), 527–536.

Stanley, S. M., Markman, H. J., and Whitton, S. W. Communication, conflict and commitment: Insights on the foundations of relationship success from a national survey. *Family Process*, 41 (2002), 659–675.

Stanley, S. M., Rhoades, G. K., Amato, P. R., Markman, H. J., and Johnson, C. A. The timing of cohabitation and engagement: Impact on first and second marriages. *Journal of Marriage and Family*, 72, 4 (August 2010), 906–918.

Stanley, S. M., Whitton, S. W., and Markman, H. J. Maybe I do: Interpersonal commitment and premarital or nonmarital cohabitation. *Journal of Family Issues*, 25, 4 (2004), 496–519.

Stith, S. M., Rosen, K. H., Middleton, K. M., Busch, A., Lundeberg, K., and Carlton, R. The intergenerational transmission of spouse abuse: A meta-analysis. *Journal of Marriage and the Family*, 62 (2000), 640–654.

Strom, B. Communicator virtue and its relation to marriage quality. *The Journal of Family Communication*, 3, 1 (2003), 21–40.

Sullivan, O. Time co-ordination, the domestic division of labour and affective relations: Time use and the enjoyment of activities within couples. *Sociology*, 30 (1996), 79–100.

Sweeney, M. M. Two decades of family change: The shifting economic foundations of marriage. *American Sociological Review*, 67 (2002a), 132–147.

Sweeney, M. M. Remarriage and the nature of divorce: Does it matter which spouse chose to leave? *Journal of Family Issues*, 23 (2002b), 410–440.

Tasker, F. L., and Richards, M. P. M. Adolescents' attitudes toward marriage and marital prospects after parental divorce: A review. *Journal of Adolescent Research*, 9 (1994), 340–362.

Teachman, J. D., Tedrow, L. M., and Crowder, K. D. The changing demography of America's families. *Journal of Marriage and the Family*, 62, 4 (2000), 1234–1246.

Tesser, A., and Beach, S. R. H. Life events, relationship quality, and depression: An investigation of judgment discontinuity in vivo. *Journal of Personality and Social Psychology*, 74 (1998), 36–52.

Theiss, J. A. Modeling dyadic effects in the associations between relational uncertainty, sexual communication, and sexual satisfaction for husbands and wives. *Communication Research*, 38, 4 (2011), 565–584.

Thibaut, J. W., and Kelley, H. H. *The social psychology of groups*. New York: Wiley (1959).

Thompson, P. Desperate housewives? Communication difficulties and the dynamics of marital (un)happiness. *The Economic Journal*, 118 (October 2008), 1640–1669.

Topham, G. L., Larson, J. H., and Holman, T. B. Family-of-Origin predictors of hostile conflict in early marriage. *Contemporary Family Therapy* 27, 1 (March 2005), 101–121.

Trudel, G. Sexuality and marital life: Results of a survey. *Journal of Sex and Marital Therapy*, 28 (2002), 229–249.

Twenge, J. M., and Campbell, S. M. Generational differences in psychological traits and their impact on the workplace. *Journal of Managerial Psychology*, 23 (2008), 862–877.

Twenge, J. M., and Campbell, W. K. Isn't it fun to get the respect that we're going to deserve? Narcissism, social rejection, and aggression. *Personality and Social Psychology Bulletin*, 29 (2003), 261–272.

Twenge, J. M., and Campbell, W. K. *The narcissism epidemic: Living in the age of entitlement*. New York: Free Press (2009).

Twenge, J. M., Konrath, S., Foster, J. D., Campbell, W. K., and Bushman, B. J. Egos inflating over time: Across-temporal meta-analysis of the Narcissistic Personality Inventory. *Journal of Personality*, 76 (2008), 875–901.

Umberson, D., Chen, M. D., House, J. S., Hopkins, K., and Slaten, E. The effect of social relationships on psychological well-being: Are men and women really so different? *American Sociological Review*, 61 (1996), 837–857.

Umberson, D., Pudrovska, T., and Reczek, C. Parenthood, childlessness, and well-being: A life course perspective. *Journal of Marriage and Family*, 72, 3 (June 2010), 612–629.

Umberson, D., Williams, K., Powers, D. A., Chen, M. D., and Campbell, A. M. As good as it gets? A life course perspective on marital quality, *Social Forces*, 84 (2005), 493–511.

Van Lange, P. A. M., Rusbult, C. E., Drigotas, S. M., Arriaga, X. B., Witcher, B. S., and Cox, C. L. Willingness to sacrifice in close relationships. *Journal of Personality and Social Psychology*, 72 (1997), 1373–1395.

Van Laningham, J., Johnson, D. R., and Amato, P. Marital happiness, marital duration, and the U-shaped curve: Evidence from a five-way panel study. *Social Forces*, 79 (2001), 1313–1341.

Ventura, S. J. Changing patterns of non-marital childbearing in the United States. National Center for Health Statistics, U.S. Department of Health and Human Services. *Data Brief*, 18 (2009), 1–8.

Verhofstadt, L. L., Buysse, A., and Ickes, W. Social support in couples: An examination of gender differences using self-report and observational methods. *Sex Roles*, 57 (2007), 267–282.

Vernon, V. Marriage: For love, for money . . . and for time? *Review of Economics of the Household*, 8 (2010), 433–457.

Vogler, C. Cohabiting couples: Rethinking money in the household at the beginning of the twenty first century. *The Sociological Review*, 53, 1 (2005), 1–29.

Voorpostel, M., van der Lippe, T., and Gershuny, J. Trends in free time with a partner: A transformation of intimacy? *Social Indicators Research*, 93 (2009), 165–169.

Voorpostel, M., van der Lippe, T., and Gershuny, J. Spending time together—Changes over four decades in leisure time spent with a spouse. *Journal of Leisure Research*, 42, 2 (2010), 243–265.

Waite, L. J., and Gallagher, M. *The case for marriage: Why married people are happier, healthier, and better off financially*. University of Chicago Press: Chicago (2000).

Watson, D., Klohnen, C. E., Casillas, A., Nus Simms, E., Haig, J., and Berry, D. S. Match makers and deal breakers: Analyses of assortative mating in newlywed couples. *Journal of Personality*, 72, 5 (October 2004), 1029–1068.

Weger, H., Jr. Disconfirming communication and self-verification in marriage: Associations among the demand/withdraw interaction pattern, feeling understood, and marital satisfaction. *Journal of Social and Personal Relationships*, 22, 1 (2005), 19–31.

Weller, J. E., and Dziegielewski, S. F. The relationship between romantic partner support styles and body image disturbance. *Journal of Human Behavior and Social Environment*, 10, 2 (2004), 71–92.

Whitson, S., and El-Sheikh, M. Marital conflict and health: Processes and protective factors. *Aggression and Violent Behavior*, 8 (2003), 283–312.

Wickrama, K. A. S., Lorenz, F. O., Conger, R. D., and Elder, G. H. Marital quality and physical illness: A latent growth curve analysis. *Journal of Marriage and the Family*, 59 (1997), 143–155.

Widmer, E. D., Treas, J., and Newcomb, R. Attitudes toward nonmarital sex in 24 countries. *Journal of Sex Research*, 35 (1998), 349–358.

Wiederman, M. W. Extramarital sex: Prevalence and correlates in a national survey. *The Journal of Sex Research*, 34 (1997), 167–174.

Wiederman, M. W., and Hurst, S. R. Physical attractiveness, body image, and women's sexual self-schema. *Psychology of Women Quarterly*, 21, 4 (December 1997), 567–580.

Wieselquist, J., Rusbult, C. E., Foster, C. A., and Agnew, C. R. Commitment, pro-relationship behavior, and trust in close relationships. *Journal of Personality and Social Psychology*, 77 (1999), 942–966.

Wilcox, W. B. The evolution of divorce. *National Affairs* (Fall 2009), 81–94.

Wilcox, W. B., and Dew, J. Is love a flimsy foundation? Soul mate versus institutional models of marriage. *Social Science Research*, 39 (2010), 687–699.

Wilcox, W. B., and Nock, S. L. What's love got to do with it? Equality, equity, commitment and women's marital quality. *Social Forces*, 84 (2006), 1321–1345.

Wills, T. A. Downward comparison principles in social psychology. *Psychological Bulletin*, 90 (1981), 245–271.

Wolfinger, N. H. Beyond the intergenerational transmission of divorce: Do people replicate the patterns of marital instability they grew up with? *Journal of Family Issues*, 21 (2000), 1061–1086.

Xinhua, S. R. Marital status and quality of relationships: The impact on health perception. *Social Science and Medicine*, 44, 2 (January 1997), 241–249.

Xu, X., Hudspeth, C. D., and Bartkowski, J. P. Role of cohabitation in remarriage. *Journal of Marriage and Family*, 68, 2 (May 2006), 261–274.

Yabiku, S. T., and Gager, C. T. Sexual frequency and the stability of marital and cohabiting unions. *Journal of Marriage and Family*, 71, 4 (November 2009), 983–1000.

Yeh, H. C., Lorenz, F., Wickrama, K. A. S., Conger, R. D., and Elder, G. H. Relationships among sexual satisfaction, marital quality, and marital instability at midlife. *Journal of Family Psychology*, 20 (2006), 339–343.

Zeki, S. Mini-review: The neurobiology of love. *Febs Letters*, 581, 14 (June 2007), 2575–2579.

Zimmerman, T. S., Holm, K. E., Daniels, K. C., and Haddock, S. A. Barriers and bridges to intimacy and mutuality: A critical review of sexual advice in self-help bestsellers. *Contemporary Family Therapy*, 24, 2 (June 2002), 289–311.

INDEX

abandonment: anxiety attachment and, 56–57; fear of, 56, 115–116, 195

absolutes: irrationality of, 204–205, 206, 208, 224; negativity of, 224–225; self-destructiveness of, 224

abuse: mimicking parents and, 117; verbal, for control, 190–191

acceptance: of power and control, 193–194; relationship work and, 225–226; self-reflection and, 226. *See also* social acceptance

accommodation, 130–131

accusation, 6

activities: beneficial, 95–96; emotion work in, 96; importance of joint, 94–95; men and women differences with, 97

affairs. *See* infidelity

age: divorce and, 42; infidelity and, 54; live-together relationships and, 18; marriage related to, 2–5, 18; marrying, significance, 35–36; sex and, 18, 73, 73–74, 80

agreeableness, 108, 112. *See also* accommodation

alternatives. *See* options

ambivalence, 113

anger: in bad marriage, 20; in divorce, 9, 10; expression of, 119; justification of, 208; as non-adaptive emotion, 202. *See also* hostility

anxiety: emotional instability and, 109–110; as non-adaptive emotion, 202

anxiety attachment style, 56–57, 115–116

arguments: agreeableness and, 108; attack-counterattack approach to, 6, 127, 130, 207; benefit of, 30–31, 123; about children, 25; commitment and, 47; communication styles in, 124–131, 134; constraint in, 113–114; control of partner behavior and, 37, 38; demanding behavior and, 37; emotional stability and, 110; financial issues and, 175, 176–177, 184–185, 186; forgiveness and, 155–156; frequency of, 20–21, 124; global perspective influencing, 144–145, 146–147; honesty in, 136; hostility underlying, 46, 127–128, 207; housework, 170, 171; improving, 134, 138; irrational beliefs and, 30–31, 207, 211; listening issues in, 131; marriage counseling and, 213; mimicking parents in, 116–117; misunderstandings in, 133–134; parenthood and, 165, 169, 170; personality influence in, 103, 106, 107, 108, 109, 110, 111; power and control, 179–181, 186–187, 191–192; problems unveiled in, 121–122; pronoun choice in, 129–130; reciprocation in, 131–132; responsibility for, 226–227; rumination and, 155–156; about sex, 76; social

ABOUT THE AUTHORS

Rob Pascale received his BA and PhD in research psychology from Hofstra University in 1980. Upon completing his education, Dr. Pascale began his career as a market researcher, a field which utilizes polling techniques and quantitative research methodologies borrowed from the social sciences to assess consumer attitudes, interests, needs, and behaviors. In 1982, Dr. Pascale founded Marketing Analysts, a consumer research firm. Dr. Pascale has since departed the business arena and the world of the consumer to concentrate on researching social and psychological issues.

Dr. Lou Primavera is a licensed psychologist trained in behavior and rational emotive behavior therapies, maintaining a private practice for more than twenty-five years specializing in marriage counseling. Dr. Primavera is currently the dean of the School of Health Sciences at Touro College. Previously he was the dean of the Derner Institute of Advanced Psychological Studies at Adelphi University, held the department chair and served as associate dean of the Graduate School of Arts and Sciences at St. John's University, and has held full-time faculty positions at Hofstra University, St. Francis College, and Molloy College.

Dr. Primavera has published extensively in the social sciences, and his work has appeared in a number of prestigious professional journals in psychology. He was a consultant to the Department of Psychiatry and Behavioral Sciences at Memorial Sloan Kettering Cancer Center and has held a number of other consulting positions in medicine, business, and education. He has been a member of a number of professional organizations and has served as president of the Academic Division of the New York State Psychological Association, and the New York City Metro Chapter of the American Statistical Association. Dr. Primavera is a fellow of the Division of General Psychology and the Division of Evaluation, Measurement, and Statistics of the American Psychological Association, a fellow of the American Educational Research Association, and a fellow of the Eastern Psychological Association.